*Praise*

Too Much *of*

D1488957

"Jane Pollak writes with candor—and a healthy dose of humor—about the paradox of growing up in a middle-class Jewish family that looks to all the world to be ideal, but is far from it in all the ways that count. The story of her determination to define herself on her own terms both as an independent woman and as an artist makes for an absorbing read."

—Fred Hersch,
author of *Good Things Happen Slowly: A Life In and Out of Jazz*

"Jane Pollak, a successful artist, businesswoman, and coach, courageously takes us on an intimate journey. She shares her inner struggles due to the fallout from her childhood with a narcissist mother, and then a distant husband as she quests for connection and love. She plunges early into personal development courses and a twelve-step program, where she digs deeply and finds friendship and community. Pollak breaks out, discovering what went wrong, shows us the importance of being true to ourselves and asking for what we want. Brave, inspiring and relatable, Pollak leaves the reader feeling enlightened and empowered."

—Gayle Kirschenbaum,
documentary filmmaker of *Look At Us Now, Mother!*

"*Too Much of Not Enough* completely captivated me. On the surface, it seems like a conventional story, but within a few pages you realize it's an extraordinary one. Jane pulls you in with both tragedies and triumphs in her search for love—leaving you wiser and more self-compassionate for having had the experience."

—Ann Randolph, performer and award-winning writer of
*Inappropriate in All the Right Ways*

Too

Much

*of*

Not

Enough

# Too Much

# of

# Not

# Enough

*A Memoir*

by

# Jane Pollak

SHE WRITES PRESS

Published 2019
Printed in the United States of America
ISBN: 978-1-63152-527-8 pbk
ISBN: 978-1-63152-528-5 ebk
Library of Congress Control Number: 2018959802

For information, address:
She Writes Press
1569 Solano Ave #546
Berkeley, CA 94707

She Writes Press is a division of SparkPoint Studio, LLC.

*Book design by Stacey Aaronson*
*Chapter illustrations by Oksana Didkova*

*To my future self*

## It Felt Love

How
Did the rose
Ever open its heart
And give to this world
All its
Beauty?
It felt the encouragement of light
Against its
Being.
Otherwise,
We all remain
Too
Frightened.

—HAFIZ

# Author's Note

The defining moment of this memoir occurred thirty years ago when I ended a significant friendship. I had no idea at the time in what direction my life would go, but that action, looking back, tipped over the first in a long row of dominos that had been lining up in my life since birth.

I had a recurring dream back then that I was in a house trying to find the exit. The rooms and hallways were continually narrowing. I had to turn sideways while walking between rooms and scrunch my body up as small as possible, even trying to exit through a shrinking skylight above. When I finally said "no" to that friendship, I had a new dream, only once, where that friend handed me a key. There were no diminishing exit dreams after that.

Though everything I've written is true to the best of my recollection, those closest to me might debate a fact, location, or phrasing. I bow to their memories and hope they will accept artistic license and not mal-intention as my rationale.

I have changed the names of institutions and key players to protect their identities. I've made up names for my fellowships out of respect for the tradition of anonymity.

# Chapter One

*A*fter thirty-seven years of marriage, Ben and I are meeting in a therapist's office in Wilton, Connecticut. My theme song throughout the marriage has been "We Can Work It Out." But at this session in March 2010, Ben takes out a typewritten memo stating that another woman has become "very important" to him.

The cliché of going cold at bad news is actually happening to me. I hear only silence. The sounds in my brain are a *whoosh* of nothingness and an inner dialogue. *Did I just hear what I think I heard? Did he say he's in love with someone else? Was it love I once felt, or did I want to believe that so badly I pretended it was?*

These thoughts are drowning out whatever ambient noise is actually around me. There's only a dull hum sending pulsing sensations between my ears.

I'm aware of the texture of the couch I'm sitting on. The weave of the herringbone scratches my palm as I tug at a fuzz ball that's nestled between the threads right next to my thigh. The diagonal lines of beige and brown intersect to form the pattern. I stare at these woolen marks and sink into their repetitiveness for what feels like an hour.

I pull closed my sweater, the gray, button-less cardigan we bought in San Francisco on a chilly August night so many summers ago, and I tuck my hands under my legs for additional warmth.

Present again, I note that this statement by Ben signifies the end of my marriage because infidelity is a bottom line—nonnegotiable. I am also aware, for the first time, that another woman finds this man attractive.

In our early coupledom, I tried to tell Ben how good-looking he was—the glory of his speckled, gray-green eyes and the water-moon curve of his sweet smile. But after years of his deflecting my compliments—"I wish I were taller" or "I hate my hair"—not to mention gravity's downward pull, this beholder could no longer see that original beauty.

All I can think when I hear his words is, *Where did I go wrong? How did I miss this? Was there evidence I overlooked?*

I'm glad my mother is already dead, because her shock and disappointment would have been an additional burden. "How could you let your marriage slip away, Jane? Your father and I stayed together for fifty years, and God knows we weren't that happy." I could imagine her holding up her wedded heights as a hurdle she expected me to leap over as well. After all, she was the one who gave me the set of commandments I thought would get me through life: Remain a virgin till you meet The One. Check. Marry a nice Jewish boy. Check. Teach so you have something to fall back on. Check. Have children. Check. It will all work out.

*What's the opposite of "check"?*

I must be at fault.

SPENDING TIME IN a therapist's office was not new to me. I'd sought out rounds of guidance throughout our marriage, at least a dozen years' worth before I got into recovery, and more after. A twelve-step counselor I met with twenty years into my marriage asked me to share about my past. I revisited my privileged background, our four-bedroom home, sleepaway camps, and a liberal arts education. He caught me up short after I'd recited the many gifts I'd received as a child and echoed back what I'd just spoken: "You said, 'I *should* have been happy.'"

"I did?" I couldn't remember saying those words, but who would make that up? There was too much truth in his recollection for me to deny it.

My sisters, brother, and I were brought up in a house with live-in help. "Good custodial care," my current therapist tells me. There are pictures of me, gingham-clad as a toddler, in our fenced-in backyard, six feet away from a dark-skinned woman I don't recognize. My untested theory is that a series of indifferent caretakers, whom my mother oversaw and instructed, raised me. When I looked over my shoulder to be sure someone was watching me, there was evidence of supervision but no love object to attach to.

I read a lot about how families interact when I started having children of my own because I wanted to raise mine differently. I heard the expression "looks good, feels bad," which defined my family perfectly. It was important to my mother that her children be well-dressed: pinafores with crinolines, ruffled socks, and black patent-leather Mary Janes for dress-up occasions like visits to Grandma and Grandpa on the Upper East Side. How we appeared ranked higher than how we felt.

"Hold your tummy in, Janie," Mom cautioned me at eight. "No potbellies!" I wasn't sure what that meant, but I wanted to please her, so I learned to tighten my stomach muscles and view my profile in her full-length mirror to be sure nothing bulged. By twelve, I was wearing a girdle to hold up the stockings required for sixth-grade dance classes.

We lived on Easton Avenue, a gracious street of deep lawns edged with white stones in White Plains, a bedroom community of New York City. Our house sat on one-third of an acre, where my mother often imagined and talked about a swimming pool that never materialized. I grasped as early as elementary school that our city wasn't as fine as the neighboring towns of Scarsdale and Larchmont. That my mother was not satisfied with her lot, even though it was worlds more bountiful than her Bronx roots. That we children would have to fill in what was missing.

I couldn't comprehend this while I lived in that house, but as I got older and explored the self-help shelves of bookstores, I devoured volumes about our lives. John Bradshaw, a popular author back then, labeled my experience. He described the exchanges between parents and children as though he'd been peeking through our dining room window. We interacted like a mobile, a hanging sculpture seeking balance, he explained. Each of our behaviors contributed to the workings of the whole. As one of us took an action, the others moved this way or that to maintain the balance.

If Dad came home annoyed by traffic, and Mom failed to respond to his upset, Mom might yell at my older sister (the Scapegoat in Bradshaw's model) for arriving late to the dinner table, just to shift the focus away from my father's bad mood. My younger sister (the Mascot) would act more adorably during dessert. I (the Lost Child) became extra quiet, no trouble at all, and disappeared from notice. My brother (the Hero) would make a remark demonstrating his quick wit and diffuse the thick air. The dangling family unit made up of multiple pieces was thus recalibrated.

We were not unique, according to the literature. Discovering this gave me hope. I was not the first young adult to express unhappiness about how she was raised. It felt un-American and ungrateful to criticize one's upbringing. If I were to remove myself, I read, from our family's mobile, it might cause imbalance at first. Eventually, it would right itself again without my hanging by a thread.

Complicated families existed before Bradshaw characterized them in his book, and I felt understood. I was just beginning to allow outside sources into my awareness. For the first two decades of my life, my parents were my ultimate authorities. I chose Ben as my guide once we got married, but when I became a parent, that changed, too.

Chapter Two

My mother, Anita Siegel, a virgin, and Larry Goodman, a nice Jewish boy, were both native New Yorkers growing up in their own orbits. Mom was raised in the Bronx, a detail my father brought up more than occasionally. "You can take the girl out of the Bronx, but you can't take the Bronx out of the girl," he'd say when my mother appeared less than perfect, human. She might spill something or miss a punch line of his. Dad would tease her, but it didn't feel loving. Mom would let out an audible "ha," an acknowledgment that might have been heard as a laugh. A lot of her mannerisms reflected her desire to appear as the competent wife, but it was thin armor, given her background.

Before little Anita was two years old, her mother had died in the 1918 flu pandemic. This was a piece of history that never got talked about in our family. What would there have been to say?

Anita's father handed her over to her maternal grandparents to rear. My mother's grandparents were well into their forties when she arrived in their household. It's accepted today to have babies in one's fifth decade, but in the early twentieth century, it was uncommon. How much energy could this couple have had? Who could give this small child the attention a little one needs? What would it be like not to receive that loving devotion?

They'd already had their family, now grown and reproducing. I can't imagine how it must have been for them to lose a daughter and gain a toddling little girl. Was my mother a joyous bundle for them or an additional burden after their loss? I think about this only now, years after my own mother's death at eighty-eight.

As a young child myself, I never questioned my mother's presence in my earliest years, even though there was photographic evidence to make me wonder. She answered with authority every concern I brought to her. Her responses were the truth. Life was black-and-white then. Her certainty made me less fearful.

"No one will rob our house, Janie. You don't have to worry about the atomic bomb. You are perfectly safe." It was good to know that this parent had the answers. I wouldn't go to my father with these matters. He would have scoffed. "Nonsense. Don't worry about that." I often had nightmares and would come into their bedroom, if the door was open, crawl in on Mom's side, and snuggle into the warmth of her arms and belly.

She went to Hunter College High School, a New York City secondary school for intellectually gifted students. She didn't continue her formal education after that, although she attended college classes somewhere in Oregon, near where Dad was posted before he went overseas to the war.

After high school, Mom said, she modeled. I know she worked in a fur store and would try on coats that husbands intended for their wives. In her mind, that was a modeling career, not a sales job. That was the extent of her runway experience.

I learned from my father's example to diminish my mother like I did just now. Maybe she did model, but the only one mentioning her accomplishments was Mom. Because she had no parents, siblings, or cousins to support her claims, it was her voice alone filling the void. By necessity, it got louder and grander in order to be heard.

My father, on the other hand, was surrounded by family. The oldest of four children and the only boy, he was brought up in Manhattan, graduated from Townshend Harris High School, then City College, and then went off to New Haven for graduate school. Dad got his master of fine arts in scene design from Yale School of Drama in 1940.

For years, a quartet of his framed watercolor set renderings for the Eugene O'Neill drama *The Great God Brown* hung in our living room. I thought these pieces were true Art, the way my father captured the textured folds of the velvet drapes and the solidity of the wood furnishings. But those paintings were relegated to the attic years later, when my mother hired an interior designer to upgrade our decor. I claimed them for myself and hung them proudly in my college dorm room, where I chose to split my major between studio art and theater. Like my father, I, too, designed sets for plays.

My parents met in their twenties, fixed up by my mother's schoolgirl friend. Photos capture their early courtship at a beach club on Long Island. Even though the pictures are in black-and-white, you can imagine Dad's khaki pants paired with a white cotton T-shirt. A muscle shirt for some, it hangs loosely on my father's slim, tall body. Mom's one-piece bathing suit reveals no cleavage but does outline her smooth, ample curves. She has a broad smile on her face. Her eyes, fastened on Dad's, are darkly alive. He's smiling, too.

They were a young, attractive couple. Looking at the photograph, you'd think they'd live happily ever after, not fifty unfulfilling years of matrimony. They played out their marital and parental roles, but my father rarely acknowledged my mother, at least not that I could see. I have no memory of loving looks between them, except when a camera was present to record the moment.

You wouldn't need a degree in psychology to understand that my mother suffered from feeling abandoned, first by her mother's untimely death, and then by her father's having relinquished his duty and passed her on to those well-meaning grandparents who didn't have the capacity to dote on her.

Even though I knew my dad's parents and sisters, I'm less sure about his emotional needs. He never spoke in those terms. Somehow the two attracted each other. My mother, with her unfillable well, complaining to her hardworking, unemotional husband that a sizable plot of land in White Plains was not enough. If only we had a pool. Maybe she was just trying to get a rise out of him. Any reaction would do.

My parents' wedding photograph captured my dad in uniform, ready to go off to World War II, and Mom, a beautiful, raven-haired bride in a rented white satin gown. Sometime after the ceremony and reception, my father shipped overseas to fight. My mother stayed behind to help the war effort in the United States, serving for a time as an interpreter because her knowledge of Yiddish was helpful in understanding German.

Neither spoke at length about the years between their wedding and the end of the war. Like my mother's upbringing, it was an off-limits subject. World War II seemed in the distant past by the time I was old enough to comprehend its significance. A German soldier's gun stashed on an upper shelf in my mother's closet was revealed to us once. When I snuck into my parents' bedroom again, months later, to have another peek, it had disappeared. Asking questions would have re-vealed my misdeed, so the mystery remained. Even as a young child, I knew not to probe any further.

It wasn't just my family. Nobody talked about the war ex-perience. This was the 1950s, Eisenhower and television. People were busy booming with babies, upward mobility, and suburbia.

I was the second-born of four children to this veteran-turned-department-store-executive and his wife. My father's role in theater never materialized but instead translated into retail showroom displays—a more profitable career path. My mother regularly moved our expanding family, as my father's corporate climb had us relocate five times in nine years.

My sister Meredith, older than I by two years, was born in 1946 in Hartford, Connecticut. My younger sister, Barbara, followed my arrival in Columbus, Ohio, by nearly three years. Three moves later, the family arrived in White Plains, New York, where my brother was born and my parents lived the rest of their lives.

Before I had children of my own, I never considered what it must have been like for a young couple reuniting after a traumatic war, not to mention all the relocations and expanding family, and having to act like raising children was as attainable as the cover of *Good Housekeeping* made it look: contented boys and girls putting puzzle pieces into place, perfectly dressed and coiffed, while the grown-ups tried to muddle through the complexities of a long separation, bloodshed, and getting back to normal, whatever that was.

I try to envision my mother uprooting her growing family from house to house, enrolling us in schools, finding new pe-diatricians and synagogues, and then being transplanted back East soon after she had happily grounded us in the Midwest.

I was born on July 4, 1948, a firecracker baby, at a Catholic hospital, even though we were Jewish. Drugs were taboo there, but an anesthesiologist was present at my birth, perhaps in the event that something went wrong. Dr. Jerry Jacobs became a close family friend and was someone my mother held in high esteem. I'll never know for sure what it was about their relationship that was so soothing, but I came to suspect that it may have been the monthly supply of amber vials with child-proof tops that showed up in my mother's bathroom cupboard, prescribed in Ohio and fulfilled in a pharmacy in New York for as long as I continued to peek into her cabinet.

I didn't know until my own children were born how much it meant to me for my husband to be present. Ben was there not only for the birth of each of our three children, but also for our Lamaze training classes beforehand. He witnessed every minute of my labor and delivery, patting my head with damp washcloths, feeding me ice chips, and coaching me through the breathing techniques we'd learned and practiced in my final month of pregnancy.

My father, like other fathers of the late 1940s and '50s, sat in a waiting room for my sisters' and my births. There flitted an oft-repeated accusation throughout their marriage that Dad was not even on the premises for my brother's arrival. Mom would retrieve that old hurt and lob it over the net, perhaps when he mentioned her Bronx roots one too many times.

I do remember that my father brought us girls to visit Mom at White Plains Hospital. Maternity stays were closer to a week back then, not the two-to-three-day ones of today. But the closest we got to her was standing in a small garden patio below the maternity wing. We tilted our heads back, looking up to a balcony where Mom stood in a pink chenille bathrobe, her newborn son swaddled in a receiving blanket and embraced in her arms. To an outsider, we looked like a typical family, a perfectly balanced constellation of six stars.

Those were the days—the 1950s—when long sedans and wood-paneled station wagons crawled slowly down neighborhood streets as children lined both sides, creating a wake as the driver interrupted an in-progress game of Spud or running bases. We four kids joined the dozens of neighborhood children outdoors after dinner, lined up for Good Humor treats, and melted into the dailiness of suburban America.

Life at 19 Easton Avenue seemed like that of other households on the block. My father commuted daily to his job in the city. After driving Dad to the train station in the morning, my mother stayed home, shooed her brood out of the house for the walk to school, awaited our return at lunchtime, and repeated the cycle again at 3:15 p.m. when the day was over.

After we became a two-car family, Dad drove himself to and from the train. At the end of the day, we kids lined up, in age order, for kisses on the forehead when he came in from the garage. Was that something we did every night? Or was the fact that my mother staged this tableau of domestic tranquility so unusual that I remember it because it happened only once?

It reminded me of a scene from *The Sound of Music*, the first Broadway show my mother took my sisters and me to in New York City. In it, Mary Martin, playing Sister Maria from the convent, lined up the von Trapp children to greet their father, the captain. Did my mother take her cue from the Rodgers and Hammerstein musical, thinking that it represented the ideal family? I think she may have been inspired by the way those well-behaved children, in matching outfits, stood in a row according to height. There was something impeccable about the stage-worthiness of it all.

Dinner was a family event. I loved its routine, helping to set the table, getting to lick a spoonful of sauce before the meal, anticipating dessert—my favorite course—and listening to everyone talk and laugh.

Mealtimes were when being good and being quiet came into the picture for me. I sat silently, observing everything around me. What was Mom's mood? How was my father reacting to what Meredith said? Was Andy being funny? Was Barbara the first to offer to clear the table? Taking it all in. Judging. Evaluating. Hoping to be noticed or called on.

"Jane's so good," my mother would say. "I don't have to worry about Jane." (Lost Child!) I heard this as praise and kept my status by never speaking up or expressing an independent thought. My *I'm here!* muscle shriveled from disuse.

If I were good, what could be bad or go bad? I carried this belief with me for longer than it was useful. Being good and doing the right thing festered into righteousness.

Why did my mother remember my sister's April wedding anniversary years after her divorce but rarely think to acknowledge Ben's and mine, whose marriage endured? If this was what being good got you, I'd signed up for the wrong plan.

My mother wanted us to believe she was the perfect homemaker. Maybe she needed to believe this herself. She enacted the roles of charity volunteer, hostess, nurturing mom, and beautiful wife. To her credit, she got a lot right. We were high-achieving, likable, well-turned-out children. We thrived in the system. She signed us up for activities, schlepped us to our extracurricular lessons, and attended our recitals and awards ceremonies. She applauded our home-choreographed performances to show tunes played on the Victrola.

But it was mostly bravado. If we looked good, she gloried in our reflection. That made me angry. "I *knew* you'd get an A," she'd say, reducing my deed by calling attention to her intuitive power. The older me aches for her, needing that momentary evidence that she was okay. The younger me longs for the missed acknowledgment. "An A! You worked hard to get that, didn't you?"

Sitting around the dining room table, eating Mom's cooking, was what it meant to be a family. Dinners like this were as good as it got. I was part of something even if I felt as if I were just on the edge, looking in. We were together. We ate well. There was laughing and conversation, until eventually my father said, "Everybody's excused," ending dinner and signaling his departure to fill his pipe, turn on the TV, and put his feet up on the couch.

This was love, I was taught. If I could arrange my own version of this Norman Rockwell illustration, everything would be all right. When I got married to Ben, this became my job, as it had been my mother's.

Chapter Three

*I* met Ben at a ground-floor mixer for residents of Whittier Hall, a Columbia University Teachers College (TC) dormitory. It was the fall of 1970, and I'd just graduated from Mount Holyoke College in May. Ben was returning to academia after having dropped out of a dental-school program a year earlier.

Having so recently been in an all-female college environment for four years, I reveled in the attention of the men at Columbia. Ben's appearance—his scraggly beard, unkempt hair, and hippie-ish leather vest—did not invite me in. In fact, it masked his intelligence, humor, and sweetness. I barely noticed him in September.

Before I considered Ben romantically, I dated several graduate students at Columbia. Jonny, another resident of Whittier Hall, had curly, jet-black hair and a smile that lifted the right corner of his mouth. He invited me to see a play at the Public Theater and the next day slid under my door a poem he'd written. On our second date, we went to a party at his sister's place in New Jersey. We made out a few times, but I was steadfast about maintaining my virginity, and he soon lost interest.

There was the med student I met at a mixer, named Bill. He had potential, a future doctor. His last name, Herman or something similarly Jewish or German, depending on the number of r's and n's, made me pay attention. In the back of my head, I carried my mother's judgment about who I might bring home. This intern's credentials would have impressed her, but it never took.

By midyear, my social life revolved around a gang, several guys and I, including Ben. We'd smoke pot in a dorm room as a prelude to whatever came next—a walk to Baskin-Robbins, a beer at the West End, or a dance. My first experience with this gateway drug, which led no further, happened on a date at Williams College in the late '60s, behind a dorm-room door, which paranoid underclassmen, especially me, barricaded with a bureau and a desk. Though I managed to inhale, I failed to get high.

At Columbia three years later, weed smoke wafting through the halls was ignored as commonplace. No one, including me, worried about getting caught. I mastered the intake and enjoyed the effects without concern. Ever the Good Girl, I never allowed it to become habitual.

Although we were high, Ben didn't participate in dancing but watched while I shimmied around Dan, a curly-haired Adonis whose attention I sought. Ben never initiated these evenings but came along if he wasn't working on a paper or lesson plan. I admired his work ethic and decision to stay in and complete an assignment. He was beginning to leave an impression on me as someone who valued his education. Not that I didn't, but socializing was a higher priority for me that year.

TC was easy after the rigors of Mount Holyoke. Besides, no one would ever ask about my grades in graduate school.

Without that motivation, I was content with the B's I received. At Columbia, I had marriage on my mind. Following my mother's playbook, I was on track for her vision of my future.

As an undergraduate, I was aware that every senior in my dorm was engaged to be married and had a subscription to *Brides* magazine. There were comparisons of diamond rings over dinner and engagement showers held in the parlor of our dormitory. Getting one's MRS was more a reality than a joke in the late '60s. For you younger readers, the facetious MRS degree, like a master's (MA), was another way of saying "Mrs.," the honorific (another antiquated notion!) for a married woman. It was part of what you did when you went to college: you found a mate.

I was able to postpone that requirement for another year, but by the middle of 1971, the time had come. The next step, after I earned my master's to become a teacher, would be finding a husband.

When only a few days were left in the term, Ben asked if I wanted to catch the new Robert Altman film. This was the first time he had invited me out, just the two of us. When he showed up outside the movie house on Broadway, he was clean-shaven and had had a haircut. I saw him differently than I had before. Once he shed the hippie look, he was very attractive.

We dated throughout the summer. His job that July and August was as a day-camp counselor, which he loved. His days were full, but he never complained about crossing the George Washington Bridge to be with me every night.

I liked having a boyfriend, finishing my master's degree, and living in the city. Going out each evening erased any loneliness I might have suffered. Ben particularly enjoyed my long, wavy hair, though not as much when I had to stack it on top of my head in a bun during that summer's heat wave.

We held hands as we walked, and our legs rested against each other's on the long subway rides to the East Village. A place on campus distributed cheap tickets to cultural events throughout the boroughs. We scampered onto the express train and rode underground in the heat to attend plays.

We fell in love and did the deed. We weren't engaged, but there was predictability and consistency in my life, which I clung to. My time as a coed was dwindling, and I soon put pressure on Ben to get married. I thought that that was what we were supposed to do. I didn't know what other options there were.

I should mention that I had had one serious boyfriend at Mount Holyoke starting at the end of my sophomore year. Matthew, a junior at Yale, was my first real love. We dated steadily through my junior year (his senior), slept in the same twin dorm bed, and fondled each other passionately but never consummated our union. Matthew graduated that May and returned to his Chicago hometown to begin law school. Continuing to date would have been inconvenient from Mount Holyoke, so I selfishly broke up with him.

Besides, I knew it would never work because he was too different. During college, you saw a person only in their current milieu, surrounded by the choices of an institution. When I visited Matthew at his home during the first summer we were dating, I noted startling differences in our upbringings. His Midwest house had Venetian blinds on the windows, instead of draperies, and area rugs on the wood floors, rather than wall-to-wall carpeting. My vision was so narrow that something as foreign as alternate window treatments could change my opinion of someone I loved. The mercury in my romantic thermometer dipped below normal and never climbed back to the heat I had once experienced in his company.

After finishing my degree at Columbia, and having been to Ben's fully carpeted home in Fair Lawn, I determined that this would be it. I loved him, thought he was funny and smart and would make a good teacher. What else was there?

Up until then, my life's milestones, other than my college major, had been decided for me. It was time to become a wife, and Ben fit the part. It surprised me that, for a novice decision maker, I was unyielding.

By the end of graduate school, I had played it cool but was inwardly desperate. Who would I be after I got my degree, if I were alone? Who would take care of me? Where would I live? I shudder to admit that those were my unspoken, unacknowledged fears about not fulfilling my mother's prescribed formula, which had now become mine. I had no inner resources because, prior to this, nothing had tested them. A failed exam, of course. Wine spilled on my prom dress, yes. But no genuine life choices needed to be made.

I'm sure I would have figured it out if I'd had to, but not getting married at twenty-three made me feel like I might die.

The most realistic comparison I can make to the pressure I felt inside happened a few years later. A friend of mine and I were both due with our first babies the fall of 1974. Tragically, she had a stillborn a month before our close delivery dates. I could not fathom how she could go on another day when all of the expectations were geared toward what was supposed to be the next step in her life: motherhood, the nursery, diapers, and feedings. How humiliating not to deliver according to the script!

My marital status felt that dire. I am ashamed to admit it, but it appeared that big to me then. What was a humbling and devastatingly sad experience for her counted in my mind as a shameful failure. That's how wrongheaded I was in my twenties.

Ben and I started dating in June 1971. By late August, he hadn't proposed yet. At the time, it felt like an eternity. It wasn't even a season.

I soon realized that I was going to have to move out of my Columbia housing and make a decision about the next step in my life. Marriage had seemed like the obvious answer. It would solve all my problems. I wouldn't have to make my next choices alone.

But Ben had a semester of student teaching ahead of him. Even though we had declared our love for each other, he wasn't ready to make a commitment and resisted my moving the conversation in that direction.

I had no perspective. I simply wanted to reel in my man. We took a short break—two weeks, maybe—no dates, no telephone calls—before I dialed him up to say I'd be willing not to discuss marriage again. We resumed dating.

When Ben's term at Columbia was over that December and we'd been a couple for six months, it made more sense to talk about a future with each other. Though we never revealed our innermost fears, he might have had the same uncertainty about his future as I had about mine. Planning the next step as a couple suddenly felt more urgent for him as well.

I didn't have a best friend then whom I trusted enough to discuss this romance with. My mother wasn't an ally, even though I was living my life to please her. Speaking to a therapist was years beyond consideration. Though I had lived my life independently, I didn't recognize how alone I was.

Coaxing Ben down the wedding aisle gave my story its next plotline. Crafting this fictional drama was where my best thinking had brought me. My older sister had been engaged for several months and was planning her nuptials for April 1972. Ben and I chose August 26 as our date to be wed, based primarily on our fall semester's teaching calendar.

My mother was a party planner before event planning became an industry. Listening to her and my sister argue over minutiae, like their screaming match about the color of the groom's shoes, alarmed me. Wasn't this supposed to be a fun and magical time? The happiest day of a girl's life? Why were there only tears and raised voices?

I wanted to be a bride but resisted having to select bridesmaids or parade down a petal-strewn aisle with a hundred guests watching. I did envision wearing a pretty gown, having my hair done, and getting my picture in the *Times*. But kissing everyone in a receiving line and tossing a bouquet had no appeal.

Ben's and my opposite needs for our families' attention were beginning to be revealed. As the apple of his parents' eyes, he often felt overattended to and shunned their gaze. The idea of having only our two immediate families present when we married was even more than he desired. But he loved me and was willing to go along. I'm sure I gave him my permission and blessing just to show up. I'd do all the necessary planning.

Chapter Four

*E*very other Sunday, because it was the maid's day off, our family would go to Cook's, a hamburger place about five miles from our neighborhood. This gave my mother a break in her household routine. Our live-in domestic help washed the dishes and cleaned the kitchen, but Mom oversaw the menu and supervised food preparation.

Cook's, located in Mamaroneck, had a large Dutch windmill as its architectural centerpiece. Our whole family would pile into Mom's white Tempest station wagon, we four kids scrunched together in the backseat—there were no seat belts then—Dad driving, Mom on the passenger side. She'd drape her left arm over the seat back, reaching for one of our hands. I would grab her fingers. I loved holding on to her like that. She'd pat my knee and say my name: "Janie."

For many years, those times we spent as a family were what I looked upon as love.

Cook's had two wooden counters, one where you ordered your hot dogs, hamburgers, and fries, and the other for beverages and desserts. The limited menu made it easy. We'd enter en masse. We kids would make a dash for a table while my parents divided up and got the drinks and meal items. We'd play clapping games, like "I am a pretty little Dutch girl," or pinchies, a variation of a game I can't find a name for. We made up lots of games in our alone time together. Some were to keep ourselves occupied while the grown-ups played their roles, like at Cook's. Other games were made up to help us understand our lives.

Every Saturday morning, when my brother was still too young to participate, we three girls produced elaborate scenarios with our Ginny dolls. These eight-inch plastic figures were precursors to Barbie dolls but still resembled little girls.

Barbara and I shared a second-floor bedroom that had wall-to-wall, spring-green carpeting and twin beds with matching spreads. Across from where we slept was a wooden cabinet with sliding doors that housed our doll collections, and a patch of empty broadloom in front of it for game playing.

Meri, our nickname for our older sister, would come into our room, still in her pajamas. The three of us would sit cross-legged in a circle with our dolls and their outfits arranged in piles around us to allow for frequent wardrobe changes as the scenes required.

She always took charge and claimed our family name, Goodman, for her dolls, assigning Goodwin to me and Goodson to Barbara. Her dolls' father earned the most money, had the best job, and was the smartest. Down the ranks were Barbara and I, getting the second and third place in each category, based on birth order. I learned that by obediently following my older sister's lead, I was allowed to dwell in her realm.

The attributes we claimed were around money, success, and brainpower, I notice now, not kindness, love, and generosity. Also, there was no mention of the doll children's female parent. Were we simply mouthpieces for our mother's view on the world? Or Meri's perspective as the oldest?

Stories unfolded, and we dressed and redressed our dolls for school, parties, and home. I wish I could listen to our interchanges from those games. We entertained ourselves for hours this way, until Mom opened our bedroom door to announce, "Lunchtime!"

I think that many of the ideas I had about how the world should be were formulated during those weekend re-creations according to the Goodman sisters: that being rich and having nice outfits to wear and places to go equaled happiness, equaled love.

Cultural influences from the television shows we watched, like *Father Knows Best*, *Leave It to Beaver*, and *Ozzie and Harriet*, helped imprint what relationships and love in families should be. Every episode wrapped up its conflict in thirty minutes, give or take commercial breaks.

I don't remember feeling like the way the Andersons, Cleavers, or Nelsons looked. I couldn't articulate that gap for another thirty years. On inspection, the rooms of our house could have been TV backdrops. They were nice enough and contained all the trappings of comfort in suburbia. But the happy scenarios featuring parents with their arms around each other, chuckling over their offspring's mishaps again this week, were more Norman Rockwell than John Bradshaw.

"Oh, that Beaver," June might say, winking at Ward. My father never called us girls anything like Kitten, the Anderson father's affectionate nickname for his youngest. Mom and Dad didn't team up to help their kids solve this week's crisis, the way Ricky and David's parents did. I wanted the closeness I saw on the small screen. We looked like we had it. In the pictures.

"We're rich in love," Mom often said, summing up our family's time together. I believed her back then. We'd laughed, eaten, traveled in each other's company and arrived safely home. It's odd that she would have put an emotion into economic terms. By any standards, we were well-off.

Dad rarely used the *l*-word. He didn't concur when my mother made that statement. When I asked my father if he loved me, he replied, "You know that I love you."

"That I love you" became a joke among my siblings in adulthood. "That I love you!" I said to my brother, Andy, some years ago, after staying at his place in California soon after Ben and I separated. The three little words alone were too intimate in my relationships with males especially. I wanted to express my affection to him, to say simply, "I love you," but the emotion was too powerful to be allowed to escape.

There's a song in the musical *Fiddler on the Roof* in which Tevye, the patriarch of a Jewish family, asks his wife, Golde, "Do you love me?"

Her response to him is, "For twenty-five years I've washed your clothes, cooked your meals, cleaned your house, given you children, milked the cow," and, in a later verse to the audience, "For twenty-five years I've lived with him, fought with him, starved with him, twenty-five years my bed is his. If that's not love, what is?"

I can hear my father imploring, "I've paid for your college, taken you out to eat, bought you clothes, and kept a roof over your head. If that's not love, what is?"

As I got older, my understanding about love evolved. It wasn't until my mid-thirties that I sensed a different and new awareness. When someone looked directly at me, heard and reflected back to me what I'd said, or responded with a gesture that made me feel visible, I felt like I existed as never before.

This form of love was nothing like what my mother declared us rich in. This form of love was about being seen.

Moments after my first child was born and I lay on the delivery room table, shivering from the postpartum release of hormones, a nurse saw this and placed a heavy, preheated blanket on top of my entire body, up to my shoulders. Immediately, the chill diminished and my body relaxed. That's what this new kind of love felt like: embracing, vital, and healing.


BEN AND I were friends first. We often had lunch together in our dorm. There was a social area in Whittier, up two stairs and to the right of the reception desk. It had sturdy, square tables and wooden chairs where students sat for card games or meals, and leather banquettes lining the walls so we could watch TV. It was never crowded and a good place to meet someone casually.

His routine was to pick up a sliced-egg sandwich, along with a copy of the *New York Post*, from the blind woman's newsstand that was tucked in between the deli and Whittier. Back in the student lounge, he'd flip the paper over to get to the sports section first. I frequently ate there, too, having a container of yogurt and a piece of fruit. Ben knew that I enjoyed doing the crossword puzzle and tore that page out for me and left it waiting on the table if he'd gotten there first. I'd feel bad if I had other plans at lunch. I imagined him sitting at the table alone, watching for me and tossing away the ripped-out crossword puzzle page, along with his leftovers.

I liked him, but as a friend. I had never had more than one person at a time interested in me before graduate school. I enjoyed this new dating-around phase of my life.

Ben "sat bells," a term used for the job of answering the

phone at the front desk of Whittier. This was before cell phones. Outsiders, friends or family, would call the main line of the dorm, and the person sitting bells would connect the caller to your room. He often had the 8:00 p.m.–midnight shift. I thought it was virtuous that he held a job on campus. My parents provided my tuition, plus room and board. It made me wonder if he was on financial aid.

Coming in late one night, I passed by the front desk. Ben stopped me and said, "I made something for you." He handed me a sheet of paper with a neatly inked grid consisting of ten squares across and ten squares down, forming one hundred boxes. After drawing that structure, he'd written the number three in each of the boxes, except for the one near the center.

"It's a quiz," he said. "Find the nine."

The times I've been picked out of the crowd for recognition have left an impact on me. Maybe it was because of my family position as the second of four children and the middle girl, but when I'm singled out for special consideration, it stays with me.

Someone noticed me, selected me, and handed me a gift that made me feel important. That's how touched I felt when Ben stopped me as I passed the main desk in Whittier Hall that night. He'd created this amusing challenge for me because he liked me. It was a small enough gesture that I wasn't frightened. I began to appreciate his subtlety and dry wit.

When we went out in a group, Ben made us all laugh, and I began to miss his presence if he stayed in the dorm to complete an assignment, instead of joining us.

By second semester Ben and I had begun sitting together in a literature class. A passionate reader, he'd won a cash award for excellence as an English major at Lafayette College. He'd promptly lost it in a poker game there, he proudly confessed, showing how little the honor meant to him. He shunned any kind of accolade or attention. His attitude was so different from mine. That he didn't cling to an honor as if it defined him, as I would have, attracted me.

I was grateful for and valued his explanation of our homework assignments. Reading was not a strong subject for me, and I needed a guide. Ben was generous with his time. He helped me appreciate a Melville short story our professor had assigned. I couldn't believe that writers struggled over word choices until I started writing myself, and thought it was pure coincidence as a twenty-two-year-old that a particular word had been thoughtfully selected.

"My eleventh-grade English teacher made us go through a book, word by word, underlining symbols the author had used," I told him. "I thought it was a waste of time. I'll never forget in *Red Badge of Courage* how Stephen Crane wrote that a cloud looked like a wafer in the sky. What if it really did look like a wafer? Is that brilliant writing?"

"But he didn't say it looked like a cookie. Wafer has a Christian meaning. He's alluding to that through symbolism," Ben said, without any judgment. I noticed his desire for me to understand. I knew he would make a great teacher. He loved literature, and he conveyed that to his pupil. As the one in front of him at that moment, I felt his warmth.

When we started going out that June, 1971, we saw each other almost every night. On our first date, when we watched *McCabe & Mrs. Miller*, our shoulders touched, and I didn't move away. I might have, if we'd been hanging out in a group, thinking the closeness simply accidental.

At the end of the movie, Ben leaned over for a kiss. On the lips. His were soft, and they lingered on mine for a few seconds longer than I expected. It sent a shiver down my spine.

That moment redefined our relationship. We were now boyfriend and girlfriend, and it felt good.

Picking me up for a date one June night, Ben looked at me admiringly. I wore a new red-and-white mini dress with platform sandals. He put his arm around my waist and kissed me, smiling and holding himself more upright as he did. I wore high heels sparingly, since Ben was just my height when I had on flats. I was self-conscious about being tall, particularly when dating.

That summer, we went to lots of movies and shows, played tennis in Riverside Park, and ate in different restaurants throughout the city. I loved being in his company as we laughed, competed, and thrived on being young and in New York.

One weekend in July, I took Ben to visit my alma mater in South Hadley, Massachusetts, where we attended a play put on by the Mount Holyoke College Summer Theatre. Ben was getting to know more about my background, witnessing my recent history, and seeing me in the place I'd been prior to our meeting at Columbia.

We spent the night in the upstairs bedroom of a two-family house, sleeping together on a futon that was on the floor. After we'd made love, Ben, lying on top of me, leaned up on his elbows, his face close to mine, and said softly, "I love you."


IN THE FALL, I took an apartment share on Seventy-Ninth and Riverside Drive. My new roommate, Cheryl, had posted its availability on a three-by-five-inch card pinned to a bulletin board at the Mount Holyoke Club of New York. I hadn't known this woman in college but trusted that a fellow alum would offer a safe place. It was a large, two-bedroom, ground-floor unit. I was given the smaller bedroom, which had bars on the windows and its own bathroom. Cheryl worked downtown as a computer programmer in the days of mainframes. Her work hours started late in the day and went till early morning, so we rarely saw each other.

I took a job in the art department of an independent textbook publishing company in the Flatiron Building downtown, on Twenty-Third Street. I wanted the glamour of living in New York City and shunned teaching even after earning my master's in education. I lived frugally on my salary of $125 a week and had no concept of what I'd do with only a two-week vacation.

I commuted from Seventy-Ninth and Riverside to the Flatiron building in a packed, hot, rank subway car and got only half-hour lunch breaks. Though I didn't have big dreams back then, I knew this wasn't the way I wanted to live and responded, a few months later, to a *New York Times* classified ad looking for a stagecraft and art teacher at West Hill High School in Stamford, Connecticut, starting in the fall. The job description fit my qualifications perfectly. I applied and was hired. After only six months of working-girl life, I was ready for a school calendar with shorter days, multiple vacations, and summers off.

Ben still needed to finish his degree and had a semester of student teaching remaining. He continued to live on the Columbia campus. We spent occasional weeknights together at my place and every weekend in each other's company.

Commuting to work in early September, getting into an overcrowded, un-air-conditioned subway car, I felt light-headed and was overtaken by nausea. I wasn't sure if it was the heat or the uncomfortable press of bodies against me, but after several days of being sick to my stomach, I had the even more upsetting thought that I might be pregnant. Ben and I had taken no precautions during sex. Inexperienced as I was, I wasn't sure we'd even had real intercourse. There were bent limbs and breathless panting, but I wondered, after all that time protecting my virginity, was that it? Why would my mother have been so uncompromising about a mediocre gymnastics workout?

Only years later, and it was years—six, to be precise, when I'd finally experienced orgasm—could I look back on this sex act for what it was: a first attempt by two amateurs ending with only one climax, not two.

I'm sure I'd never been to a gynecologist, but I must have located one, where I dropped off a urine specimen and waited for the results. I didn't tell anyone except Ben what I was experiencing. The nausea continued. I had a secret and no one else to tell. It was out of the question to mention this to my mother. I didn't have a best friend. My coworker in the art department was someone I'd just met. I barely knew my roommate.

Unlike the instant outcome of today's pregnancy tests, it was a full week before I could call for results. My test was positive. To put it clinically, intercourse had indeed occurred, orgasm or not, and something had taken hold inside me.

"Congratulations," the technician said when I gave her my name. I was too upset and scared to say anything. This was not on my agenda, not the right time to be pregnant. I hung up without responding.

There was nothing resembling the Internet then. No Google search for "what do you do if you're pregnant," like there is now. Somehow Ben and I found Wickersham Hospital, where abortions were available and legal.

I scheduled an appointment to terminate the pregnancy as soon as possible. Ben offered to be by my side and escorted me to the hospital, at 133 East Fifty-Eighth Street. I knew that neighborhood from shopping at Bloomingdale's, a few blocks away. It was odd to associate that area with a medical procedure now—like the way my thoughts about the World Trade Center and lower Manhattan altered after 9/11. It would be years before I could walk on Lexington Avenue without also thinking about how much more real life became after that experience.

No shoppers were on the street when we arrived early on a Saturday morning. We entered the waiting area of Wickersham, where Ben learned that he could not be present during the procedure itself. He asked what time he could come pick me up and then left.

The room was full of young women, dozens of them. I was ashamed of myself and whispered to the receptionist, "I'm here for an abortion." She looked at her list, checked my name off, and asked me to take a seat. "So are they," she replied cocking her head to indicate everyone else seated in the waiting room and pointing me to an empty cushioned bench near the window.

I had no moral misgivings about my decision to terminate the pregnancy. I was barely out of school, underemployed, neither married nor ready to bring new life into the world. Having a child then was not an option I even considered. Ben and I had had no conversation about having this baby or raising it. The Right to Life Movement was barely a concept in 1971, and abortion, though not taken lightly, was an alternative form of birth control if you got in trouble. I might have chosen differently after delivering my children, but back then, there was no contemplation, guilt, or misgivings.

This dilation and curettage (D and C) was my first surgical procedure ever, minor as it was. I didn't feel afraid, went out easily under anesthesia, and came to quickly when it was over. I woke up in the recovery area, rested awhile, and then put my street clothes back on and found my way out to reception.

Ben was there when I was ready to leave the hospital.

"How was it?" he asked, his hand touching the middle of my back as we walked out the door. I rested my head on his shoulder and circled my arm around his waist. "I'm okay," I told him.

"Are you hungry?" he asked. "You didn't get to eat anything before you went in. Did they give you something after? Do you want to stop for lunch now, or would you rather we go right home?"

We were a couple. Two people who could rely on each other. There was now more to our relationship than taking advantage of the city. We had been through a life experience together and supported each other.

It was shortly after the abortion that we were lying in bed, maybe even the weekend it happened, when Ben, his arms wrapped around me as we spooned, said, "We should get married." I agreed and snuggled closer.

I'd just come through an event that had changed me. Something had happened in my life that was bigger than I was. A force of nature, getting pregnant, humbled my sense of control, order, and destiny. Beyond my own expectations, life had happened in the way that it does, and I'd moved through it. I had done this with Ben and clung to him with new appreciation.

SEVERAL MONTHS LATER, Ben was scheduled for an interview to teach at Brigham Woods High School in a small, affluent suburb of New York City. The career placement department at TC had informed him of this opening in Westchester, the home of IBM families and other wealthy residents, and encouraged him to apply. He asked if I would accompany him.

Beyond the interview with administrators, Ben would also have to teach a sample class. He spent days agonizing over what lesson to bring to a group of teenagers he'd never met, something that would both demonstrate his abilities and capture their attention.

He had to be there first thing in the morning, so I spent the night before his tryout with him in his dorm room. He reviewed his notes several times, packed his briefcase, and put out the pants, jacket, and tie he'd selected for the occasion. I watched as he organized. We barely spoke. Because he provided most of the conversation in our courtship, this was unusual. I knew he was nervous but had never felt its effects personally.

"Is this outfit okay?" he asked. "Do these pants need ironing?" I assured him everything was fine.

Wanting to avoid traffic, we left the dorm even before the sun came up. As we stood on the softly lit sidewalk, waiting to cross the street to get to his car, Ben suddenly doubled over, his body racked with convulsions. He dry-heaved for a long while. I had never witnessed someone else's anxiety at such close range. All I felt was compassion and love for this man who had become completely vulnerable in my presence.

I had no previous experience with another person's frailty but instinctively put my hand on Ben's back, alternately patting and rubbing. "It's okay. It's okay," I repeated. He had been so caring to me when I'd needed him a few months earlier. I was happy I was able to respond when he was in crisis.

The moment passed. I could feel a pleasant fullness in my chest. My sense was that I had done the right thing. Up until this point in my life, there had always been a parent, a teacher, or some superior witnessing my growth and development. I was used to looking elsewhere for approval, recognition, and love. This private moment was just between Ben and me, and I had to measure my own performance. With little experience at self-assessment, I thought I'd done okay.

We got in his VW bug and drove to the suburbs, the sun

rising as we rode the thirty-plus miles north to our destination. Once parked in the lot in front of the school, Ben went inside to fulfill his obligation. I remained in the car. I had picked up on his nervousness, and as the minutes and hours ticked by, I couldn't stop thinking about him being scrutinized by students, faculty, and administrators and wondered how he was doing, if he'd covered up his nervousness while giving his sample class, and whether he liked being there.

It was midmorning when he finally came back to the car. He was practically strutting as he yanked open the driver's side door. He put the key in the ignition, adjusted the rearview mirror, grabbing a glance at himself in it first, sat up straight against his seat, and stretched his arms out in front of him, hands firmly gripping the steering wheel.

"How'd it go?" I practically shouted with curiosity and excitement.

"Great. They loved me. Let's get back to the city," was all he said. And I didn't probe further, because I picked up his cue that there would be no more conversation on the subject. My father used to make a noise with his tongue, kind of a clicking sound; then he'd look down to signal his departure from connecting any further. Ben's absenting himself was more elusive. He simply stopped responding, and, because I feared being too parental, I didn't ask anything more.

I came to understand that his mother and father's well-meaning attention overwhelmed him to the point of his retreating. Anything resembling that curiosity from me was rapidly squelched. I learned to be very careful about how far to go. Ben liked an audience, so long as they stayed on their side of the curtain he'd rigged up.

I had to repeatedly remember that Ben didn't like a certain type of spotlight. After his audition, he had no need to relive his performance. The students' attention and administrative approval sufficed.

I would have wanted to give my companion a play-by-play of my success, but not Ben. We had different needs, which I didn't understand back then. I might have reacted differently if I'd had that insight.

I would have known that his reaction wasn't an evaluation of me or the job I was doing as his girlfriend. Today's Jane would have noticed his dismissal of the event, not taken it personally, and suggested we put on sports radio.

Shortly after his audition, Ben was offered the job. He spent his entire career at Brigham Woods, first as a teacher and later as chairman of the English department. He was a beloved faculty member and administrator there for thirty years. I was both proud and envious of his talent as a teacher and the love his students and colleagues had for him.

Each year, there was a special arts day at Ben's school where experts in a variety of creative disciplines shared their passion with the students. During his second year at Brigham Woods, Ben let the founders of the program know about my particular talent, Ukrainian Easter egg decoration, which I'd learned teaching art at West Hill. I was invited to offer a workshop there. I loved it! I gave several classes, received great admiration for my work, and made connections with faculty members and kids. When it came time to sign up to participate the next year or any year after that, Ben was vague about the details, and I missed one opportunity and then another, until I stopped asking.

Looking back, I have the distinct feeling that Ben didn't want me taking away any of his spotlight. I believe he wanted to keep certain things just for himself. Even the way he behaved with our kids showed that he wanted to be the star. On vacations, he'd wait until I'd gone to bed in our adjoining room before watching TV and entertaining them with his antics. They would never smother him or ask too many questions, so he must have felt completely safe in their company.

BEN MET MY family a few months before I was introduced to his. My sisters and brother embraced him immediately during a Sunday-afternoon visit to our home in White Plains. They saw his intelligence and wit, and they fell into easy conversation with him. I slept in my old bedroom that night, but Ben had to return to New York before supper.

During our family dinner, my mother sized up and dismissed my boyfriend in one sentence.

"He looks like a pickle-barrel salesman," she uttered, without glancing up, as she sliced her meatball in half with the edge of her fork. Long sideburns and granny glasses were the trend back then. He was not the image of what she'd had in mind for her daughter. She would have preferred trimmed hair, a clean shave, and a medical lab coat, even on a weekend. My eyes burned with tears, but I said nothing.

I sensed it was a more significant occasion when Ben invited me to meet his family in New Jersey. I had an idea about his father before we were introduced. Prior to going to New Jersey, I'd heard Ben talk to him on the phone one night while I kept him company as he sat bells.

When I arrived at the dorm's front desk, Ben had the phone receiver pressed to his ear. Slumped at an angle, his head leaning heavily onto his right hand, Ben acknowledged my entrance with a slight eye roll toward the receiver, then nodded and mumbled to the person on the other end, "Uh-huh, uh-huh."

In front of Ben was a notepad covered with his circular doodles. He lifted the pen-holding hand, cupped it over the receiver, and mouthed to me, "My father. He's drunk."

After he hung up, there was a pause as he continued to mark the pad. The loopy circles he'd sketched during their conversation were now cross-hatched with heavier strokes, the pen deeply engraved through to the sheets below.

As though coming to, he looked away from his drawing, then toward me. I'm not sure he actually saw me. When his eyes found their way back to the inked pad, he said, in a tone I'd not heard before, "He gets disgustingly mushy when he's had too much to drink. Tells me how much he loves me. I hate that." His mouth stretched downward into a sneer, and he murmured, "Ick."

My first thought was *He tells you he loves you?* At least his father could open up, even if it took some lubrication. I would have loved any expression of affection from my father. I remember little phone time with him. He would accept my Sunday-night collect calls from college and quickly hand the receiver to my mother. I envied Ben's relationship, the fact that he had a relationship, no matter what his father's state was. I never had the feeling that my father even had me on his mind.

But this focus seemed to annoy Ben. "When I was little, my father used to play ball with me in the backyard. He'd hit fungoes—you know, high pop-ups—that were easy for me to catch." I noticed Ben's shoulders relax and then heard a long exhalation. "He never missed a Little League game I was in. My mother, neither. I felt smothered." What I saw as great luck—his father's expression of love—he distrusted and regarded as a burden. The ways in which we are shown affection and attention as children shape our future relationships.

I had never heard of a fungo and tried to envision a father

and son playing in a yard. On the rare occasions that my father came outside, he stood near our swing set, arms folded across his chest, watching us. I don't have a memory of him pushing me higher or playing ball with my brother.

When I flash back to other performances in my life, it is my mother who is always there. Alone. I've never considered, until I wrote these words, how that might have been for her. It seemed normal at the time. How could my father have attended? He was a commuter. He'd get home too late for a back-to-school night, a dance recital, or an after-school assembly. I never expected that he'd be there. It never occurred to any of us that he could leave work early.

"Impossible!" he would have responded, if I'd ever asked him to take an earlier train. "I can't. I have to stay until six, when the store closes."

My mother relished her four kids' performances. I could spot her wide-eyed gaze from wherever she sat in the audience, her hair freshly coiffed by Miss May at the beauty parlor earlier in the day, her applause louder than the others'. She'd even, much to our embarrassment, shout, "Bravo!" if she was particularly moved, which she often was.

It was our achievements that were recognized and celebrated—A's on report cards, solos, curtain calls. That left the ordinary activities of my daily life largely ignored. I learned to anticipate neglect.

When Ben's glance didn't take me in the night of the observed phone call, after I'd arrived to keep him company, it was not an unfamiliar sensation. I'd grown accustomed to not being seen.

I FELT EXCITED to meet Ben's parents as we drove from Manhattan to his house in Fair Lawn, New Jersey for the first time. We'd been dating a few months at that point. I leaned toward him as we crossed the bridge that night.

"Nervous?"

He'd been quieter than usual on the car ride, tuning the radio dial to find a Mets game and not talking to me. I knew that meeting a boy's parents is a big deal but wasn't sure if Ben was feeling anything. He slid his hand across his hair from the crown to his forehead and cleared his throat.

"Nope."

His house was smaller than I expected, but on an attractive street with sidewalks and manicured lawns.

From the moment he ushered me in, I entered a limelight I'd never before experienced and became intoxicated by the attention of these strangers. Maybe Ben's quiet was his uneasiness at the anticipated scene, or his relief that he wouldn't be at its center. He already knew how doting his mother and father could be. But I felt bathed in the sea of warmth and affection they immediately bestowed on me.

At first glance, his parents looked different than I'd imagined. His mother, a head shorter than I, had tightly curled hair flecked with gray strands, unlike the teased coifs of the Westchester matrons I'd always known. She was stocky—not fat, but more filled out than average. Bob, his father, stood six feet tall, wore a thin cotton, short-sleeved shirt, and had a slight paunch. My first impression was that they were plain.

I soon saw beyond that superficial judgment. His mother, Bunny, treated me like a princess. "Did Ben mention to you that we're the Four B's? Bunny, Bob, Ben, and Billy!" she told me, as she escorted me up the stairs for a tour of the house. "Ben and I are the real B's in the family. Nicknames from Benjamin and Bernice. Bob and Billy are just derivatives of Robert and William. But we let them into the club," she said with a wink. I wondered briefly if being a "J" would diminish any of her love for me.

"This is where Bob sleeps," she said, as we arrived on the second floor. "He gets up a lot in the middle of the night and doesn't want to disturb me, so I sleep downstairs." I loved hearing her thoughts and the intimacy her sharing them created. Their sleeping arrangement made sense to me until I mentioned the layout to my mother when I called her to debrief my visit.

"What? Separate bedrooms? That's not good, Jane," she declared. "Something's not right there."

"I don't think so, Mom. They seem very loving. He lights her cigarettes, pulls her chair out for her at the table, and opens the car door. I'm impressed with what a gentleman he is."

"Nonsense! It's a cover-up. Mark my words."

My father rarely performed those gestures for my mother. Maybe she was jealous or angry that I might be comparing Ben's family to ours. She never said that. But she planted a seed in my mind that I would have preferred left untilled.

With two grown sons, Bunny had never gotten to dote on a girl. I was the first. Maybe even the first girl Ben had ever brought home. He was unclear when I asked him if that was so, and I didn't press the matter.

In a short amount of time, the Pollaks made me feel cherished, special, and seen. I hadn't had to achieve anything other than attracting their son's heart, I believed.

BEN NEVER WENT to my father to ask for my hand in marriage. After the Wickersham incident, when we agreed that we should get married and began talking about where we might live and how many children we wanted to have, we shared our news with my parents, announced our intention for a small event, and circumvented the drama we'd witnessed so recently.

"I don't want a big wedding," Ben said, as we walked along Broadway late one night, heading back to my apartment. We stopped at the corner newsstand to pick up the *Times*. If it was past 11:00 p.m., you could get all the sections of the Sunday paper late Saturday. Ben riffled through the thick pile to make sure everything we wanted was there—sports, arts, the magazine. He handed the guy a dollar and got two quarters back.

"Neither do I," I said, taking the magazine section out of the pile. I opened to the crossword page to check whether it was going to be hard or easy.

"Let's elope," he said, as I unlocked my apartment door with the key.

"That's fine with me," I replied, excited at the fantasy of his throwing pebbles at the second-story window of my parents' home in White Plains to wake me up, climbing up a ladder on the side of the house, and carrying me off into the darkness. "But I have no idea how you do that. If that's what you want, tell me my part, and I'll play it. The only way I know how to get married is to ask my mother to plan it for me."

Although Ben said he preferred eloping, he took no steps in that direction. Eloping would have been okay with me. I couldn't envision myself walking down our synagogue's aisle, following a half dozen gowned attendants.

I knew that Ben hated having that kind of spotlight on him. Being in front of a classroom of adoring students was fine. He had earned that right. Simply being prized as the groom may have felt invasive to him, though he wouldn't have said that and maybe didn't actually know it.

My father even offered an impetus. He repeatedly told us

three girls, knowing what weddings cost, "If any of you are interested, I'll give you five thousand dollars and a ladder." But no scheme was hatched.

I could kill two birds with one stone—please Ben by not having a spectacle of a wedding and annoy my mother by not allowing her to plan a second extravaganza. Since Ben didn't seize the opportunity to arrange our elopement, I went with the default of letting Mom do the work. If I couldn't make them both happy, this time I chose my mother. I cringe now at that self-imposed dilemma. Making myself happy wasn't even on the list.

What Ben lacked in planning skills, his mother compensated for. Two months before our wedding, Bunny mobilized, quietly but strategically, to make sure our household would be properly established. She hosted a shower for me, inviting only New Jersey friends from her bridge and golf clubs. She purchased several items from our bridal registry so we'd have the tableware we'd need. Additionally, she arranged a day trip for us to Long Island, where a relative owned a linen shop.

"What do you like?" she asked me, gesturing toward shelves full of colorful towels and bedsheets and indicating with a nod that I was free to choose. I'd never been given that sweep of permission before. "You'll need three sets of each pattern," she instructed. "One on the bed, one in the linen closet, and one in the laundry." I was grateful for a formula.

She picked up the entire tab and then bought several additional items off the Bloomingdale's registry I'd filled out. Ben's parents also bought each of us a Volkswagen. I felt taken care of, tended to, and loved. Treated in a way I had not known before. I never questioned his family's financial status again. I did begin to wonder, though, if there was something I needed to do or give in return.

I was excited to share his mother's largesse when he arrived at my apartment after his day of teaching. "Ben, let me show you what your mother helped me pick out," I said, pointing to the tall pile of folded towels and sheets on my desk.

"Maybe later," he said. "I'm tired." He knew how generous his parents could be. Although it wasn't stated, I think his disinterest stemmed from an unspoken annoyance about having been over-given to. Something unnamed might be required of him.

I had spent a day with his mother picking out bedding and towels for our new home and thought it warranted a glance or acknowledgment. I believe I wanted the same love and approval from him that his mother dished out. The truth was, I had attracted a partner who couldn't give that to me. I also know that I wouldn't have been prepared to receive it even if he provided it.

Intimacy once removed was delicious. Too close, and it felt like a burden.

The next day, I put the goods back into the shopping bags and stored them on the floor between my desk and the wall. I'm certain I ate my way through any offended feelings I might have had that day. If I couldn't yet speak up, I could always eat up.

I KNEW I wanted to get married in a Mexican wedding gown. As a subscriber to *Seventeen* and *Glamour* magazines, I kept up with what was fashionable. Coming from a family in retail, I cared about what I wore and knew where to find it.

I went to Fred Leighton, a small shop in Greenwich Village. He was, in 1972, what Vera Wang is to brides today—the go-to designer for wedding apparel.

I spent an hour trying on a dozen different styles. There was a platform outside my dressing room door. A bride-to-be could stand on it, see her entire reflection in the three-way mirror, and complete the ensemble with sample shoes the store provided.

I wanted to dazzle Ben, something I came to understand was not possible in our relationship, though not until our marriage ended.

My saleslady declared, "That's the one!" when I walked out of the dressing room in my favorite. It was fitted on top; had a wide sash, a square neckline, and long sleeves that gathered at the wrists and draped over my hands in graceful folds; and fell to the floor in rows of pin-tuck cotton alternating with crocheted lace insets. More than the flattering figure it gave me, my beaming smile must've assured her I'd take it.

It was $125, and I felt like a happy, hippie Princess Grace wearing it. I'd made my selection and had the woman in black wrap it up for me. I was proud of myself for taking this step on my own and felt the sun beam down on me as I emerged from the store. The praise and attention of paid strangers—teachers, saleswomen, camp counselors—often substituted for what I really wanted: my mother's and then Ben's loving reflection of me.

Chapter Five

The rabbi from my synagogue married us. Our Jewish service was a ten-minute ceremony which concluded with Ben stomping on a napkin-wrapped flashbulb—the traditional breaking of the glass—and a hearty round of *mazel tov* from the assembled.

Mom had set a flower-laden table in our dining room and hired a staff of two to serve the twelve of us a menu she'd chosen and I'd approved. I'm sure there were toasts, clinked glasses commanding kisses, but nothing stands out from that night, other than that it was pouring rain and I was concerned about my hair frizzing.

Ben and I spent the night at the White Plains Hotel, whose guests were more often businessmen than newlyweds. Our bridal suite was suitable but hardly lovey-dovey. Besides, we were amateurs in that department.

Our real weeklong honeymoon to Puerto Rico was postponed until February, when we both had a winter break. Because my faculty orientation at my new teaching job was the

Monday after our nuptials, we drove on Sunday morning from the hotel to our apartment in Stamford, where I proceeded to lie sobbing on the pullout couch we would sleep on until our bed arrived.

"What's wrong?" Ben asked.

"I don't know," I wailed. "Maybe it's that we got married and moved and I'm starting a new job all in the same week. I can't explain it," although I just had. I didn't know what was wrong, and I didn't have the tools to decipher my upset. Now married, I still felt alone, but I couldn't say those words. I'd never known what it was like not to feel alone. Maybe I'd hoped that marriage would magically relieve that inner hunger.

THE SHOCK OF all the changes in my life subsided. Those early years of marriage felt effortless and fun. We were a young, working couple with little responsibility other than to our jobs, to which we were both devoted. We ate out most nights, never argued, and played together. There are photos of us as a smiling couple clapping tennis rackets over the net at our club, toasting each other by the pool on Paradise Island, and celebrating Passover with my family in White Plains. Every Friday after the school week ended, Ben and I played a set or two of singles tennis at Stamford Indoor Racquet Club, and then came home to relax and watch mindless TV, like *Bowling for Dollars*. Ben would get up to turn off the TV set and entertain me by standing erect, with his arms flat against his sides, and jumping sideways across our bedroom until I made him stop because I was laughing so hard.

In February of that school year, we went on our prescheduled honeymoon to Puerto Rico. We had just bought a set of soft-sided luggage, which our airport limo driver commented on. "I'll be able to recognize you at the airport when I come back next week to pick you up. Those bright blue bags will make it easy." Ben and I cracked up. We both knew we had no idea how to appear as grown-ups. Being called out on our less-than-adult choices made us giddy.

We got into San Juan late the first night. We had never traveled together before this trip. You learn a lot about a person when you go on a journey. We both liked to be punctual, so we gave ourselves plenty of time to get from our place in Stamford to the airport in New York City. So far, so good. I noticed Ben clutching the armrest between us as we took off and landed. I was not a comfortable flyer back then, either. But he was more anxious than I.

Leaving the airport after landing in Puerto Rico, we found the taxi line, which was bustling. I pictured myself standing with our royal-blue luggage while Ben hailed a cab, and then fetched me and our pieces, tucking them into the car's trunk in even rows. The way Ozzie Nelson would have.

That didn't happen. Instead, I watched as he joined the crowd waiting for cabs. He raised his right arm slightly, opened his hand in a partial wave, lowered it as cab after cab passed by, and then lifted it once again, to no avail. After fifteen minutes of trying, he came back to me and the bags and said, "Let's just stand here until the crowd thins out. I'm not doing this. It's embarrassing."

Something shifted inside my body. My cheeks and neck reddened, and my heart tripped downward in my chest. "Okay," I lied. Both my parents were native New Yorkers and knew how to aggressively get the attention of a driver. I must've thought everyone was born with this skill, though I surely wasn't. Seeing Ben withdraw from this challenge scared me.

Who was going to take care of me now? Wasn't that the

job of the person who said he loved you? I globalized disappointments like these. They helped me be the passive sufferer time and again.

I didn't know it then, but the mythology I'd written in my mind was being dismantled. It would take years of therapy, self-help books, and twelve-step recovery to learn the answer to the first question: Who's going to take care of me is *me*. The answer to the second question is *no*. No other human, after age eighteen, needs to caretake another. Others, spouses especially, will love us and care about us but not take care *of* us.

Some of the deepest, most touching love I've experienced has come from people I least expected it from. I was nearly two decades shy of that awareness.

Ben picked up on my expression, which must have telegraphed a trace of disillusionment. We had not argued at all during our first six months of marriage. We had rarely even had a stressful situation to test our ability in conflict. Life was a seeming parade of honest work at our jobs and fun at home. Here we were now in a foreign country where neither of us knew how to manage as tourists, and I was unable to accept Ben's not knowing.

As we finally strapped on our seat belts in the backseat of the cab that night, Ben said, "If you were expecting something different, that's not who I am." He had read the twisted expression on my face and told me what was true for him. At least he knew what he was capable of and admitted it. I had no idea who I was back then. I hated everything about that moment. Neither "serenity" nor "acceptance" was in my vocabulary.

Between piña coladas, tennis games, and swimming in the tennis racket-shaped pool at the Racquet Club Hotel, I put the airport upset aside as the enjoyment of our vacation increased. We spent a couple of evenings at a nearby casino, joining a dressed-up crowd, playing at the dollar tables, and sipping our umbrella-rimmed drinks. We both noticed and imitated the dealer's pronunciation and repetition of the word "insurance" whenever he dealt himself an ace. It sounded like *in-shuuu-raaaance* with a French accent, the *r* being swallowed as it was spoken. It became a running joke throughout our marriage whenever the mention of a guarantee came up. "Insurance?" we'd ask the other, meaning, *Do you want to take a chance on this?*

On our final night in Puerto Rico, I'd hoped for a leisurely dinner and time in our room afterward, for passion. But after we'd eaten, Ben asked, "Do you mind if I try my luck one more time at the casino?" I didn't think he should be asking me that question, but since he did, I guessed I should say yes.

# Chapter Six

*B*en and I wanted to start our family when I turned thirty, but Mother Nature had another plan. I became pregnant at twenty-five, midway through my second year of teaching at West Hill High School. This time it made sense to bring a child into the world, when a couple of years earlier it hadn't.

The chairman of the art department stopped by my classroom at the end of a school day in early spring 1974, just as he had done the previous year. "Can we expect you back in the fall?" he asked, clipboard in hand, ready to make the designated tick to let the administration know if this faculty member would continue on the payroll.

I was cleaning up the hooked-rug project my students were working on. There were strands of colored wool on several desks, fuzz balls on the floor, and a stack of half-hooked canvases in a pile on the windowsill. Even though this wasn't a messy activity, like papier-mâché, I'd begun wearing a smock to school every day to conceal my expanding waistline. I wasn't yet ready to announce my pregnancy at work.

"As a matter of fact," I began, "I'm expecting in August. I'd like to take a six-month leave, so I will *not* be back this coming September."

His eyebrows lifted slightly. He penciled a checkmark on the sheet of paper and extended his right hand toward me for a congratulatory shake.

"Best wishes," he said. I had the feeling he was more concerned about filling an unexpected vacancy in his staff than about absorbing my momentous news.

At home, it was an exciting time for us. Lying in bed at night, Ben and I tossed around potential baby names.

"I like Sarah for a girl," I said, to kick off the discussion.

"No! I have an aunt Sarah who was awful to my father. How about Molly?"

"I love Molly, but Molly Pollak?" I asked. Then we'd go through a round of increasingly silly combinations and end up laughing. These were the times when I felt closest to Ben, especially when I made him laugh. I wanted to please him, make him happy. During this naming game, I could relax for a minute. Ultimately, we chose Lucy as our girl's name.

The grandparents-to-be on both sides were equally excited. This birth would provide each of the four of them with their first grandchild. Bob, Bunny, and my father were all happy for this offspring to call them Grandma and Grandpa. Only my mother objected, thinking it made her sound old. She preferred Nana, which we went with.

I could get away with wearing pants with the zipper open under my smock for just so long. By my fourth month, I needed a new wardrobe. My mother offered to take me shopping for maternity clothes.

In the dressing room, she scanned my expanding, underwear-clad body and asked, "How much weight have you gained,

Jane? You look bigger than four months. Susan is due about the same time as you, right?" she asked, referencing my cousin, whose delivery date was within days of mine. "She's carrying beautifully small," she commented, with a disapproving wag of her head. My mother had always feared that her daughters would get fat and become unattractive. In pregnancy, I'd thought I'd be spared being assessed in that way.

"Seven pounds last month," I said.

"That's too much! Your breasts are enormous. It looks like you're carrying your pregnancy up there," she said, pointing at my chest. "You'll get stretch marks if you continue to let yourself go like that."

I blinked hard and bit down till my jaw hurt. I wished she'd told me I looked radiant and lovely, not heavy and ignorant of the consequences of weight gain. Shopping in public minimized her criticism. Also, maternity clothes are intentionally forgiving. Her words still stung.

I gathered the outfits we'd chosen to take to the checkout counter. While we walked to the front of the store to pay, Mom said offhandedly, "Oh, remember to give me the name of your obstetrician before we leave. I want to be sure you have the top man."

I often felt a twisting sensation in my stomach at the same time my mother was providing something generous. Before she completed an act of kindness, she'd extract something I was reluctant to hand over.

"Did you know that your mother called the hospital to find out who the chief of obstetrics was?" Dr. Banfield, my ob-gyn asked, while holding my chart during my next appointment. He was in his fifties, graying at the temples and handsome in his white coat and horn-rimmed glasses.

"She does stuff like that" was the only defense I could offer.

I was unaware that I could say no to her request. The term "boundaries" had not yet entered my vocabulary. I knew I didn't like her interfering in my life but didn't know then that I had a choice of whether to respond to her question or not. Who would have taught me that skill?

It wasn't until several years later that I heard Wayne Dyer say, "If you can't say no to the person, you have to say no to the relationship." I was an obedient and dutiful daughter. Saying no would have felt like a transgression when I was twenty-five.

During a subsequent visit with Dr. Banfield, he asked if I had any questions. After I'd reviewed the pro forma ones about heartburn and frequency of urination, I ventured a more personal one, hoping for some paternal wisdom.

"Is it typical for mothers of pregnant daughters to be mean to them? My mother berates everything I'm doing—what I'm eating, how quickly I'm gaining weight, whether it's okay for me to be playing tennis."

He glanced at the wall clock as he snapped on a latex glove for my internal. Even though he was medically equipped to access the most intimate parts of my body, he may not have had the training, experience, or desire to answer questions about emotional intimacy. He shook his head, shrugged slightly, and demurred.

I was desperate for outside validation—*Your mother is overstepping! This is most unusual and inappropriate!*—and hoped, wrongly, this Father-knows-best look-alike would provide the consolation and comfort I sought. That he would stand up for me when I couldn't.

As most women did in the mid-'70s, I attended each prenatal appointment by myself. It wouldn't have occurred to me to ask Ben to come along. As a pregnant woman, I had become part of a vast, nonexclusive sorority that had a singular entrance requirement. We mothers-to-be were easily identified and brought into the circle. I was getting a sliver of what it must feel like to be a part of something. I hadn't felt a part of my family, and I didn't feel a part of my marriage. I might have told you I was happy, but I hadn't experienced real happiness yet.

My pregnancy was the first time I fully embraced membership in any association. I began reading every book on the shelf about childbearing and motherhood. Unlike today's profusion of online and mega-bookstore literature on what to expect when you're expecting, there were only a handful of titles on the shelf, one shelf, in 1974. I read them all.

I learned that I wanted to have an unmedicated—this was now labeled "natural"—birth experience, and that I would breastfeed. Although I immersed myself in the literature, I could advance only one chapter to find out how my insides were shifting to accommodate the growing fetus. Midway to term, I was not ready to find out about the episiotomy, the stitches sewn in a woman's perineum after her baby is delivered. I knew I would be more open to that information when the time came, but I protected myself by minimizing the flow and ingesting it in bite-size bits. It was too scary.

Throughout my life, I have followed this pattern, taking in only as much information as I can handle in the moment. It's a form of self-preservation. I would not allow anyone to think my marriage was anything less than perfect, especially me, as we traveled together through our lives. Maintaining that deceit, chapter after chapter, year after year, kept me in it all that time. Emotionally, my insides shifted around my fears and resentments.

No need to start worrying now about something inescapable but not present. This mindset made adapting to the "one day at a time" mantra of recovery a natural for me several years later.

On my way out of a doctor's appointment one afternoon mid-pregnancy, I picked up two pamphlets, one about Lamaze training and the second about breastfeeding, to find out what support was available locally on those subjects.

La Leche League (LLL), an organization devoted to helping mothers learn about breastfeeding, offered a monthly series of topics that covered the basics of the mother-infant relationship. New mothers attended to meet and bond with other women. It was recommended that mothers-to-be also attend before giving birth so that they could become familiar with this natural process.

The first meeting I went to was on a weeknight in May, when I was in my sixth month. It was at a member's apartment in Stamford, close to my own. There were a dozen women in attendance, most of them with infants and a few with older babies. I felt like I was in a foreign country. I had never seen live nursing and had no idea how it worked. That may sound unbelievable, but, other than an image in *The Family of Man* or an issue of *National Geographic*, nursing mothers were not prominent subject matter in the mid-'70s. I had no relatives with babies and no memory of my mother's ever having breastfed my brother, even though I was seven when he arrived.

"I nursed all of you," my mother told us when we were younger, but I hadn't been interested in the details then. Now I was hungry for information.

"For how long?" I asked, only after I'd begun breastfeeding Lucy. I had already made my decision, when my mother was still my role model, to suckle my babies, based on the fact that I wanted to be like her and do what she did.

"I nursed each of you on the table," she responded. A delivery-room nurse must have held each of us to her breast to encourage lactation immediately after delivery, which helps the uterus contract and get back its original shape. After that, she received an injection to dry up her milk, a common occurrence post-World War II. She may have offered her breast once more to relieve the accumulation. But I would never have claimed I was breastfed if I'd known the brevity of the experience.

I became a regular at the La Leche League meetings to better understand the nursing relationship. My role at these sessions was that of the quiet observer, particularly while I was still pregnant. I felt I had nothing to contribute, so I was mostly silent. I waited to be asked if newcomers had any questions. The good-girl, rule-follower thing continued to play out in this group setting. But it mattered more to me now than ever before. It was here that I began the journey of learning who I was. It started with understanding my own pregnant body and how it was created to nurture my offspring.

I didn't know anything, including in what position to hold the baby to the breast, or how often to alternate sides. Seeing women so nonchalant about exposing their intimate anatomy surprised me. They appeared comfortable lifting their blouses, unfastening the flap of a nursing bra, and allowing anyone present to see their exposed nipples.

These young mothers would become leading players in this act of my life. Rosalea, still a dear friend today, forty-plus years later, was the La Leche League leader presiding over that first meeting. Seven years older than I, she carried a vast knowledge of the mother-child relationship, which she generously shared with those of us in attendance. A tall, confident mother of a three-year-old son and four-year-old daughter, Rosalea was someone I looked to for advice and comfort. She understood about invasive grandmothers and offered a generous ear without commenting on or criticizing my mother's behavior.

An aristocratic-looking, Prince Valiant-coiffed woman sat on the floor, leaning against an upholstered chair behind her. This was not someone I would have encountered in any other area of my life. She supported her newborn's head by stacking cushions under her arm to bring his tiny face to breast level. "I believe that breastfeeding is the best thing I can do for Allistair," she said during her turn to talk. Allistair? *Who would name a baby* Allistair? I had so much judgment but was willing to learn from all of the women who had walked this path ahead of me. I never saw her and Allistair again. I would have remembered.

I realized that my choice to breastfeed crossed socioeconomic classes and that my new teachers might come from unexpected backgrounds. As my membership in La Leche League lengthened, I found new friends and role models.

Women were being encouraged to have their voices acknowledged and reinforced regarding their birth experiences. The fact that we were even asking questions and making requests of our physicians was unexpected and often unwelcomed. My doctor was in practice during the pubescence of women in society.

Some physicians became more rigid. Those names circulated fast, even without the benefit of the Internet. At one monthly La Leche meeting, Lynn, a model-height, slim blonde with a perfectly centered basketball of a belly, spoke up about a recent checkup. She was an assertive, creative intellectual, dressed in a long, gray-and-black-striped jersey dress that accentuated, rather than hid, her protruding midsection. She was someone I would have admired and envied from a distance, but our shared nursing challenges and triumphs gave us common ground. Lynn explained that she had admonished her ob-gyn on a recent visit, before she adjusted her legs in the stirrups on his table, "Word on the street says that you give rough internals. That can stop with me."

I had never heard a woman speak to a man in this way. Not my mother to my father—my most intimate role model—nor any others that I could think of. Lynn spoke assertively but with humor, stating her case. And not just to a mere mortal but to a professional, a doctor. That made her story more impressive to me.

It took a therapist's homework assignment, five years into our marriage, to ask Ben, "Will you please let me finish my sentences?" That may have been the first time I ever specifically asked any man for consideration. You may be shaking your head in bewilderment, but that's how remedial I needed to get.

Ben's response was not an immediate "Oh, of course, sorry!" Rather, he told me that he didn't want to have to be so careful around conversations and that this could make him tiptoe around how we spoke to each other.

I questioned myself. Was I being too demanding? Should I retract my appeal so he wouldn't feel uncomfortable talking to me in the future? After that day, he did wait until I finished my sentences, but in my heart it felt like a battle, not a simple petition.

We LLL-ers all laughed at Lynn's story and wanted to know that physician's name and whether he had changed his ways. I wanted her confidence and self-assurance. If I couldn't have it, I could imitate it.

Similarly, the "good" doctors who accommodated the new demands of informed women saw their practices blossom.

Lynn delivered a Down syndrome baby a few weeks later. At future LLL meetings, we watched her nurture that tiny little girl, put her on a special nutritional regimen, and research the best ways to help her offspring develop and thrive. Although grieving the absence of a "normal" child, Lynn dove into her role as a special-needs mother, and I witnessed grace in action, not something I would have been exposed to at such an intimate level except by virtue of La Leche.

I wondered how I would have turned out if I'd been mothered like that child.

By late June of my pregnancy, I was referred to a Lamaze instructor who educated expectant mothers and their husbands in a series of classes starting six weeks before the due date. Back then, you would not hear a proud father-to-be declaring, "*We're* pregnant." Men's participation in the birth experience was increasing but was not yet like today, where it's all but assumed that the couple will share every experience, from pre-natal checkups to registering together at Buy Buy Baby to co-hosting a gender-reveal party.

The year our daughter was born, there were no same-sex couples we knew of, no single moms-to-be. Everyone in our Lamaze class looked like us. I requested that Ben read *Thank You, Dr. Lamaze*, a slim volume, in preparation for our classes. I was pleased that he did but wasn't sure if he was joking or not when he said, "I understood most of it. But tell me: What's a uterus, and what's a placenta?" I burst out laughing. I guess if you're not going through it yourself, those words would be mysterious. Still, I appreciated the supportive action.

I attended the first July training session without Ben because he'd gotten sun poisoning and was suffering from a list of symptoms, including blistering, chills, and nausea, the night of that class. Even though everyone else was part of a couple that night, I didn't mind showing up alone because I wanted to hear every word about this next stage of my pregnancy and the all-important birth experience.

By the next week, Ben had recovered and joined me. We

sat next to each other on the floor and, along with the other couples, rehearsed the different postures for labor and delivery and practiced breath techniques and sequences that would ease labor.

Our instructor showed us diagrams of a baby in utero, projected movies of childbirth onto a blank wall in her home, and instructed us on how to have conversations with the professionals who would help us through the birth process. She encouraged us to consult our doctor to review our choices. For instance, she recommended against putting silver nitrate, a preventive measure against venereal disease, into the newborn's eyes, explaining that it interferes with the earliest bonding.

"Are you certain you'd want the responsibility of a blind child on your conscience if you're not a thousand percent sure?" was my doctor's response when I mentioned that I was instructed to withhold that procedure. Going to a doctor with a list of desires like these was like climbing Mt. Everest in sneakers—I had no idea how to even begin approaching base camp. I bumbled my way through the first half of my list of "demands," then crumpled it up after his reply.

I was being swept up in this movement as a new mother and guided by the women I met in my Lamaze classes and in La Leche League. We had the opportunity to make choices that were different from my mother's and those of her generation. In this process, I was becoming a woman with my own opinions and ideas about what was right for this new stage of my life.

On the more sensible heels of the women's-lib movement, consciousness-raising groups, and the aftermath of the Vietnam War and Watergate, old bastions of authority were being questioned every day. Hippies and yippies raised their voices. There were examples of the world as we had always known it shifting on its axis: our country losing a war, Watergate, and a president leaving office. It was a different time. Playing the role of the quiet, don't-make-waves woman was losing its appeal. Women like me were being pushed to the rear by others of my gender who had discovered their voices and were not afraid to use them. Or maybe I was attracted to Helen Reddy's message, "I am woman, hear me roar!" and no longer wanted to be associated with the good girls waiting to be called on.

If I wanted to be seen and known in this new age, I would have to "use my words" even before I'd heard my kids' nursery school teachers recite that phrase in the late '70s. I had never learned how to speak up for myself. Beginning to do that at twenty-six was a daunting prospect for a Lost Child who'd been rewarded, albeit sparingly, for being quiet.

I had always kept a low profile politically, but aspects of the women's movement seeped into my awareness regardless. I wasn't going to run for office, but I eagerly corrected anyone who referred to females over eighteen as anything but women. I cringed at the word "girls" and noticed how entrenched it had become in our society to minimize my gender. I got angry when I heard the term "infantile uterus" applied to a woman's body part. Inch by inch, my mindfulness was raised. My front line was motherhood.

Between my fullest expression of who I was becoming and me was Ben. What was happening to the obedient, submissive woman he had married and, perhaps, preferred?

I didn't have to argue against many of the procedures other women had warned me about. I was a somewhat young primipara, a twenty-six-year-old woman giving birth for the first time, which meant that I wouldn't require the multitude of tests older primips needed, like amniocentesis or ultrasound.

The pregnant women and new mothers I met were reporting back from their medical fronts that when they made the request and got the treatment they wished for, they felt better and their delivery went better. At our final Lamaze class, a yuppie couple who'd "graduated" from our instructor's previous group gave us expectant parents details of their successful labor and birth experiences. Daniel, whom I could imagine in a three-piece suit, commuting to Wall Street, had cut the umbilical cord, and Susan, a lawyer by day, had nursed on the delivery-room table, they told us, beaming. That these brave men and women were living out my dream provided hope and role models. Mere mortals, here in my presence, told of risks I hadn't even dreamed were possible. I trusted their experience and wanted to be like them. I had a long and arduous road ahead of me, not only in my own labor and delivery, but also in trying to get Ben to see the wisdom in a path I wanted to embrace.

When our Lamaze training was complete, and with a few insights learned from attending La Leche League, we were ready for the birth process to begin. My due date was August 25, but my labor didn't start until nearly two weeks after that.

Ben offered consistent support and coaching during my thirteen-hour ordeal, which began when my water broke at home the morning of September 5. He called the doctor when the contractions were the right number of minutes apart, and we were instructed to head to the hospital. Ben had hoped to speed me there, ignoring red lights and dodging other cars, but we left the apartment before dawn, and there was no traffic en route to Stamford Hospital.

In the labor room, Ben fed me ice chips, pressed a cool compress to my forehead, and patted my back when I threw up bile. He reminded me of what breath sequence to use and urged me to look at the photos we'd been instructed to pack, to take my mind off the pain. Instead, I stared at the clock on the wall, exactly what our instructor had told us not to do, where I watched the second hand crawl around the Roman numerals, letting me know exactly how long the contraction lasted. Though he teased me about this, I'm not sure I ever gave Ben enough credit for his support during that painful process. I wanted all the glory, but he was right there with me. Did I have the partner I wished for? Would I have been happier with a Daniel? I doubt it. Ben was exactly who I needed to be with then for everything else that would come after.

When it was time to move into delivery, Ben left the labor room to put on scrubs. Two nurses came in to transfer me. I took offense when I heard one complain, "Why do I always get the big Guernsey?" I thought she was commenting on how gigantic I felt and was referring to me as a cow. I learned later that she was talking about the transport used to move hospital patients—the gurney. The one in this particular labor room was old, outdated, and strenuous to push. I laugh now with understanding affection for my ultrasensitivity then.

The only smile I remember during the entire labor and delivery process was when I saw Ben march in to join me in the delivery room, wearing his green uniform and the matching head covering they made him put on to come into the sterile area. Ben confessed that he'd have been just as happy sitting in the waiting room as our fathers had been in the '40s, anticipating news of the baby's arrival and handing out cigars. I was grateful he'd agreed to participate.

"What're you laughing at?" he joked, as he deliberately shuffled toward me, his shoes covered with a pair of elasticized, light green paper booties. He grinned in partnership. Here were the two of us, who considered ourselves sophisticated and above it all, in embarrassingly compromised states, for the sake of this little person about to enter our lives. We were both onboard the same vessel and sailing off into the same sunset.

At 4:14 p.m. on September 5, 1974, our beautiful baby girl, Lucy, was born. The delivery-room staff weighed and measured her, cleaned her up, and laid her on my chest. When we were assembled as a family for the first time, Ben rested his head next to mine to take in our brand-new offspring and said to me, "You were amazing!" I was exhausted but content.

When Lucy and I were alone that evening, staring into each other's eyes in my hospital room, I whispered to her, "I know you're going to change my life, but I don't know how."

On that day, I had fulfilled my mother's list. *This must be happiness.* I had done it all right, according to the Talmud of Mom.

Having a baby, though, was a distraction from my marriage. An infant's needs, by all counts, trump an adult's. My constant attention and devotion to our infant began a long, slow process of eroding the foundation of our marriage. Where was the rule about that?

ALTHOUGH I'D BEEN to La Leche League meetings in the four months before I delivered, it was news to me that a baby may want the breast for hours at a time. My uninformed, made-up thought was that babies latch on for ten minutes per side, then nap for a couple of hours. That never happened. It was more like twenty to thirty minutes on one side; snooze, snooze, snooze; play for a while; twenty to thirty minutes on the other side; fuss, fuss, diaper change; fuss, fuss, nurse again and again. No one, other than the supportive women in my new sorority, understood.

"You're nursing her *again?*" my mother asked, incredulous.

"I think you like it more than she does." I never told my mother that her statement hurt my feelings. I was defensive and insecure. She wouldn't read any of the literature I offered her and wouldn't take my word for it that what I was doing was normal.

Ben picked up on her cues. He never doubted me in front of company, but after a particularly challenging day he might ask, "Do you think a supplemental bottle would do the trick?" He wanted only for Lucy to be happy and for me to have some relief. It would have been more helpful to hear, "This must be hard, but I believe in you and know you're doing the best thing for Lucy." I don't know if any of my LLL friends heard those words I yearned for.

I can see how unrealistic this wish was. I had no perspective then on my husband's role as a father. How could I expect that objectivity from him? We were two unskilled young adults in charge of a new human being who, rightfully, had her own, infantile agenda.

I read that mothers should trust their instincts. When Lucy wanted to be attached to me more frequently than Dr. Spock recommended, I sensed that it was the right thing for her. It was reinforcing to hear my new friends say, "I felt that way, too. I kept her in my arms the entire day."

I looked forward my La Leche meetings more and more, not only to educate me in better caring for my daughter, but also to support me as a new mother. I knew little about taking care of an infant and less about taking care of myself after the massive changes that had occurred in my body. The mornings we breastfeeding moms gathered were highlights on my empty calendar.

During any given session, the women and their babies sat on chairs or the carpeted floor while toddlers roamed the room, trying out push toys, occasionally climbing onto their mother's lap for a quick sip from her breast. At first I was shocked to see an eighteen-month-old still nursing, but after a few months of exposure, it became normal and comfortable. We were taught that babies will wean themselves when they're ready, if you allow them to. I could trust my eyes and heart that these children and their mothers were thriving.

I believed it was my job, my responsibility, to convert Ben to this approach. If he saw and heard what I was witnessing, surely he'd be convinced of its rightness for our daughter and stand behind and encourage me.

At each meeting, we addressed the topic of the month—bringing the baby home after birth, adding solid foods or weaning, for instance—and then had an open discussion. I learned the most from these conversations—ways to cure your baby's ear infection (a peeled bulb of garlic works miraculously!), how to deal with a cranky older sibling, how to soothe a husband's sex drive when you don't want to be touched any more that day. It wasn't like school, where answers are given to impress a teacher in charge. Here was genuine, clear, and honest sharing among peers. I never wanted to succeed at any subject matter as much as I did at being a new mother.

Susan, the yuppie woman who had shared her birth experience during my final Lamaze class, was a regular at my LLL meetings. One winter morning, she related an incident that happened in her gynecologist's office. "During my exam, I told him that I'd discovered a small lump on the wall of my vagina," she said, surprising me with her candor. It felt like reading three chapters ahead in a book I had not yet opened. "I was concerned about it, and asked if he would give me his opinion. You know what he said to me? He said, 'What were you doing with your hands down there?'"

The other women gasped at his response, but I was wondering the same thing myself. I had not yet read *Our Bodies, Ourselves*, a volume that would have better prepared me for Susan's self-assurance. I had never touched myself or even felt around my female parts. It wasn't until I was expecting my son a few years later that Mary, the midwife overseeing my pregnancy, invited me to have a look "down there" during one of my prenatal appointments.

I had little curiosity about my body and wondered what kind of permissive family this new acquaintance had grown up in. Rather than acknowledge my own naïveté, I had judged what I deemed her sexual boldness. In order to continue to feel good about myself, I had established my own code of ethics, in which my conduct was at the top.

Ben and I were rank beginners sexually, and I was intimidated by anyone who threatened my thin grasp of carnal knowledge. My ears were open, but my narrow mind was hardly ajar.

"Would you like to see your vulva?" my nurse-midwife inquired.

"How would I do that?" I asked, as I lay on my back, legs bent, my feet in stirrups. If it required too much energy, I might pass.

"Here," she said, and offered me a long-handled mirror. I raised myself up on my elbow, positioned the mirror between my legs with her assistance, and glanced at this body part.

I don't know what I was expecting to see—a dark, crumpled pile of tissue or something vaguely unpleasant. Instead, I saw a smooth, glistening pink area that was quite beautiful.

"This is your vulva, and if your eyes go more deeply, where the speculum is," she said, "you can see your cervix. Look, see! Right there?" she said pointing with her forefinger in the direction I should look.

"Wow!" was all I could say.

Slowly, with the guidance of these knowledgeable instructors, I began to stretch my mind and accept concepts that were new to me but that felt true and right.

The universe inside me whispered, *You are a fertile, feminine being.* Taking ownership of my body, viewing my own anatomy, seeded my curiosity. I delved into *Our Bodies, Ourselves* and began to read about masturbating and the female orgasm. I followed my friend's example of feeling inside myself. At age twenty-nine, I gave myself my first orgasm.

You do the math. I must have felt some unexpressed frustration at Ben in the six years between when I lost my virginity and when I started a path to my own sexual fulfillment. This was ten years before *When Harry Met Sally* hit the big screens, but the concept of faking orgasm was not new to me. I was no Meg Ryan, but Ben bought my act.

I CALLED ROSALEA, my La Leche leader, to find out what to do the day my breasts became engorged when Lucy was about six weeks old. I had also developed a fever. My mother and Ben both said, "Maybe you should stop nursing." By that time, I was just getting the hang of the process. Other mothers told me this was normal and not unexpected. They recommended that I put cold, wet compresses over my breasts and encourage the baby to nurse as long she wanted. There was also the suggestion of using cabbage leaves, instead of washcloths, but I was too afraid of Ben's reaction to try that one.

Being prompted to nurse Lucy through the mastitis felt like the right thing to do. I survived the discomfort. The swelling went down, and she continued to thrive. I was glad I had heeded the advice and wisdom of these women.

After I delivered my child, something else took root inside

me. Not only had my organs been displaced during my pregnancy. My relationships—with myself, with doctors, with other women, and definitely with my young child—were transforming as well. I had become part of a conversation that felt true in a way I had never known before. My tiny voice grew stronger, and I risked using it more often to speak up to Ben on my own behalf.

*What do I have to change now so that Jane will be happy?* I imagined Ben thinking each time I spoke up.

I had a hard time viewing myself as anything but an imposition on his way of being. Would a more self-assured woman —Lynn, for instance—have expressed herself without apology?

*To be a thriving mother to our child, I need this. To be a sexually satisfied woman, please do this.* I was still a world away from believing I deserved to say anything like that. And if I had spoken with that confidence and authority, would Ben have stayed?

Up until Lucy was born, I was on a clear, prescribed path: twelve years of public school; four years of college; a year of graduate school to zero in on a profession; a job; and marriage. There were structures and systems that the world I grew up in supplied: guidance counselors, college advisors, and career service departments to point me to my future as an adult.

But once you leave those establishments, unless your workplace acts in loco parentis, you're on your own. I had to find my own educators to trust and listen to. There are no guideposts for the average citizen once formal schooling is complete. Families or religious institutions might provide this, but I'd reached a fork in the road once I declared my choices. My parents favored Western medicine and procedures and didn't understand my newfangled ideas, which took me down a different route. Their Little Jane was separating herself from their pack. Ben may have been afraid to express his concerns about my mothering choices, but my parents never edited theirs. The battle toward my own self-awareness was being fought on two fronts now.

My allegiance had moved from trusting my parents as a source of infinite wisdom to doubting their motives and questioning their authority. I had begun to select my own teachers and guides. Often, these new ideas conflicted with what I had learned at home. Frequently, they were in conflict with Ben's ideas, too. I would have to instruct him on what was true for me.

I had never stood up to my parents on my own behalf. I was still years away from confronting Ben. Although I didn't know it then, I was latching on to troops who held the same beliefs and truths I was just discovering.

I was also beginning to appreciate and cherish my body in a new way. It was producing every drop of nourishment for my baby. There was evidence that by trusting my anatomy and the wisdom and support of my La Leche League friends, I could count on having a thriving child. Lucy's dimpled pink cheeks grew chubby, her body lengthened and filled out, and she looked at me with deep trust and love in a way no one else ever had.

"Look at those *pulkas!*" an elderly aunt commented, squeezing Lucy's chubby thighs. *I did that. I made that happen.* I had discovered a new form of love and a new place to look for support.

My confidence as a mother grew as my chosen teachers nurtured and encouraged me. They served as role models I wanted to emulate. They embodied the chapters ahead I had been afraid to read. Now, I had living examples to guide me. I followed their lead through the birth experience, nursing, and motherhood.

In 1978, nearly three and a half years after Lucy's arrival,

Ryan, our son, was born, making us a family of four. This expanded both the joys and the challenges of daily life. You can
tote an only child along for a few years, but having two kids
made us more family-centered and homebound. By the time
Lily, our youngest, came along in 1982, fissures that had begun
appearing earlier in the marriage became cracks.

Chapter Seven

*A*n image perpetuated in the mid-'70s was that of a housewife taking care of the kids all day long, keeping a spotless home, preparing gourmet meals, and greeting her hardworking husband at the front door with a cocktail in hand. There she'd be, completely naked save the Saran Wrap she'd sheathed herself in sometime between washing the dishes and getting the kids to bed. After that, her job was to be multiorgasmic all night long. This was an airbrushed representation of womanhood that we mostly laughed at but still referenced, always falling short.

I believe on some level, though, that my mother held up this fictional view of how it should be, citing how good her sex life was with my father. What I witnessed on a daily basis—the bickering, belittling, and lack of mutual support—belied what I imagined a close physical bond would create.

Rare is the child who wants to know more on this subject. "Ew, you did *that* four times?" was my reaction after learning how babies were made. But years later, once we daughters had all married, we looked to Mom for her wisdom on the subject.

Leaning against the padded arm of the yellow-striped couch in the living room, our mother held court as Barbara sat beside her, Meredith and I cross-legged at her feet on the carpet. "Twice a week is standard," Mom declared knowledgeably, "and daily when you're on vacation." We sisters glanced at each other, silenced by this pronouncement and how our marriages fell short of its measure.

There were evenings when the door to my parents' master bedroom was closed and others when it wasn't. I could now put this together with her statement. I must've known not to enter then, even if I'd had a nightmare, though I'd never been conscious of their being a sexual couple.

Ben and my sex life never came close to Mom's metrics. Was it me? Us? There were so many areas where I would not live up to some expectation.

BECAUSE I WAS so busy with our brood, I no longer dropped off or picked up Ben's dry cleaning for him. The living room might be strewn with toys when he arrived home from work, and that upset him a lot. "The house is a mess," he'd complain. He was right, but I'd counter that the kids were happy. That was as much as I could manage.

Though I became better at running the household as the kids grew, I now focused my two precious hours between nursery school drop-offs and pickups on accomplishing a project of my own, like my artwork, not vacuuming or folding laundry. I wasn't always at the door to welcome Ben when he came home from teaching. There were no lineups of offspring waiting in height order to greet Dad. I'd often fall asleep putting the kids to bed and crawl back into ours only late in the night.

None of this would I confess to anyone other than a therapist, and that was after five years of barely coping. I couldn't tell another soul that Ben hadn't wanted to be seen pushing the baby carriage with me when Lucy was an infant. I was too ashamed that he didn't deem us worthy of walking together. I made that up to be true and believed it.

Like my mother, I attended our kids' school functions alone more often than not. Months, even a year, might go by without sex. I was embarrassed and felt responsible that all was not bliss. When Lily was three, I insisted that Ben see a therapist himself. By that time, I'd been seeing a mental health professional and we'd gone to a few couples' counselors to work on our marriage. But my gut was telling me more than ever that something was not right.

Ben's lips avoided mine when we kissed. There was more of a puckered-up peck than a meeting of our tender flesh. This lack of touch created an undefined distance between us. Fewer hugs, less hand-holding at the movies. Conversations focused on the kids. I felt avoided. It's hard to name all the small desertions, mine and his. The absence of any one of these would be negligible, but the repetition of them created a Sahara inside me.

I'd heard the term "emotionally unavailable" and could point to my father's behavior as an illustration. Dad's routine of excusing himself from the dinner table and retreating into the den to read the paper or watch a TV show was never questioned. I could walk by his stretched-out figure on the couch three times in a row and not be acknowledged. Even sitting next to him and watching his favorite shows with him, *College Bowl* or *Bonanza*, it was as if he were someplace else. His arm rested across my shoulder in a symbol of affection, but I couldn't feel anything besides its weight.

My father used to quote a snide remark from a magazine

article critiquing Katharine Hepburn's acting skills. "Her emotions run the gamut from A to B," he would say, with a snort. I wonder if it was a projection of his own limited emotional state onto the famous celebrity, pointing the finger at her, rather than at himself.

I can only speculate about why he was like that. My mother harped on the fact that she'd been his rebound love after his parents objected to his marrying "the shiksa," perhaps his true love. Or was he haunted by the World War he'd returned from? Though a dutiful son to my grandparents, had he felt loved, seen, and nurtured as a child? Was it all of the above?

It was easier and safer to put a label on my father's lack of attention. Even twenty-five years after his death, we four kids continue to remark about Dad's inability to express his love. That's how deep that scarcity went. I knew he was there, that he cared about me as best as he could, but not as much as I wanted or needed as a child.

Ben could also seem far away. Learning that there was a term for this behavior actually made me feel less alone. It was like saying he had the flu. Sometimes the symptoms were worse, and other times they went away on their own. It was unpredictable, the emotional distancing, but I recognized a flare-up. Averted eye contact. Less engagement in conversation. Dwindling awareness of me as a separate human being sharing space in a home. I always thought that if I were somehow different, he wouldn't act like this. Did I need to be funnier, more thoughtful, cook better? Be more orgasmic or wrap myself in Saran?

Ben did go to see a psychiatrist for a few sessions. Things got better briefly, and our busy lives filled in and smoothed over the tensions we had most recently experienced. "Things are good," I told friends. Mostly they were. By all outward measures, we looked as normal and happy in our marriage as the household of my youth had.

Ben got busier with the side business that had begun when Ryan was about two. A math teacher from Scarsdale High School had invited him to begin offering an SAT prep course in Greenwich, Connecticut, for extra income. He'd present the verbal training; she'd handle the math section. Within a few years, the business went from a once-a-week class for twenty students to multiple nights and locations for hundreds of students. Our kids got used to dinners without Dad. Lucy was in college by then. I picked up the slack, overseeing homework and getting Ryan to band practice several evenings a week. Lily and I snuggled up to watch *Blossom* episodes together in my bedroom.

Eventually Ben's weekends were fully taken up with back-to-back courses Saturday and Sunday mornings and afternoons. Because of his full schedule, I expanded my studio hours. My egg-decorating hobby morphed into a full-time cottage industry. When the kids were small, I'd rush to my work area and try to get one piece finished. With so much time alone, I expanded my product line to include jewelry pieces made from eggshells and note cards with photos of my colorful work, and filled my calendar with regional exhibits and workshops.

Ben and I were at our best when we joined forces for an event like my annual studio sale at our house. I had his time and attention, or at least the occasion did. I arranged it for a weekend when Ben and our two kids still at home would be able to participate.

For days, I converted the downstairs into an art gallery for my work, rearranging bookshelves in the living room to accommodate display cases. My studio was scrubbed top to bottom. I'd hired a cleaning lady by then, because I still detested dusting and vacuuming. I took inventory of my work and prepared a schedule of demonstrations.

Lily baked cookies with my business assistant the day before the show. Ryan put signs out on the front yard and pointed to where customers should park their cars on our cul-de-sac. Ben worked the sales desk during our open hours in the dining room, Lily by his side. He tallied up the goods on the calculator. My daughter wrapped them carefully and handed them to the buyer with a receipt.

Once we added up the day's take, we all celebrated over pizza at Via Sforza, our favorite neighborhood trattoria, with its imitation-grotto interior and piped-in violin music. The waiters knew our family and brought Ben his Diet Coke and me my glass of chardonnay.

"The usual?" Andre asked, knowing our preference for their Margherita pizza, extra crispy, please. We often recognized a neighbor or school parent there, and exchanged hugs. Our family unit looked good, and I felt happy but also worried that I was using something up—though what, exactly, I couldn't say. Now that they'd done this for me, what was my debt back? I never considered that this may have been my family repaying my past service. I always felt as if I needed to contribute more, that I now owed them back for their help. Were we rich in love, as my mother had claimed when I was the child? Had I learned to put my relationships into monetary terms? What was I measuring?

LATER, ONCE THE kids were independent, driving, in college, or out on their own, Ben and I still went out to dinner regularly, saw movies, and shared family gatherings for birthdays and weddings. But we led parallel lives. That was okay with me, because playing our assigned roles outweighed personal happiness. It always had. That was the scripture I clung to. I remained optimistic. *Ben knows how steadfast I've been, what a good mother I am. How hard I'd worked on myself. It will all be fine.*

But by late 2009, thirty-seven years into our marriage, I knew something was definitely wrong. Days would go by without a meaningful conversation. Ben's kiss would be a peck on the cheek, from which he withdrew as though he'd received a shock. That fall, he avoided planning a trip with me to California to see my brother over Christmas, something we'd had fun doing in the past.

On a cool October night, we'd taken two cars to the Lime, another restaurant in town where we were known. Ben had to pick up printed class materials at Kinko's after dinner, and I was going to a meeting in another direction. We sat at our favorite table for two in the nook by the front door. There were no diners on either side, just a two-seater at Ben's back. I liked to sit against the windowed wall. Our glass-covered table displayed local merchants' business cards under its surface. I noticed my chiropractor's card as I examined the collection during the extended silence before Lisa, our waitress, arrived at the table.

She handed us the laminated menus and asked, "Diet Coke, Ben? Tea, Jane?"

Once we ordered, I opened the conversation.

"I think we should start planning our trip to Andy's this December. I know it's early, but flights get so expensive as the holidays approach. When are your classes over for the semester?"

Ben stirred his drink with its straw and concentrated on the swirl of the ice cubes in the glass. Without looking up, he responded, "There's something I've been meaning to talk to you about."

I'd never heard these words from my husband. That he'd been mulling over something he wanted to tell me. I was hopeful. What could he reveal about himself that I didn't know? I was blank and expectant.

"I don't think I can plan the trip this year. I started seeing a psychiatrist, and I'm feeling too anxious to go."

"Oh, honey!" I said, with genuine concern but also a mild thrill that his internal condition had caused him to seek help. He was finally realizing how much his nervousness was holding him back. I saw this as a good thing and encouraged him to reveal more. He must have been feeling the same lack in the marriage that I was and now was seeking help to do something about it.

"On my birthday next month, I'll be sixty-four, the same age my mother was when she died. I can't stop thinking about that."

This was not the direction I had expected the conversation to take.

"Okay," I said. "I'm glad you have someone who can help you." I'm sure we continued some form of conversation after that, but none of it stayed with me. His seeing a psychiatrist on his own was the headline I remembered. We left the Lime to go our separate ways after he paid the check.

No plans got made for us to fly west.

During the next few weeks, our empty nest felt emptier still. Fall got colder with each shortening day. The distance between us lengthened, and I felt as though I were on a remote island in my own home.

Shortly before Thanksgiving, our thinning tie unraveled. "Would you like to come upstairs and watch something with me?" I asked, my indirect way of offering to have sex. It had been a long time since we'd made love, and even though I didn't really want to, I thought that it might be helpful.

But Ben said, "I'm done with that. I can hardly even get it up anymore." Later that same night, I heard sounds to the contrary coming from our bathroom after he thought I'd fallen asleep. When I got up on Wednesday and saw him, I said, "This isn't working."

"Should I move out?" was his swift response.

That was the second time I'd heard that memorable question. The first time had been nine months earlier.

Throughout our marriage, I was always the one seeking help and solutions, maybe because Ben was satisfied with the way things were, or was able to find his own happiness through his career and outside interests, like golf, reading, and the Red Sox.

I believed there must be something more, better, or different, and I was on a mission to find it. I enrolled in workshops at Kripalu, a yoga and meditation center in Lenox, Massachusetts, studied transcendental meditation, became a certified coach through the Coaches Training Institute (CTI), and went through their leadership program—all this, I believe, to seek a better understanding of what could be.

During the fall of 2008 and into the winter of 2009, I invested in a course of study called ORSC—Organization and Relationship Systems Coaching. Many coaches I knew had gone through the training and raved about it. It would expand my coaching market and also give me tools I thought I could apply to my own relationship.

The classes met in the Boston area, which meant being away from home for three nights at a time, usually with one-month study intervals and fieldwork in between.

Ben and I had been in an okay place for a few years, but I'd recently felt a widening in the space between us. I could use scenarios, as we called them in workshops, from my own life to get added benefit from the coursework I was studying. I paid attention to my eagerness to leave for those Boston stays and increased reluctance to come back home.

I couldn't define it. I kept describing Ben as unavailable. He wasn't deliberately hurting me. It was more that I didn't feel as though I existed when we were in the house together. How do you confront neglect? I was hoping to find the answers.

Hamilton, my twelve-step counselor, and other therapists had asked me in the past, could I accept that this was who Ben was?

"Focus on the doughnut and not on the hole" was an expression I heard in the rooms of recovery. For weeks after that, I'd notice all the positive things about Ben—what a good father he was, how much his students loved him, and how hard he worked. How lucky I was to have a successful husband who shared his paycheck and slept next to me every night. That he was giving me as much as he had to give. Was there enough doughnut left for me to even look at? Or had it crumbled beyond recognition?

I left for the fourth of my five-weekend ORSC classes in late February 2009. Ben leaned over the computer in his office as I wheeled through with my turquoise carry-on. "Where're you going?" he asked, as I reached the door close to the staircase.

"Remember?" I asked. "I've got my coaching class in Boston this weekend. I told you about them the other day."

"Oh, right," he said, not looking toward me. "Have fun."

"The Oscars are this Sunday night," I said. "Do you want to watch together when I get home?"

"Okay," he said still focused on the Facebook page in front of him.

"Bye."

"Bye."

Using my own relationship examples throughout the weekend, I went through the various exercises with an increasing awareness and heaviness that something wasn't right. It was a feeling that I couldn't articulate.

"The body is the midwife to the mind" was a quote from our learning manual that we discussed during our study. Borrowed from Arnold Mindell's teachings, the phrase tells us that sensations we experience internally provide information our brain has not yet detected. You have physical sensations you can't define.

In the movie *What the Bleep Do We Know!?*, one story described how Native Americans were drawn to the coastline and predicted impending danger as European explorers neared the shore. Because they had no vocabulary or concept for large ships, or the threat to Native American society those ships posed, it was a premonition that they felt yet could give no language to. The message stayed with me.

Driving back to Connecticut after the ORSC classes the last Sunday in February, I felt a similar sensation growing in me as I neared my exit. It was a combination of resistance, fear, and dread. I had nowhere else to go, but pulling into our driveway felt impossibly hard. I knew that Ben and I had a date to watch the Oscars, but it seemed forced and wrong.

Coming up the walk, which had been shoveled but was still icy, I saw Ben's silhouette through the dining room window. He was seated on the banquette, leaning over papers on the table in front of him. A cardboard carton filled with stapled test booklets was to his left. A smaller stack, presumably of corrected exams, lay to his right.

He didn't come to the door when I put my key in the lock, and I didn't enter the dining area.

From the hallway I asked, "Are we going to watch?" using

the marital shorthand that minimizes niceties and gets to the point. But it felt different this time. The bridge spanning our individual lives was flimsy and insecurely tethered.

"What?" he asked, turning his head in my direction. "Watch?"

"The Oscars. They start in ten minutes."

"I can't," he said, gesturing to the paper-laden table.

*You had the whole weekend to do this*! "I thought you'd be finished. That we'd have this time together. We always watch the awards," I reminded him.

"Maybe we should talk," Ben said. This got my attention. It was always I who pointed out the rifts in our marriage.

We went into my office for our discussion. Ben leaned on the black Formica desk where my assistant sat to work on my eggs.

Whenever I'm in a difficult conversation, a piece of my awareness faculty goes away. I hear something that rearranges my thought patterns, and time and details evaporate. The only other quote I remember from that night was Ben asking for the first time, "Should I move out?" I said nothing but felt blood pooling in my feet. Once those words were spoken, their devastating reality surprised us both, and each of us was in tears.

We had fought many times in the past, had long periods before normalcy was restored, but neither of us, in our history of disagreements, had ever verbally suggested a next step to alter or end the relationship.

Back in our thirties, when I angrily contemplated a life apart from Ben, I didn't know how to accomplish that. There was no "going home to Mother" in my dysfunctional family. That would have been worse than whatever was my current crisis. I doubled down on therapy and got by.

Now that we were in our sixties, the kids grown and gone,

the suggestion startled me, and I didn't welcome its implications. By this time, we had the resources to split households. No one else's lives would be disrupted. But I'd never contemplated separation as a possibility.

As we finished talking that night, we agreed to try another form of couples' counseling. I admired the coach who'd co-founded the ORSC program. We hired her and had several sessions by phone, completing assignments in between.

Again, things got better, but it felt as though we were treading on a rug grown lumpy from all that had been swept under it.

We were scheduled for our next phone session at a time when conflict in our house of two had peaked. Our mutual annoyance was at an all-time high, and none of the coaching tools was working. Though we'd consulted calendars when we made our appointment with the coach, for some reason, Ben said he'd have to be late for the 5:00 p.m. time slot we'd agreed to. Punctuality was a badge of honor for both of us, so I called him on this. After some unpleasant words, Ben found a way to be in my office at exactly five, though not in a happy mood. I was hoping our call could deal with what was present and that things would improve once again.

We dialed the coach's number, but no one picked up. After four or five rings, we got a recorded message. I felt guilty, since I was the one who'd hired this woman and insisted that Ben keep his word to attend this appointment. Though our coach accepted full responsibility for her absence, that was the end of our therapy with her.

The ships sailed closer to the shore, but I still couldn't describe what they looked like.

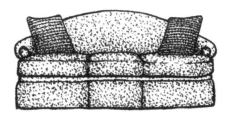

Chapter Eight

"What's going on?" my son, Ryan, asked when he arrived home the Thursday morning of Thanksgiving weekend. He had noticed the unmade bed in the guest room and Ben's clothing lying on the floor in what had once been his bedroom.

I don't know how Ben and I worded our new status, or who delivered the news to whom, but by midday each of our three kids knew that Dad would be moving out. They were all grown and living on their own at this point. Ryan, thirty-one and married, worked at a law firm and lived in Manhattan. Lucy, thirty-five, was successfully running her own business as a consultant and author, was also married, and lived on the Upper West Side. Lily, still in her twenties, shared an apartment with a college friend on the Upper East Side and was freelancing as a translator (Japanese was her second language) and working at a clothing store.

Our family divided up later that afternoon and drove in separate cars to the hotel in White Plains where my siblings and cousins would gather for our annual Thanksgiving dinner, an event I never looked forward to but dreaded more than ever this year. Since the plans had been in place for months, and the situation between Ben and me was barely a day old, we hadn't considered canceling.

Ryan took the wheel of my car, pointing us west on I-95.

"This is awful," he said, barely able to keep his voice from cracking.

"I'm sure this is the worst of it, honey," I offered falsely, trying to comfort him and myself. To my way of thinking, breaking the news to the kids was the most devastating aspect. They knew the marriage wasn't perfect, but having the premise of your whole existence pulled out from under you was world-shattering. Once we'd gotten through that, I'd imagined, nothing could be as hard.

Divorce opened the door to a world I had never wanted to explore but that was enveloping me. Initially, I was unable to see anything but the end of our storybook appearance.

What's awful about separation and divorce is not so much the fact of it as the everydayness of its impact. Quite simply, instead of four addresses, we would now have five. Our original unit, now grown to seven and more with marriages and babies, ceased to be. Every future birthday, holiday, and special occasion would be different.

That day, without having to say anything otherwise to our kids, Ben and I acted as if everything were as it had always been once we arrived at the ironically named Renaissance Hotel. No one was the wiser. We all faked our way through turkey and the trimmings. Not even my sisters or brother sniffed a difference.

Children of all ages sense when not to ask questions. Reflecting on a night in my own childhood when dinner was marked by raised voices between Mom and Dad, I remembered having watched the volley of their emotions. I turned my head to see my father leaning across his place setting and rubbing the red patches where the nose pads of his glasses left angry indentations. I turned back toward my mother as she cowered in her seat at the opposite end of the table. She didn't fight back. I wanted to make whatever had happened unhappen. I wanted not to feel the turbulent void in my body.

There was no formal announcement that everyone was excused from dinner that night. My father stormed out of the dining room, took up his pipe, and reamed out the remaining ash from last night's smoke. Mom retreated to the kitchen to cope with the aftermath of the meal.

I sidled up to Dad.

"Are you getting divorced?" I asked, with as much seriousness as a ten-year-old could scare up.

"Ridiculous! No!" he replied. That shut down any further investigation on my part. I dropped the subject. Their marriage continued.

There was no visible conflict between Ben and me for our children to witness, but the climate our relationship created must've been as thick as the one my parents had when I realized that something wasn't right and that no further conversation would be of use. I thought I'd been a better communicator than my folks, but, in this moment of crisis, I knew I had not. I was my own version of my mother, recoiling from my wound. My father hadn't left her. What came after Ben's departure was virgin territory for me. I was on my own to create a new act.

After Ben moved his things out, we didn't speak for several months. He would email me to find out when he could stop by to pay household bills or pick up a book he needed or a piece of clothing he'd left behind. During those visits, I'd stay in my studio or leave the house. I had no frame of reference for how to behave.

In late February, Ben contacted me saying he'd found a marriage counselor, Elaine Cooper, for us to see together. *He's now the one who wants to work on the marriage*, I thought. I had always been the one to instigate the next step. I felt a whisper of optimism flutter in my chest—for what, though, I wasn't sure.

Our first appointment was in early March. It had been three months since we'd seen or spoken to each other. Ben's MINI Cooper was in the parking lot when I pulled off River Road in Wilton by the office building where our therapist held her sessions. Even though we were both ultrapunctual, he usually beat me to a destination when we arrived separately.

That first session, I didn't know the right greeting for an estranged husband. Should I offer him my cheek? A hug? A nod? He was sitting in an armchair, a book in his lap. He remained seated but looked up when I walked in. I waited for his cue. With none forthcoming, I hung up my parka and sat down in the chair against the opposite wall. "Hey," he said.

"Hey," I responded.

"Ryan's job is going well. He seems to like it there enough," Ben said, referring to our son's recent work as a lawyer.

Small talk. I didn't feel like chatting when our relationship was hanging by a thread. "Good," I said, so as not to be rude.

"You can have Charlie stop making the seltzer deliveries if you want" was his next gambit.

"Okay," I answered, and glanced at my watch. Did the therapist's closed door indicate that she was in session, or was she just waiting for the top of the hour to open the door for us? I flicked a piece of lint off my pants.

"Can I come by tomorrow to pick up the mail?" Ben asked.

He was more talkative and engaging in those few minutes than he'd been in months. I found it hard to maintain my detached facade when he seemed to be trying so hard.

Finally Elaine Cooper opened the door to her inner sanctum and gestured us in. A tall, slim woman, she was outfitted in tones of beige. She held a legal pad in her left hand, a finger keeping a pen in place. Her hairdo was simple. She called little attention to herself.

During this session, she defined the rules. She would be the listener, ask questions, direct the discussion. Neither of us was to communicate privately with her by phone or email. Anything she might hear in that capacity would be brought up at the following session, not kept secret, okay?

We both nodded in agreement. I respected order and felt safe knowing what was and wasn't okay. For better or for worse. Till death do us part.

Each of us had met with Elaine once on our own before this first joint session. After that consultation, I initiated a practice I'd learned in recovery: bookending. I called my good friend Doreen before and immediately following that session with the marriage counselor and vowed to repeat this sequence throughout our therapy—meaning that she and I would speed-dial each other to "bookend" difficult tasks in our lives. That day, I had called her from the parking lot before heading upstairs for our appointment. "I'm scared," I'd said briefly. "I have no idea what to expect." My hope was that Ben would have missed the comforts I had provided him all these years and that this separation would make him long to be back with me. I gave little thought to what I wanted.

I dialed Doreen again when it was over, expressing my frustration and disappointment. I didn't think we had covered any new territory, that it had been a rehashing of every other marriage counseling appointment we'd ever had. Doreen assured me that I was doing what I needed to do in the equation. Time would tell. "You showed up, Jane. That's important."

The second session was a couple of weeks later, the afternoon he would deliver the news of the other woman. I again saw Ben's car in the parking lot, but he was not in the waiting room when I opened the door from the hallway. Instead, Elaine's office door was ajar and I could see him already seated inside. His wool overcoat was off, draped over the back of the couch. He had on a navy cashmere sweater, dark twill pants that looked like he'd just picked them up at the cleaner's, and the tan suede desert boots he'd gotten at the fancy store in South Norwalk where Sammy, the owner, treated him like a god because he always dropped a thousand dollars when he shopped there. Ben prided himself on his expensive, classic wardrobe. No European tight-fitting shirts or slacks for him. He preferred a high-end, professorial look, which he achieved.

His eyes didn't meet mine when I entered. His right hand was smoothing a strand of hair across the top of his head, a familiar gesture. Dealing with losing his hair had been a theme throughout our marriage. He shuddered at the thought. When we were first sleeping together and I spent the night at his apartment in the Bronx, he told me he wanted to show me something. He opened the drawer in the nightstand next to his bed and took out a crumpled-up swatch of nude-colored, stretchy nylon. It was the cut-off toe piece of what must've been his mother's pantyhose. To demonstrate its purpose, he spread the fingers of both hands as he stretched the thin, flesh-colored stocking and lifted it over his head, put on this flimsy knitted cap, and pointed at himself.

"I hate my hair. This helps me keep it straight. I thought you should know I do this." His tone was sincere, and his lips suppressed a smile as his cheeks flushed. As I had a roommate help me iron my own frizzy hair on an ironing board to straighten it, the Jewish-hair thing Ben and I now shared touched my heart. That day, early in our courtship, I was receptive to this lovable quirk. Now, much of his hair was gone, as were any warm feelings I used to have about his idiosyncrasies.

"It looks like you've started without me," I commented, taking my seat on the same couch but on the end closer to the door.

His body, though seated, seemed to be in motion. His right foot was tapping the floor. There was a small stack of documents on his lap. Envelopes? A folder? A couple of loose pieces of paper? Nothing registered. I was still musing about why he'd gone into her office without waiting for me to arrive.

A noise came out, as though from the back of his throat. It sounded like a grunt but wasn't quite a "hey" or a "hi"—more like a "heh."

I drifted back to my first day of French class at Mount Holyoke, not a strong subject for me, but a requirement. The teacher called my name—"Jeanne," for Jane—and gestured for me to come to her desk. She made a remark in her native French, a language that I was not fluent in. I smiled politely, nodded, and went back to my seat.

A deep silence engulfed the classroom.

I knew something was wrong, but I didn't know what I'd done. The other students fastened their eyes on me. One girl, seated in the front row, raincoat on over her flannel pajamas, put her hand over her mouth to conceal her smile. Another classmate—I had no friends in that room—muffled a giggle. I wanted to disappear and have whatever had just happened be over with. I wasn't in danger of dying, but I would have traded death for the humiliation of that moment.

Madame Whatever Her Name Was asked Flannel Pants to translate. "She told you to take the packet on her desk that has the syllabus in it," she said slowly, in English.

It may seem amusing in the retelling, but living it was excruciating for this girl, who always needed to get things right. I know now that I had made a mistake. In that moment, I believed that *I* was the mistake.

I felt a similar tension in the air in the Wilton office where I now sat, not knowing what was going on and why Ben was in there already. I was doubly surprised when this therapist, who had spelled out the rules, began the session differently. "Ben called me last night. He wanted to notify me about something important he would be sharing during today's session," she said.

This confused me. I had thought there wouldn't be any behind-the-back communication. Wasn't this a breach of our agreement? Shouldn't she have told him that when he phoned? Why did she get to know anything before me?

I wanted to make her wrong. They were now bringing up the issue that had been discussed. There was no breach there, no matter how much I wanted to feel superior to the situation.

My eyebrows creased toward each other, my thoughts blurred, and my stomach shifted a notch.

"Ben?" she prompted. I looked in his direction. I stared at this man, in profile, about to read a document to me in a near stranger's office. He opened the manila folder that had rested on his knees. I noted that for someone who frequently reused a folder over and over again, crossing out a student's name and penciling in a fresh one, he was about to share something that warranted a brand-new sheath. From this covering, he removed a typewritten page. It was printed on an eight and a half by eleven-inch sheet of plain white copy paper. I could see it was single-spaced, dense.

He held up the memo, the edges resting lightly between the fingers of each of his hands. Those fingers had always intrigued me, with their dark hairs resting between the knuckles. Long and slender, but masculine because of the black tufts. Short fingernails, clipped, but not filed, so their edges were sharp and pointed.

I tried to follow along as he spoke, but I couldn't seem to focus my attention. What was this thing he had in his hands? When had he written it? Was it a letter to me? An essay on how he felt? I was adrift on a couch as the words spilled forth. He wasn't reading it to me. He was reciting it to the room, to Elaine. What was happening?

The Starbucks decaf with soy I'd had at lunch lingered, its bitter, slightly creamy taste still on the roof of my mouth. I sucked at it with my tongue to see if there was one swallow left before it disappeared entirely.

I flashed back to being among the masses at the County Center in White Plains, a makeshift cavern of a synagogue used for the High Holy Days. I sat with my family, rising when the rabbi directed us, swaying to the Hebrew chanting, not understanding a word but obediently following the congregation's rhythm. Eventually the familiar *sh'ma*, the first prayer we were taught in Sunday school and which I knew by rote, began and I was able to join them in singing from memory. I became present again.

I felt similarly lulled while Ben read his statement in an unmodulated voice, until not the *sh'ma* but an unexpected line startled me into awareness: "A woman in Maine has become very important to me." Everything before and after those words dissolved in midair.

I had put up with his neglect, moodiness, and lack of passion because that's what a good wife does. Even when I was unhappy, divorce was never a consideration. Good girls don't divorce. When my brother and his wife had separated early in their marriage, they'd worked it out and gotten back together and were still married. I believed that could be our happy ending, too. It never occurred to me that we weren't both working toward reconciliation.

But now that infidelity had been unveiled, I knew this was the end.

In that moment, thirty-seven years of a once-sacred union evaporated from the center of my well-ordered universe and drifted into particles that floated willy-nilly throughout a marriage counselor's office in Wilton, Connecticut. There we sat. A truth that changed everything in an instant had been revealed. It was all different now. This man I thought I knew was a foreigner. The woman I thought I was had no land.

Elaine's voice emerged, asking if the following Wednesday at 2:00 p.m. suited me for the next appointment. I must've nodded, fumbled around to gather my belongings, and gotten myself back into the car. Out of force of habit, I dialed Doreen to bookend this most difficult occurrence as my car's engine warmed up and heat began to blow out at me through the dashboard vent. I had called her earlier to say I didn't know what the purpose of this session was. Now I blurted out the result: "Ben has another woman. He didn't even look me in the eye when he told me. He read it off a piece of paper."

Who was I, if not the good girl for whom things worked out by waiting patiently, enduring? But what had being good gained me? This wasn't supposed to be happening to me. I thought I had done it right. I had married the Jewish boy, taught, procreated, visited parents while they were alive, and worked to keep our relationship intact for nearly four decades. Although divorces had happened all around me—both of my sisters and several friends—I never thought it would happen to me. This wasn't supposed to be fucking happening to me.

No, not to me. I had imagined that we would be that unique couple at weddings where everyone was on the dance floor and the emcee announced, "Stay dancing if you've been married for more than ten years." Slowly, younger couples would leave the floor. He'd announce five-year increments— fifteen, twenty, twenty-five, thirty. We'd made it to thirty-five. I wanted to be the last couple standing. It didn't matter if we weren't that happy together. What mattered was that the people at the party would see that we were still married. I wanted the look of it. The feeling had died a long time ago, yet I kept dancing.

There was a long pause. Words were choked in my throat, and Doreen's silence allowed me to feel her warmth, holding the space open for my tears. After a minute passed, she said, "You're not alone."

Chapter Nine

*W*e guess at what normal is," read an item on a checklist to determine whether one qualified for a particular twelve-step program. I had no idea what a "normal" family should feel like or how a marriage was supposed to be. What I did know was how hungrily I responded to affection and attention when outside sources offered it, particularly older women or authority figures.

Jack Canfield, coauthor of *Chicken Soup for the Soul* and a motivational speaker I respect, advised his listeners: A surrogate mother is *any* woman who nurtures you. A surrogate father is *any* man who nurtures you.

During my children's early years, I identified and cultivated nurturing women, surrogate mothers, who supported me in a way that was different from what I knew as a child and even as a young adult. Growing up, I was criticized and compared—the well-worn question asked, when a grade of 98 was brought home, "What happened to the other two points?" and other phrases that left me feeling not quite good enough.

Ben wasn't openly critical. Rather, he asked me a lot of questions that left me feeling insecure. "Are you sure she's getting enough to eat?" "Shouldn't she be sleeping through the night by now?" "What did the doctor say about how heavy he is already?"

Granted, there weren't the online forums there are today for keeping up with a baby's early development, but I had all the books that existed on infancy and was doing my best to learn as much as I could on the subject. I wanted my mothering decisions to be sufficient evidence, without having to defend them.

The women I met postpartum offered me softer, non-judgmental places to turn than I found at home. I understood that Ben couldn't be my only source of comfort and advice, but I needed more than he had to offer me.

Even though I knew these sympathetic women existed and where they showed up, I had trouble seeking them out. Rather, I would wait, hold my breath, until my calendar gave me permission to be in their presence. I was too shy to pick up the phone, preferring to be sought out, though that rarely happened. God forbid I should appear needy, even though that's exactly what I was.

My pediatrician offered a "new mothers" call time from seven to eight o'clock every morning, but I rarely took advantage, thinking my issue too small to concern this busy man. Had it been available, I would have liked a twenty-four-seven hotline to an unconditionally loving and approving source. Truthfully, I didn't even want to have to dial. What I craved was someone who could read my mind, swoop down to lovingly care for and nurture me, and provide whatever I was missing.

Rather, I hobbled from one monthly La Leche League meeting to the next, too shy and embarrassed to reach out for guidance in between. I felt ashamed that I didn't know how to handle each new situation as it arose and too prideful to let anyone else see my insecurity. When Lucy's bottom tooth broke through the gum at nine months, I suffered her unintentional biting until a fellow sufferer at a LLL meeting instructed me on how to alter her nursing position for relief.

Sharing my fear with Ben would only have added to his own distrust of my methods, so I avoided the subject. I wanted to be held and soothed, not interrogated.

I always believed that my situation was unique and had no remedy. A dish of mint chocolate chip ice cream was my refuge more often than not. My immediate feeling of inadequacy and shame went away. I savored the comfort of food and went on to the next moment. This pain-relieving shortcut was only a stopgap solution, I discovered, as weight piled on after I'd reached my thirtieth birthday. My misery was becoming visible in my widening hips and thickened middle.

It wasn't that I was without friends. In each area of my life as a mother—La Leche League, the Community Cooperative Nursery School (CCNS), and SoNo Magnet Elementary School —I found women to talk to and become close with. What I wished for was a built-in structure for plugging into support on an as-needed basis, kind of what I'd dreamed my marriage would provide.

With a friend, you had to pick up a phone and call, make a date, or know that you'd run into her carpooling or volunteering. When there was a project to work on, like the holiday fair at SoNo Magnet, my support quota was met predictably and I felt full. But as we moved toward Christmas break or summer vacation, I could sense my level of anxiety rising, knowing that I'd soon have nowhere to turn with my own personal crises. Though I couldn't define it then, my emotional tank was becoming empty.

My relationship with Ben didn't provide that safe haven where feelings could be discussed and sorted out. That emptiness couldn't be filled by another human being. Neither Ben nor I knew how to provide a soft place for the other. Rather, we both looked elsewhere to be soothed, or at least I did.

As dependent as I was, I was loath to let it show. "Looks good, feels bad" summed me up perfectly. It was important that I appeared and sounded fine, and much of the time, I was. At least, I was FINE: *f*ucked up, *i*nsecure, *n*eurotic, and *e*motional.

Every five years, I'd show up at my college reunion with success stories about my artwork, growing family, and lengthening marriage. At Passover and gatherings with relatives, Ben, the kids, and I mingled and played our roles. The externals were shiny and attractive.

FOR MY FORTIETH birthday party in 1988, I invited twenty close friends and family members—all women—to a dinner party and sleepover hosted by Maggie, a good friend and steady walking partner, who had offered her home in Norwalk for the night. It had been a long time since I'd had an official celebration like this, and I invited everyone to dress up, prepared recipes from the *Silver Palate Cookbook*, and arranged an icebreaker so that everyone could meet each other. It never occurred to me to have a couples' party. Ben and I didn't have a circle of friends.

By 11:00 p.m. my mother, sisters, and other guests who weren't spending the night left. There was one activity I wanted those who'd stayed to be a part of. We had gotten into our nightgowns or pajamas and taken seats in a circle in Maggie's living room. *The Book of Questions* had come out the year before. I invited the remaining group to get to know each other better by opening my paperback copy and selecting a random question for us each to answer. The one I turned to read was, "If you could change one thing about the way you were raised, what would it be?"

Sandra was to my right. A pretty, dark-haired Montessori schoolteacher with a soothing voice, she was the mother of Jack, who was my son, Ryan's, age. We became close friends when Sandra had been in her last month of pregnancy and given my name by Mary, the midwife who delivered my son and later Sandra's. Having made similar choices in childbirth, breast-feeding, and motherhood, we quickly connected. She considered the question for a moment and then said, "I'd have to say that I wish my father were not an alcoholic. I think my life would have been different if he weren't."

There was a slight murmur, an audible "hmm" in recognition of her confession, a head nodding to Sandra's right. It was my friend Sue, a fellow mother, whom I'd met at nursery school. A former nurse, she had a mothering approach that took my breath away. She'd pick her daughters up from CCNS, drive them home, feed them lunch, and get them into pajamas for a three-hour nap each afternoon. I envied her discipline. Lucy and I were on the go after the morning session at school. My firstborn's nap routine had long since vanished.

Sue had shared often with me that her father was an alcoholic, so when it was her turn, I was not surprised that she said, "Same here. I believe things would have followed another track if my father weren't a drunk."

Of the ten women who spent the night and were part of this parlor game, seven of them admitted to having an alcoholic parent or relative and said they wished that that had not been so. I felt fortunate that my mother and father weren't big drinkers and can't remember the one thing I said I would have changed. What I completely missed, until a few short years later, was that my mother was addicted to prescription pills, particularly sleeping pills, and that her dependency's impact on me was similar to the way the other women at my party felt about their parents' drinking.

The majority of my closest friends, not to mention Ben, were adult children of alcoholics. This was hardly a coincidence. We were all rescuers, caretakers, and people pleasers who were assisting each other in our individual dramas. Yes, we had fun playdates with the children, but in the intimate moments I craved with these friends, it was always to complain about my mother, to get a hug, or to hear kind words that would reinforce my fragile ego-system.

There exists a "laundry" list that ticks off characteristics of people who've grown up where there's addiction, like guessing at what normal is, and I could personally put a checkmark next to every item. I would never have identified myself in that way, but that checklist was convincing.

Three items that particularly stand out when I think of my friends and me are "approval seeking," "caretaking," and "a heightened sense of responsibility." It felt good to be around women with these qualities. They were never critical, always sympathetic, and willing to rescue me if I needed them to.

Even with this core group of tender women, I had a hard time picking up the phone to ask for help. I didn't want to blow the image they had of me. They could offer what I needed, but I would have to initiate contact on my own behalf. That felt hard, and I didn't feel worthy.

My fixed idea back then was that I was a victim. Who better to associate with than nurturing women anxious to make things better for someone else? Now, at my fortieth-birthday party, I had assembled a roomful of women who suffered from the same, but differently rendered, childhoods that included liquor or pills.

If you believe the saying that coincidence is God's way of remaining anonymous, and I do, then here was a larger-than-life sign appearing before me, a veritable burning bush that I could see or deny.

I was still a year away from entering the world of twelve-step recovery, but this party stands out in my memory as the "before" thumbnail of my life, especially since I chose not to invite Ben to this significant affair.

I FIRST HEARD about recovery in August 1989, one year and one month after that milestone birthday. Until I entered the rooms, at forty-one, I'd outgrown every group I'd identified for support: Lamaze classes after the births of my children, La Leche League until the kids weaned, and the schools they attended once they'd passed through all the grades.

In the fellowship I entered in the summer of '89, they say there is no such thing as graduation. It would become the lifelong support system that I had always sought.

Without the foundation of this spiritual network in my twenties or thirties, I hobbled through my early marriage, motherhood, and relationships, doing the best I knew how to at the time. I repeated the behaviors I'd seen in my household growing up (threatening, withholding, domination) or tried out my own bag of tricks (stonewalling, passive aggression, and revenge), thinking I'd class it up a bit. I look back with compassion on my twenty-to-forty-year-old self. I enrolled in classes like Assertiveness Training and borrowed *How to Talk So Kids Will Listen* from the library, in an effort to improve on the model I'd been taught.

Ben and I hadn't developed skills for fighting fairly, listening empathetically, or resolving our differences. I had no idea how to behave with maturity. What I thought I wanted most from Ben after the honeymoon phase ended was partnership. Now, I realize that what I really wanted was caretaking. I wanted someone—well, Ben, actually—to take note of how difficult the role of new mother was and to do everything to make me feel appreciated and supported, the way my friends at my fortieth-birthday party would have in my fantasy life.

I have come to learn that expectations are premeditated resentments. I was setting up this man, this man I loved and married, to fail. It hadn't occurred to me that he, too, was undergoing big changes. Instead, I mobilized my inept strategies to further my cause. Self-righteousness: *It shouldn't be this way!* Self-pity: *Who will take care of* me *while I use every ounce of my energy to take care of our infant? Can't you see what I'm doing for our family?*

While I loved nursing, its ceaselessness was overwhelming. Where Ben had once had 100 percent of my attention at home, now I could barely eke out eye contact, let alone intimacy. But discussing this was too hard, and courage was not yet part of my vocabulary. I couldn't adequately explain to Ben the intensity of the nursing relationship, which was why my surrogate mothers in LLL were so valuable to me. They understood exactly what I was going through and didn't want anything more from me than I could give. I offered them the same compassion and consideration in return.

But friendship and marriage are distinct and separate entities. I projected all the qualities I saw with my friends and created a delusion of what my marriage should feel like.

Without a group to reason things out with, I authored and then concealed my playbook for our marriage. I crafted a powerful drama—defined in my head what behaviors I expected and desired—and then withheld the information from my costar.

Since there was alcoholism on Ben's side of the family, our insecurities clashed. His parents fawned over him, in spite of his aversion to so much attention. My parents were either unavailable or neglectful. All I wanted was for him to see me. We were at cross-purposes in our marriage. Criticism and judgmental behavior bubbled up to energize me. Negative feelings can do that. *He should know! I am so right!*

Here's a scene I wish I could restage. Before Lucy was due, Ben and I inherited a buggy from his mother, who had preserved his baby carriage as though it were a vintage automobile. The bumpers shone like silver; the canvas hood was spotless and flexed up and down without a squeak. Bunny had even kept his monogrammed baby blanket tucked away between sheets of crisp tissue to preserve the capital-lettered gray monogram stitched onto the navy wool background. I was touched by her nostalgia and desire to pass on what had belonged to her first child.

Although I thought the blanket was too masculine for our apple-cheeked daughter, I found the carriage elegant and regal. I stretched a pink cotton jersey contour sheet over the tot-size mattress and folded the afghan crocheted by Nanny, Ben's grandmother, into quarters.

A couple of weeks after Lucy's birth, I felt recovered enough to take her out for a stroll downtown. By then, the middle of September, the weather had turned crisp. I dressed her in a one-piece jumpsuit and a hooded sweater that zipped up the back, swaddled her in a receiving blanket, and tucked her under Nanny's coverlet.

I asked Ben to join us, especially to help me carry the buggy up the three stairs from our apartment house's landing onto the street. I sensed his discomfort with my request but passed it off as my having turned bossy as a new mother.

"Wheredoyouwantit?" he mumbled under his breath.

"Huh?"

"Where shall I put the thing?" he asked, more audibly.

"Up here." I gestured to the sidewalk. "Let's walk down Bedford Street and back around Latham Park," I suggested, pointing toward the small green square near our building. The sun was high in the sky. The leaves were just beginning to turn.

I was eager to show off my brand-new family to the world. I was a young mother, twenty-six, celebrating an early fall moment when my postpartum hormones weren't raging. I had a thriving baby girl and a husband. I wanted to take my place in suburban America with my bounty.

Ben reacted differently. He lagged behind us as I pushed the carriage, almost as if he didn't want to be seen this way. It's rare today to walk down the streets of New York without noticing a man carrying a baby in a backpack, but in 1974 it was unusual. My sample study was one person, who was also my husband. I expected him to be that father, but he had a different thought.

"What're you doing? Why aren't you walking with us?" I asked.

I waited a moment for Ben to reach me and the carriage. His hands were tucked into the back pockets of his jeans as he edged up beside us. "Don't expect me to be the kind of father who will be all that interested in his children when they get older," he stated.

My body must have stiffened slightly, and he continued softening his tone. "I'm happy we have a baby," he went on, and then resumed his declaration, "but when she's in high school and college, I'm not really going to be involved."

He lightly touched the chrome handlebar of the carriage and started walking alongside us. My steps slowed as I took in his words. Even though I had on a cardigan warming my shoulders, I slipped my arms through the sleeves and fastened the first two buttons around my throat.

I was stunned. I felt as if there'd been an attack on my concept of family. It was painful for me to hear his words, but, instead of inviting further conversation, as I might today—"tell me more"—I shut down, as I had in the past when I hadn't liked what had been said. Sounds ceased, and my baby seemed more than arm's distance away.

Stage direction for Young Mother role: Show signs of disappointment through body language. Internalize your judgment, but don't express it. Act sad.

This memorable scene stands out because it became a showstopper in my mind. *We're married just two years, and it's over. He's not doing what I want. I don't know how to fix this. I'm stuck.*

I'd learned in my parents' home that life was filled with events from which we crafted our history: wearing the right outfit to Grandma and Grandpa's, getting into an Ivy League school, buying the most memorable gift for Mother's Day. All my examples, I recognize, are based on how things looked, not how things felt.

*Do things correctly in the family, and be justly rewarded. Or else. . . .*

Baby's First Walk in the Park was the event I'd just produced. Now I know that life is a process. It was in making events out of processes that I created my own sadness.

The way I got rid of my negative feelings then was by smothering them with sweets. One of the great side effects of nursing Lucy when I was twenty-six years old was that I could devour as many calories as I wanted, hundreds of them, from half gallons of Friendly's ice cream, without gaining weight. This had the dual function of making me feel happy in the moment and obscuring the pain. I didn't have to delve into upsetting behaviors until years later, when I began to suffer from sugar blues and weight gain. In 1974, satisfying a sweet tooth deflected the pain.

MY RELATIONSHIP WITH Ben's parents also shifted after Lucy was born. Where once I had felt loved and looked after as the fiancée, newlywed, and cherished carrier of the Pollak line, the first time we brought Lucy to New Jersey for a visit, an almost instantaneous transformation occurred. It was imperceptible to everyone but me, mainly because it happened only between my ears.

"Ben," his mother instructed, after we'd arrived and unloaded all the paraphernalia that accompanies you once you have a baby, "you sit and watch the game with Bob. Hold Lucy while Jane and I serve you." Three months earlier, I would have been the one instructed to sit and wait to be taken care of.

Boom! In that exact moment, I realized that I was being relegated to the backseat and was therefore less loved and, by extension, less lovable. My daughter was elevated to my former status as queen. I became a lady-in-waiting.

I created an entire scenario based on one short bit of dialogue. Cue the laughter of recognition as I recite this part of my story. My ego was so fragile, and my need to be recognized so great that I instantly imagined a new drama in which I was the designated sufferer.

And what about Ben's feelings? He may have interpreted

the scene completely differently. I never asked. I was too busy feeling sorry for myself to consider another point of view. I clung to my version with all the righteousness I could muster.

Like many addicts, I saw things as black or white, all or nothing. There was no gray, no partial high. Either I got my fix—attention or ice cream—or I didn't. An apple would not satiate my hunger. It had to be Friendly's mint chocolate chip to appease the craving. *Once, Ben's parents loved me; now, they prefer my child.* There was no "and." I made this up so that I could cast myself in the role of martyr. I cherished that role, passive as it was.

I wanted the Pollaks to say, "Jane, your giving us Lucy is the best thing that's happened to us!" I needed to be in the equation because I didn't know how to love myself enough to enjoy the reflected glory.

As though there were a limit to how much love was available in the universe, I chose then to believe that their affection for my daughter diminished how they felt about me. That was what I made up, the fuel I used, to keep my world of suffering spinning.


I COULDN'T STAY miserable for long with a baby in our midst. My mother-in-law, a doting grandmother, was superb in her handling of Lucy. She got our daughter cooing and laughing within seconds of our arrival at their home. I would have loved it if Bunny had spent more time with Lucy and me, even if Lucy was number one.

It was such a gift to have someone I fully trusted caring for my infant. Every visit with her gave me exactly what I wanted: relief and pleasure. I simultaneously appreciated and envied her concern for my daughter.

If I'd had a support system back then, I would have called someone whom I trusted, told them what I was experiencing, listened to their wisdom, and heard how they identified with the need to feel loved, too. I wanted someone to affirm that feeling loved was a bottom line not only for me. To feel loved —it sounds so easy.

In lieu of experiencing that emotional security, I found that my mood improved when Bunny scooped up a large portion of the deliciousness she kept in her freezer. There was always ice cream there in my favorite flavor and brand. *She does love me*! *She remembered to stock up.* Crisis averted.

WHEN I BECAME pregnant with our second child a few years later, I felt confident enough in my parenting skills and knowledge of pregnancy to convince Ben that there was a better way to have baby number two. I had done the reading, talked to friends who'd had babies at home, a revival of the ages-old tradition, and who had raved about the experience. But, since a home birth was over the top for Ben's sensibility, he agreed to go along with only one aspect of my delivery desires: our next child would be brought into this world by a midwife, but in a hospital setting. This was another growing trend in the late '70s. Midwives were less likely to interfere medically. They viewed pregnancy and delivery as a natural process, not a medical issue. So many obstetric births resulted in cesarean sections. I wanted to avoid that at all costs.

It wasn't Ben's first choice, but he knew how much I wanted this birth experience. Sharing this decision with my parents opened up a firestorm of resistance and criticism.

"It's like crossing Fifth Avenue with your eyes closed," my father insisted, as he tamped down the tobacco in his pipe. He

must have pictured a wizened woman in a hooded cape extracting our infant's head with long, gnarled fingers. He was
unwilling to hear the statistics and data I wanted to present.

My mistake was hoping for their approval by trying to
convince them why my choice was superior. My mother was
less subtle. On a visit to their home a few months before I was
due, I asked her about a couple my parents knew on Long Island who had prepared for a home birth, hoping that their success story might alter her prejudiced view. I had been envious
of that couple's partnership, even as Mom disparaged it. I asked
her if the delivery had happened.

"Didn't I tell you?" she responded, leaning back against the
floral pillow sham on her king-size bed. I sat across from her
on their navy linen-upholstered chaise longue beneath the
window that overlooked the garden. "Not only did the baby
die, but the mother died, too."

Such an outcome in 1977! My father came upstairs shortly
after this revelation, and I shared my upset with him.

"Dad, I'm so sorry for your friends' loss. That must've been
devastating."

"What are you talking about?" he asked, having not been
in on the earlier conversation.

"Mom just told me that the Robinsons' daughter and
grandchild died during their home delivery."

Standing next to the bed where my mother sat, hands on
his hips, he looked over at me and then down at her.

"Where did you hear that?" he asked.

There was a prolonged pause. My mother finally spoke.

"I made it up," she said, glancing down at her chipped nail
polish.

She really did that.

Stunning as her lie was, it still took me years afterward not to care about their approval. Actually, that's not true. I always cared, even in recovery, although after 1989 I became increasingly conscious of how I set myself up to be disappointed.

The counselor who guided me in my step work explained to me, "Your mother will do whatever she needs to do to get what she wants." What I could change were my expectations, not their opinions, no matter how much data I provided. Eventually, I stopped offering information that could be used as ammunition.

It helped me understand that my mother's eccentric behavior was the survival skill of a woman who didn't have the support she, too, may have longed for. Instead, she made it up as she went along. She wanted her daughter in a hospital to deliver her grandchild, and it didn't matter to what lengths she needed to go to make it happen.

When I moved forward with my choice of the midwife anyway, Mom never said, "You were right. What a wonderful birth experience that must've been for you!" She simply turned her formidable attention to another event, the next cause célèbre, to get her adrenaline pumping. Hearing stories of equally shocking proportion told at my meetings helped me to accept that my mother wasn't doing this to me—she was just doing it.

I knew in my head why she did it, but my heart still wanted her to be on my side.

My son, Ryan, was born during the January blizzard of 1978, delivered by Mary, my favorite nurse-midwife from the midwifery team at the hospital. After his birth, and six months before my thirtieth birthday, I became devoted to seeking Mary's further attention.

It was the perfect setup. A nurse-midwife's role is to care for the pregnant woman. She was solicitous in that respect, seemed to enjoy having me as a patient, but made no overtures toward having a friendship with me. No problem—I'd take the lead. I invited her and the rest of the midwifery team, who'd helped me prenatally, over for a celebratory lunch, which they accepted. But I needed more. My appetite for this sort of kindness was hard to quench, and I was thirstier than ever for attention.

I wanted to create an additional thank-you gift, beyond the gourmet meal I'd prepared, that would catch and hold Mary's attention. When my son was a few months old, I tucked him into his car seat and drove to Mary's new neighborhood. I parked my car across from the house Mary and her husband had recently bought so I could make a sketch of it, have it printed on stationery featuring her new address, and present it to her.

I couldn't see then (nearly forty years ago now) how much like stalking my behavior was. That word wasn't as prevalent in our vocabulary, pre-Internet. My body was charged with energy and excitement as I anticipated Mary's surprise and pleasure receiving my gift, only to become deflated after the initial high of her telephoned thank-you but no further engagement.

Had Mary suggested an invitation to coffee or lunch, I would have felt intoxicated. Instead, her response was cordial and appropriate. There was no reciprocal offer to match my painstaking gesture. Her message was clear. It wasn't quite *do not enter*—more like *proceed with caution*.

These big feelings confused me. They also distracted me from what was missing in my marriage. If I used all my thinking time obsessing about how to attract Mary's attention, the heat was off Ben.

"I have really big feelings for this person, and I don't know what to do with them," I told Silvie, the first therapist I went to see when the ice cream was no longer enough to stuff down my longing.

Silvie's home office was decorated with artifacts from the world travels she'd taken with her husband. There were African masks and woven baskets hanging on the walls and resting on bookshelves. Silvie sat in an upholstered armchair facing my location, on a loveseat.

Her presence made it easy to talk. I was never shy in her office.

It was helpful to have a neutral person to confess this to. Silvie began to help me sort out the "spaghetti," as she called it, and gain perspective.

*Our thinking becomes distorted*, program literature says. I didn't find these words until my early forties. My ego at thirty was huge. "Humility" sounded like a dirty word, much too close to "humiliation," for me to want anything to do with it.

Seeing Silvie helped. She offered exactly what I was looking for: caring, concern, and undivided attention, albeit as a professional in a paid relationship. But I now had someplace to verbalize my issues and to better understand a behavior that was hurting my family and me.

This relationship had clear boundaries. It felt safe, and I trusted Silvie enough to admit everything that was going on inside my very busy mind. That release and her guidance carried me for nearly a decade.


LILY'S BIRTH FOLLOWED Ryan's four years later, in March 1982. Dr. Maryellen Humes, an ob-gyn, "caught" her, and our family was complete. I left the hospital twelve hours after that, with the permission of our pediatrician. By then, seven years into motherhood but not yet in recovery, I had begun speaking up, instead of hoping to have my mind read.

"You're probably right," the doctor said, after I listed the reasons I wanted to get home as quickly as possible. "Most women want to prolong their stay here and be taken care of." I was more anxious to have our family bond quickly and to recuperate in my own home, surrounded by Ben and the kids. "You know what you're doing. You and the baby will be fine," he concluded, and officially signed us out of Norwalk Hospital.

We were fine—a combination of the acronym FINE and the word "fine," meaning "A-OK." My growing family was my priority, and I rarely missed having my own work to focus on. There would be time for that.

OUR DAYS WERE beyond full.

"Do you think we'll ever have a meal where nothing spills and no one cries?" Ben called across the expanse of our dining room table at supper one night. Lily, the baby, was in a seat strapped to the table. She was still drinking from a Tommee Tippee cup, so she wasn't the culprit. Ryan had taken to pouring himself juice from the Stew Leonard's half-gallon container. And Lucy, ever the young lady, was cautious and mannerly, in imitation of Ben and me, whom, as the eldest, she considered her peers.

But inevitably, while passing the macaroni and cheese or reaching for an extra helping of sliced bread, someone would knock something over and the tears would flow.

Not that we were punishing or angry about it. But somehow, I guess, all three kids picked up on both Ben's and my need for order and precision, our hunger for their approval and love, and for them to make our marriage better. Although this was unconscious, they may have felt an urgency to get it right. Maybe they sensed an underlying yet inexplicable tension. Even at the kitchen table. Were Ben and I both reenacting what we hadn't worked out from our own childhoods? Would our insecurities be passed on to them as we had inherited our parents'?

Even without the constant nurturing I craved, I had just enough filling my well to provide my children with the attention they needed. I also got plenty back from them and adored this time in their lives. There are so many moments I recall with deep affection: reading *Pat the Bunny* or chapter books and cuddling before putting each one to sleep; watching *The Brady Bunch* together under the down comforter on our queen-size bed; giggling as we formed family sandwiches, stretching out on top of each other in a clump.

It seems like only a short time later that Lucy was applying to college, Ryan was proposing to Anne, and Lily was flying to Japan to teach English to the children there. It feels like barely a season since we went from around-the-clock daily care to hoping for a text today.

Chapter Ten

*I* longed to be the best mother I could be. I read books and attended available workshops in the hope of finding a new nugget of insight, tip, or guru to follow. One that stood out was a lecture on sibling rivalry at CCNS. I chose that nursery school because it offered an environment where parents worked in the classroom every other week and learned by doing. While we sat on chairs designed for small children one evening, I heard the social worker-expert tell the assembled parents that there are three systems in each family: the marital system, husband and wife; the parental system, mother and father; and the sibling system, the children. If the marital system is in order—if the husband and wife get along and support each other—then the other systems readily fall into place.

"The best thing a father can do for his children is to love their mother," the expert told us.

My heart sank when I heard her words. Something had shifted in my relationship with Ben. We behaved admirably in our roles as mother and father, and our children got along well. But in my core, I knew the marital system was out of order.

She had put into words what I was experiencing. Ben loved the kids and treated me decently as their mother, but I didn't feel his love for me as a wife—or, that is, the way I imagined a beloved wife should feel.

Had I been able to share these thoughts in a safe place, I might have found support and suggestions for coping. So many adult children of alcoholics feel unloved and unlovable. From the laundry list: we judge ourselves harshly and have low self-esteem.

Saying it out loud would have gotten it off my chest and out of my heart, rather than allowing it to fester and smolder. I interpreted my feelings as facts and looked no further for evidence. I was enacting a tragedy that itself was tragic. I was manufacturing my own misery.

Today I know that no one human being could have filled the empty part of my soul at that time. It would have taken a village, and even then, I would have found fault. *The village next door does it better.*

I rather enjoyed the role of victim, unaware of it as I was. Had you pointed that out to me then, I wouldn't have heard you. I couldn't. I was too invested in the attention it gave me from my caretaking friends.

Today my sponsor might ask, "What's your part in this?" And, of course, she'd be right. Relationships always involve two parties. I wanted to believe *he* was doing this to *me*. But I was a willing and eager participant. "Fool me once, shame on you. Fool me twice, shame on me."

Back then, surrounded by other active adult children, I got sympathy and collusion. "Me, too. I'm not feeling loved, either. *They* don't understand."

It was easier to stock up on resentments than to confront Ben. Like the afternoon we rented a video camera to record

Lucy's birthday party one summer. We'd just waved goodbye to a dozen of her friends as they hopped into their parents' station wagons. Ben wanted me to record him practicing his golf swing. "Can you tape me so I can see what it looks like?"

"Sure," I said, holding the shoebox-size device to my right eye.

Ben teed up a Wiffle ball, swung his wood club, and connected in a smooth arc. "Again," he requested. "Keep it rolling!"

He extracted half a dozen white and Day-Glo-orange balls from his golf bag and continued. "How do I look?"

"I'm not sure what it's supposed to look like, but I'm impressed," you can hear me say in the replay of the scene.

A few minutes later, he was finished. "Let me see what you shot," he said reaching for the camera.

"Could you first take some footage of Lily and me?" I asked. Lily had been nestled between my knees as I kept my eye on the viewer.

Ben took the camera and aimed the lens at us.

"Lily, sweetie, wave to Daddy." She obliged. She was a toddler, and I wanted to capture this brief window of her learning how to maneuver her little body across the yard.

"I want to go in now," Ben said, "okay?"

I longed for more time to be captured. But I looked directly at the camera with a smile on my face and said, "Okay. Thanks."

It wasn't okay. I had lied in the moment. I wanted more time and footage focused on Lily and me. I was afraid to ask for it. Afraid Ben would say no.

My behavior was timid and calculating. It was also the best I could do.

I stuffed the feelings with a scoop or three of ice cream and went on.

*Hello, little sadness. Sweep, sweep.* A spoonful of sugar worked its magic, and I continued my journey. I had tasks to accomplish and a role to play.

WHILE I WAS at home, tribeless, changing diapers, carpooling, and hosting playdates, Ben was commuting to Brigham Woods, taking classes at Fairfield University, and teaching his portion of the SAT prep course. He had a growing circle of admirers, students and faculty alike, from whom he drew regular support.

After Ben had been a teacher at Brigham Woods for only a handful of years, the presiding chairman of the English department was asked to step down and Ben was selected to assume that role. He had worked long hours before, but the additional administrative role increased his responsibilities. A beloved faculty member, he hosted students in his office after school and led department meetings with a group of teachers who admired and respected him. He had carved out a place for himself where he was thriving.

Occasionally, a group of his best and brightest students would arrive at our house to meet Mr. Pollak's family. Ben would beam anxiously as he introduced these teenagers to the kids and me. I'm not sure on whose account he felt apprehensive. Would they like us? Would we like them? Clearly, they worshipped him. They were all smiles and admiration.

"Lisa is going to Harvard next year," he said, introducing me to a long-haired, Asian American young woman. "She's the one whose college essay you liked so much." Ben occasionally shared a student's writing with me when he thought it was outstanding. He was always right. He was an excellent teacher who taught and inspired his protégés to be better than they'd been before his instruction. He once showed me an acknowledgment in the front pages of a student's novel expressing loving gratitude to her English teacher, Mr. Ben Pollak.

Ben and his visitors bantered, sharing inside jokes and literary references that sailed over my head. I was happy for him but also envious of the attention and affection he showed for these schoolkids. I wanted him to shine that same bountiful glow on our children and me.

"Your kids are so cute," one girl raved, as they were about to leave. Their energy filled our dining room and departed with them.

The contrast between Ben as their teacher and Ben as my husband and our kids' father was vast. He spent the majority of each day dedicated to his livelihood, teaching students, interacting with them after school, and grading their papers each night. In exchange, he received a paycheck, as well as their adulation and affection.

"Make me laugh!" Lily, at five, would say at the end of dinner on the nights Ben was home. He'd grab two straws that had come with our takeout order, peel off the thin paper wraps, and insert one into each nostril. Barely able to contain herself, Lily would break out into giggles, as would I.

But when I asked if he would read to her before her bedtime that night, he'd point to the cardboard box brimming with an uneven stack of stapled essays and say, "Did you see how many papers I have to grade?" He'd comply with my request, but having to make it and not receiving an immediate "Sure!" felt like crossing the desert for a sip of water.

Ben spent only a few waking hours each day with us at home. Even then, he devoted nearly three hours to inking comments on his students' essays or correcting their quizzes. If a sports event was on TV, he might bring his papers into the living room, where he watched and continued his schoolwork there.

"You seem so angry all the time, honey," I observed one dark winter evening a few weeks after his students' most recent visit. He'd arrived later than when I'd expected him. "I thought you would be home an hour ago."

The tension in the house felt thick. I'd heard his car's gearshift as he pulled into the driveway, the driver's side door bang shut, and the slow whirring of the garage door as it slowly descended to the cement floor. Unaware he was being watched, Ben walked slowly, head down, up the two steps to the front walk and into the vestibule, where I opened the front door.

"Some kids wanted to meet with me in my office," he replied dismissively.

"This late?" I parried.

No answer, just that gurgly sound he made when he deemed a response unnecessary.

After depositing his carton of papers and planning book on the dining room table, he said to me, "I work hard at school every day and then come home to hours of grading. When I get here, I want to relax and be taken care of. I just want to be adored."

*Who wouldn't?* I thought at the time. I worked hard, too. Taking care of three children and a household was the hardest job I'd ever had. There was no remuneration, performance review (other than the kids' hugs at bedtime), or vacation, nor did I expect any. I didn't even have a thirty-minute car ride to and from work, like he did, to have my own uninterrupted thoughts.

Ben put words to what I felt after Lucy was born but was incapable of articulating at the time. I never felt worthy of whispering that desire—to be adored—but once he'd said it, my pulse sped in realization. What I resented most that winter afternoon was not his proclamation but, upon reflection, that he had the ego to make that statement.

*I hate that he is asking for attention and love.*
*I wish that I could ask for attention and love.*

I could not imagine now letting a comment like "I just want to be adored" go unaddressed for longer than an hour. When I heard it in my mid-thirties, it was addressed exactly never.

At the time, we were both working at capacity and had little to contribute to each other's well-being. The spirit had gone out of the relationship. My confidence on the marital front had grown shaky. I felt like a drowning person with two fingers raised out of the water. I was too ashamed to bother anyone with my problems, too afraid of scaring the children by yelling or screaming, and too afraid to walk away.

Where would I go? Home to Mother? That option didn't exist, and what would I claim: *He's not paying enough attention to me?* Get in line!

Neglect is defined as a marked lack of consideration for a dependent's need for attention. I cringe at the word "dependent," but weren't we dependent on each other? Neglect is a perception. And was mine reliable? I felt so needy. Could anyone have filled that empty space? Was I doing my share to think about my partner's needs? From the perspective of knowing how to get my needs met today, I can sympathetically witness a young woman who had not been taught, struggling in a marriage with a man who hadn't been given the manual, either.

It wasn't that they didn't want to try to make it better. They simply didn't know how, and the disappointment and frustration increased the alienation.

NEVER WAS THE gap in our relationship more clear than in late June 1985, after Ben had been teaching in Westchester for nearly fifteen years. If I'd asked the universe for an illustration of how far apart our worlds were, this would have been all the evidence I needed. Mr. and Mrs. Herman had invited us to their daughter's graduation party. Ben had been solicited to attend these functions in the past but had rarely accepted. However, this particular student was a favorite, one who'd visited our house on more than one occasion. He invited me to accompany him.

"We should go in separate cars, though, in case you want to leave early to get home to the kids," Ben suggested, and went on ahead of me. This sounded more thoughtful on the surface than it felt. Wouldn't he want to get home to the kids, too? Were his students and their families a higher priority?

I agonized over what to wear to Ben's star pupil's event that summer night. The only little black dress hanging in my closet was older than Ryan, who was seven, and hadn't been worn since before Lily's birth, three years earlier. I'm sure it was out of style, as were my low-heeled pumps, which did nothing to enhance the look. But it was all I had.

The babysitter fed the kids their favorite linguine parmesan dinner, which I'd prepared, and nodded at my instructions: which chapter to read, teeth-brushing routines, and bedtimes.

I kissed the children good night and drove by myself to the gated community in Westchester where the party was held, arriving an hour after Ben. Although my stomach was empty, I felt a gripping sensation different than hunger. It was like a clenched fist right behind my belly button. Swallowing was hard.

The Hermans's yard was aglow with Japanese lanterns strung from tree to tree. Waiters in white, waist-length jackets offered canapés and white wine in crystal, not plastic, flutes. Gaggles of parents and their burnished offspring swayed in rhythmic waves to each other's witty repartee.

Eighteen-year-old boys wearing pressed Izod shirts, collars casually but precisely upturned, nestled among nubile young women overflowing from their push-up bras and spaghetti-strap minidresses. They tossed their manes of layered curls and laughed and laughed and laughed.

When I spotted him, Ben was surrounded by a group of grinning, blue-blazered fathers in contrasting primary-colored pants, and their well-coiffed wives in form-fitting black cocktail wear. The woman next to him had slung an arm across my husband's shoulder.

"It was so good of you to come tonight, Mr. Pollak," she gushed.

He had a broad smile on his face, head lowered modestly, hands in his pockets.

"Princeton accepted only two students from our district this year, and they weren't even legacies," the balding man on Ben's other side announced, as I hovered behind their circle, waiting for Ben to notice my arrival. "I'm sure it was *your* letter of recommendation, Mr. Pollak, that did the trick."

A beat later, Ben backed out of that intimate circle with an I'll-be-right-back finger lifted into the air and pecked me on the cheek.

"This is Jane," he announced, pressing me forward with two fingers in the center of my back. He introduced me to the group en masse: "These are the Harrisons, the Levys, and the Gutners," he said, gesturing with a wave of his right arm. It was too much for me to take in. I didn't even try. Small talk at cocktail parties was not part of my repertoire. I listened instead.

"Your husband is our hero!" one mother praised.

"We're completely indebted to him," said another, nodding vigorously. I did my best Miss Congeniality imitation but felt inside like a subspecies of their class.

These contestants—I viewed us as being in competition for my husband's attention, even though I didn't know it then—occupied a world of long driveways, elegant landscapes, and well-groomed children. My universe was messier, dominated by dirty diapers, takeout pizza, and early bedtimes. I loved it but felt shabby by comparison. I hadn't yet grasped the Zen concept "desire what you have." I was full of envy and longing for the gilded and sparkly lights in front of me. I knew I had made different choices, but at that moment, this scene glowed like a Shiny Brite Christmas ornament for a holiday I didn't celebrate.

I sidled away from the group in search of the buffet. Ben remained with his admirers. I wanted to criticize him for his oblivion to my feeling of exclusion, but I had earned that sentiment all on my own. I didn't say anything to him about it. I believed that a husband should know. Thirteen years into our marriage, and I hadn't learned how to open my mouth and ask for what I needed or say no to what made me feel left out. Even *I* didn't know I didn't want to be there. I must have dreamed that some student's mother would notice me, appreciate what a good helpmate I was to Ben, and be curious about my side of the journey. What was behind my husband's successful teaching? She'd escort me into the Hermans' living room, where we could be alone and she could hear my whole story and be fulfilled by my tales of virtuous support.

Talk about magical thinking.

I left the party soon after and drove back home. I'm not sure that we ever talked about the shift that happened inside me. That's how I did things then. I may have yammered to my friends about it or brought it up in a session with Silvie. She may have soothed my hurt ego. But there it lay, moldering.

Ben had appeared relaxed and confident in the presence of the wealth and ease on display at this gathering. I was more at home sitting cross-legged on a floor, surrounded by nursing mothers in T-shirts, toddlers in tow. I felt continents away from him and his existence.

I don't know if Ben saw it as I did: how different our lives had become. How do you explain the concept of water to a fish? He was perfectly comfortable there. I was the outsider visiting an alien place. Separating our worlds was a thin crack that would deepen and widen in the years ahead. There was nothing concrete for me to point at or hold on to—just a growing awareness that our individual microcosms were rotating in separate, not overlapping, orbits.

As happens in life, and particularly in close relationships like marriage and families, incidents like this bubble up and calm back down. At that time, I had no reliable support system in place, no money to call my own, and not enough courage to walk out the door with three children. So I stayed.

Time passed, memories faded, and we found our way back to a livable status quo.

Chapter Eleven

*T*he friendship that brought me into the twelve-step rooms of the Relationship Program was not what you might have predicted. Most of the people I met in CoDA were there for a marriage gone bad, an affair turned sour, or a history of short-term infatuations.

From a very early age, I unconsciously desired the attention of other females who made me feel seen in a particular way, starting with Amy, a tall, pale-complexioned girl with dusty-blond braids and light freckles across her cheeks, who was the first classmate to take special notice of me. I was the pickee, not the picker, having never had the courage to ask someone to be my friend.

We were two fourth-graders cleaning up a mural-painting project in the art room at Ridgeway School. Bold-colored tempera paints filled sectioned muffin tins with primary and secondary colors. There were small, wire-handled buckets of water for rinsing the brushes. I was squishing down the bristles of one into the now murky liquid when Amy approached, her hand tugging lightly on the shoulder strap of my jumper.

"Jane, will you come over after school to play? I want you to be my best friend."

I dabbed the nearly clean bristles onto the brown paper towels stacked nearby to absorb the moisture and remaining pigment. I swept the hairs of the brush back and forth across the thick, darkening paper. The wetter the towel, the cleaner the brush.

Amy was initiating an invitation to her house on her own, a practice I was not familiar with. Mothers made those arrangements. At ten years old, I felt liked, singled out. I was important to someone. I mattered.

I wanted more of that and allowed myself to be chosen through all my school years. But as I became older, something twisted in my heart, and simple friendship no longer filled me. By the time I was in my early thirties, the love and friendship I'd hoped for with Ben had transformed my spirit into a void of craving for what was missing.

I arrived at the Relationship Program as an outwardly happily married woman who had a crush on another woman. I couldn't define it back then, let alone ask for what I needed. Ben and I rarely found the time in our day to talk about our lives, something I craved but he shunned. He'd been with a hundred people at school. He wanted alone time. I'd been at home with three children under ten. I longed for another adult's company and acknowledgment that I still was one. Other mothers filled in between carpools and meal prep. I needed something more reliable, a regular, predictable fix.

I met my ultimate codependent partner—in recovery parlance, my qualifier—in 1981. A qualifier is the person who, when you finally admit you're powerless over the relationship and that your life has become unmanageable, assisted in that adventure.

Fran was the parent-volunteer coordinator at my daughter's new elementary school, on staff to help the mothers and fathers contribute to the Bank Street curriculum in a capacity that suited them: assisting with fund-raisers, running student clubs, or providing cupcakes for bake sales.

Ten years older than I, Fran was an inch or two shorter, slim, and sported a just-beginning-to-gray pageboy haircut. She gave me a broad smile when I walked into volunteer headquarters: the so-called Family Room at SoNo Magnet School. "Magnet" suggested that this facility, located in a depressed, largely segregated neighborhood on Norwalk's other side of the tracks, drew families from more privileged districts, who agreed to have their offspring bused in for the benefit of a desirable curriculum and improvement of the overall health of the city.

"Welcome! You must be Jane," Fran said, extending both her hands to take my right one in a warm shake. "Mary Ann has told me so much about you. She's excited that Lucy is joining us this year, and that *you* will be a great asset to our school. It's such a pleasure to meet you!"

Fran's warmth and specificity took me aback. My friend Mary Ann had enrolled her daughter at SoNo Magnet in the first lottery round and continually updated me with her excitement about the magnet school's potential. She urged me to keep our daughter's name on a waiting list, even though Lucy had happily attended first grade at our neighborhood school and excelled there.

Fran's small nook of an office housed a schoolteacher's desk and was stationed behind a freestanding screen to the right of the Family Room door. It was rare to find her seated there, though—she was always milling about, greeting parents, offering words of kindness and appreciation.

She was consistently emphatic and precise with her praise. "Jane, Ryan's costume really stood out in the Halloween parade. A baseball card! With his little head sticking through the pitcher's face! You're so creative! You must've spent hours working on that." She hit two of my sweet spots: acknowledging my art and acknowledging my child.

Parents eagerly signed up to offer their services, and the school benefited from so many extra hands. Evaluations of educational institutions often include assessments of parental volunteerism; SoNo Magnet became nationally recognized as a Blue Ribbon School, thanks in part to the robust parent support Fran's role generated. I figured all those mothers and fathers were as hungry for outside praise and notice as I was.

A few weeks into our family's first semester at SoNo Magnet, I attended a meeting that Fran led to talk about how new parents could get involved. I listened and observed the proceedings without commenting. Toward the end of the hour, Fran called on me by name. "Jane, is there anything in particular that would fit your skills? I've heard you're an artist. Would you be willing to design a poster for the Holiday Fair?"

I was flattered that Fran had learned something about me before I knew anything about her. I had observed the goings-on in the Family Room but wasn't sure how much I wanted to get involved. I was pregnant with Lily at the time and could have easily used my condition to beg off.

Most of my life, I had been a lurker, before I'd even heard the term. La Leche League provided an early scaffolding for moving away from the shy-girl choices I'd relied on previously. Unconsciously, I think I was waiting for someone to notice me. The mother thing again. I wanted to feel special and seen, the way a nurtured child does. But there was an air of entitlement to my reluctance. *I shouldn't have to make the effort. They should already know about me. Let me sit back in judgment, form an opinion, and decide if I want to participate.*

Check out the defensiveness built into those thoughts. *If I don't get picked, I won't care, because they will have missed out having me.* This is the heart of passive aggression. *I'm not going to share myself, and then you'll suffer.* It's not logical or helpful, but it protected my ego when I didn't have a more mature way to care for myself.

Being called on by Fran in front of this group of parents disarmed me. I couldn't hide. I was being asked to make a commitment before I knew which side I wanted to occupy. Speaking allowed others to know me. My cover, my mask, was being torn away. This was new, thrilling, scary. Exactly what I'd yearned for.

"I can do that!" I blurted. "Do you have a sample from last year I can look at? When do you need this?"

My response to Fran's request surprised me. It came from a place deep within and felt legitimate. I was happy to be noticed and quickly dropped my judgments. Now involved, I became a part of the school community, making a contribution. This sense of connection was what I'd wanted but hadn't been able to define or ask for before.

"People will crawl over broken glass for a thank-you," I heard at a luncheon honoring school volunteers a few years into my tenure as a parent volunteer at SoNo Magnet. I must not be the only one hungry for acknowledgment and praise. I had never offered my services so abundantly before I met Fran. Her attention and warmth were more than adequate compensation for my time and talent back when my children were small and I didn't have other outside affirmation.

"Boy, you seem happy," Ben commented after dinner one night, as he brought in the dishes for me to wash. I'd been unaware of my increased peppiness, but the fact that he'd noticed made me doubly happy.

"I'm enjoying SoNo Magnet," I replied. "There's a woman running the volunteers there, and she's good at it." I'd fill him in more as needed. He'd witnessed my attachment to Mary and how that exchange had led me into therapy. I was in an early heightened state, and he remarked on it. I thought he'd be pleased, relieved that I wasn't hounding him for more time together.

By October of that first school year, plans for the school's biggest fund-raiser, the Holiday Fair, were under way. Mothers chitchatted around the large table in front of the multipaned window at the far end of the Family Room. Their hands busily glued pine cones into baskets that would be sold as centerpieces at the upcoming event in early December. Once beribboned, the completed projects lined the top shelves of the bookcases on the adjacent wall.

I generally dislike small talk, but when parenting is the topic, as it often is in a school environment, I tune in. Like a mother hen, Fran hovered, coaxed, patted, and clucked as we produced saleable goods for the fair.

"Denise, how's Josh doing with the new allergy meds?"

"Rosemarie, your daughter's talent show performance was delightful!"

"How are you feeling, Jane? Is this pregnancy different from your others?"

Sunlight poured in, and I signed up for more hours of workshop time.

As the year progressed, I found myself frequently in the Family Room. Each contribution I made was rewarded with a short note of recognition or thanks. Fran used a child's backpack as her postal service: "To Jane, Kindness of Lucy," the envelope read. Tucked inside was her handwritten gratitude for the task I'd undertaken. Often, there was a hug.

I found reasons to drop by, even if I wasn't scheduled to

volunteer that day. The school was located on the far side of town, arrived at only by a circuitous route with several traffic lights and a bridge that might be raised when a too-tall boat needed to sail beneath. The drive never bothered me.

I even invented ways to get seen: a violin to be delivered, a field trip to chaperone, an idea to share. In retrospect, I was clearly looking for the rush I got from receiving Fran's attention. It filled up what I was missing at home. How obvious it was to Fran is a question I never asked.

She phoned me frequently in her role as volunteer coordinator. "Would you be willing to lead a workshop for stenciling T-shirts?" she'd ask. "You always have such good ideas. Parents are already asking to buy the pieces you've designed, and the sale hasn't even started. We're so lucky to have you!"

I was starving for this form of acknowledgment. My women friends and I used our time together for mutual support, not affirmation. My parents had never been forthcoming with approving words. Ben was busy with his schoolwork. He gratefully, or perhaps unwittingly, relinquished the role of attention giver to Fran. In fact, when I voiced unhappiness with that friendship later on, he was interested and, I believe, consoled that he wasn't the focus of my distress.

My first role in the early '80s was to give my time and attention to our children. I also needed to refill my own well, something I'd learn to do exceedingly well through meditation, journaling, and connecting with friends but couldn't conceptualize doing on my own back then. My only solution before that was to make an appearance at SoNo Magnet School and hope for a hit of my substance: recognition from Fran. I'd made her my source of all things positive.

Soon after I gave birth to Lily in March 1982, Fran called to ask if she could stop by. *How nice*, I thought. *Fran's making a special trip to see me.* I knew I didn't have to clean up or prepare a snack for her, but I did want to make the visit last as long as possible.

I was in the family room on the foldout couch, breastfeeding Lily, who was just a few weeks old, when the doorbell rang. I draped the baby over my shoulder for a burp, a diaper tucked under her chin in case she spit up. That's how I answered the front door.

"Oh! I remember those days," Fran sang sweetly, as she followed me back through the house to where I'd been nursing. "She looks absolutely full and content," she added, witnessing my newborn and assessing her positively.

"How are *you* doing, Mom?" Fran asked, using my role as an honorific. "Getting enough sleep?"

"I'm taking good care of myself," I offered. "Well, the best I'm able to with three kids. How did you ever manage four?"

"You know, you just keep going," she replied modestly. Then, extracting a present from her canvas tote bag, she said, "I brought you a little something."

She handed me a thin, rectangular package, wrapped in pastel-patterned paper and tied with a bow. As I slid my fingers under the taped gift wrap, I felt the familiar rush. My heart quickened, and my head was light with joy.

It was a children's book, not a standard like *Goodnight Moon*, but a volume of Mother Goose rhymes illustrated by someone whose name I didn't recognize. She'd inscribed it to our family. The perfect gift—educational, thoughtful, and personal.

"Oh, Fran! Thank you so much! I love it! I'm going to read it to her tonight," I effervesced.

After twenty minutes, Fran gathered her things and said, "I won't keep you. You've got your hands full. I just wanted to stop by and see how you were."

I wanted to be kept by her presence.

I had found the perfect crush—the person who made me feel seen and important but who also had a full life of her own and for whom I was not a priority. Like any substance people use to alter their state, mine simulated fullness, but it was an illusion. The hole it was intended to fill, mine, was actually bottomless and had leaks. No human being, not even a mother, could do that job.

GRADUALLY, I BECAME greedy for Fran's time and support. When we got together, I would think, *You're staying only an hour? Not two? When will you come again? Where do I fit into your life? What must I do next to get your attention?* My fantasy was that Fran would need me in the same way I needed her. We had shared many deep conversations about ourselves and our families in the six months I'd gotten to know her. There was intimacy and positive regard for each other, but I had a greater desire for connection than Fran did. I craved daily contact. I was the hungry one. I wanted a Lucy-and-Ethel form of neighborly access, but we lived miles apart, and our common water cooler at SoNo Magnet was less available now that I was home, caring for an infant.

As I nurtured Lily, I wanted to get nourished. The little girl inside me wanted it specifically from Fran, for her to be my doula, the woman who mothers the mother. My inner adult, whose face the world saw, was ashamed to ask for anything that would appear desperate, even though I was. I was suffering from needing to be filled by another person before I'd even heard the word "codependent."

How should one handle a needy friend?

Had Fran ever said to me, "I have limited time, and I'm

doing the best I can to be a good friend to you. How about we go for a walk twice a month?" I would have understood and respected that. Part of the attraction was that Fran's boundaries were as permeable as mine were.

The show was on. Roles had been established—Jane the Seeker, Fran the Sought—and the stage set. Another opportunity for me to play out my needs with a generous provider who couldn't say no. Would there be a plot twist this time?

Friendships are rarely suspected in infidelity, so it felt safe but unsatisfying to be infatuated in a way that was old and familiar. As a child, I longed to be teacher's pet, to be noticed and favored for my performance. I constantly looked outside myself for affirmation.

I liked being chosen by Ben back at Whittier Hall during our year of graduate school. After having children, though, and becoming more successful as a teacher, he may have felt more rewarded distributing his attention elsewhere. My focus was on the kids and on my developing art business. Fortunately, I loved both of these parts of my life enough to distract myself from what was missing—a partner who took as much interest in me as I tried to take in him. I needed a reliable source of affection. I never considered having an affair, nor was I ever the object of another male's devotion. For now, I would choose a safer object for closeness.

Part of my formula for my possessiveness in a relationship was that not only did the other person have to want to be with me, but there also had to be a touch of neglect or unavailability. Ben's unwillingness to get married the moment I was ready became catnip for my desire. Had he pursued me more actively, I might have been the one who turned away. Part of his attraction for me was being ignored. It was familiar.

"I've got to stay in to make up a lesson plan," he'd say.

*I've got to work harder, make myself more attractive,* I thought.

A therapist would name this behavior "returning to the wound."

"Dad, can you come to see my swim show?"

"No, I work Thursday nights, Jane."

Yeah, ouch. That's what it felt like. I had no words or wisdom for my behavior back then. Who doesn't want to be seen by the ones they love? To have their parents' eyes only on them?

"Crush" is a specifically chosen word, because, even though there's a puppy-dog element to it, it's also synonymous with "annihilate," "wipe out," and "undo." By the time I came into recovery, I'd been crushed. I didn't feel like Ben's favorite anymore.

*Don't be silly, Jane. That's not a husband's job. Look elsewhere to have that part of you satisfied.* I wanted intimacy with some other human. Not sex, but feeling known. I was all mixed up.

I picked someone else to do that job. But my picker was broken.

THIS WAS DIFFERENT from the way I felt about boys and men. I had the usual hormonal and physical desires for the opposite sex. I got turned on, felt a quickening when a boy called me on the phone or an attractive guy asked me to dance at a college mixer. My pulse sped up, and I spoke faster to cover up my nervousness.

I didn't have sexual feelings for the women I sought, but I did want signs of endearment from them: a compliment, a kiss on the cheek, a hug. I recognize now that I unconsciously wanted to make each of these women into a mother. Not the mother I already had, but the one I wished I had. Someone who would nurture and support me unconditionally. In return, I'd be dutiful, add value to her life, and make her proud of me.

The crush that motivated me to find my first therapist, Mary, the midwife, met those criteria. Once I had the concern and warmth of the current love object, I entered a heightened state. If you gave me a physical exam and I was thinking about one of these important women, you'd see my pulse increase and my endorphins escalate, and I might report that I was very happy and excited. I craved those sensations. I was animated, cheerful, and energized around the house. My distress at Ben's late nights, immersion in paper grading, and lack of interest in me lightened. I continued in my role as mother while my role as wife receded.

After I'd received my hit and my moment of attention-getting was over, I'd go into withdrawal, my source out of reach. I took long naps and tried to focus more on the kids and my work. But underneath that facade of productivity and nurturing, I craved my next high. I was hooked on a person.

I had to pretend that none of this was going on. Act natural, cook dinner, bake the cupcakes, tuck Lily into bed. But in the back of my mind was the drumbeat of need. I had turned a person into my higher power, the reference point used in recovery for what we put before everything else.

My fellows, the men and women I met in the rooms, described their own personal variations of what I was going through. A relationship could be with an unavailable mate, an adult child, or the car mechanic. Someone who created the same sensations in their body and mind that I felt and thought.

There was always an imbalance in the relationship that we were trying, unsuccessfully, to control. We employed a palette of behaviors to get our substance. Comparing notes on the particular means to that end was sobering.

How could *anyone* keep dialing a person who never picked up the receiver? How many mixtapes can you give your beloved without receiving a thank-you? How much disappointment can you suffer before you say, "No more"? I could see *their* craziness clearly. It was my own that blinded me.

I identified with all those others seeking to fill that same hole in the soul.

I believe I missed an important stage of bonding in my earliest years. When my kids were babies, I was fully engaged during those long, developmental days. Lily would crawl across the room and look back to be sure I was watching before taking her next action. Once she was walking, she repeated the behavior. As Ryan moved curiously toward an electrical socket with a baby-proofed plastic device plugging its opening, he'd glance back at me for a nod or a head shake. When Lucy performed in the chorus, she'd come out afterward, scanning the crowd for Ben and me.

This is how healthy bonds are formed. The child knows their parent is there and internalizes the feeling of being cared for and looked after.

The whole time I was behaving like the kind of parent I wanted, I had the gnawing awareness that I had not received what I was giving, the close attention of a mother's gaze. When, as a small child, I turned to look back for affirmation, a paid caretaker's indifference was what I got.

I am aware that I grew up in a safe home, that meals were on the table, clothes in the closet, and tuition paid for. But I never believed that if I presented a report card with a low grade, didn't buy the right gift for my mother's birthday, or wore mismatched white gloves to services at temple I would still be loved.

I can speak only for myself as a woman in recovery. I kept

looking for somebody to fill in that role of an all-knowing, all-loving caregiver the infant needs to establish her identity. Something to make me feel whole.

In my adult life, I hoped to convert someone to that part. She had to be a person I had already elevated to a custodial designation (without her knowledge, of course) to be a consistent pair of eyes focused on me. The essential missing ingredient was attachment, connection.

It's my notion that we each find our unique substance, activity, or person to fill our void. My first substance of choice was a mother substitute. Sugar and sweets were a distant second. If I could chew on an obsessive friendship, I never felt hungry.

During the times I found a woman to play the coveted role I'd created for her, I was temporarily, elusively filled up.

A book I bought at my first Relationship Program meeting I later discovered was non-conference approved, meaning it didn't have the program's blessing. Titled *The Two-Step*, it described and illustrated the out-of-balance-ness of what I suffered from repeatedly, in a style that was clear to me. Using pen-and-ink cartoon figures, the author depicts a seeker wistfully chasing a sought to begin the dance. The sought has the power and control only as long as the seeker keeps seeking. The chase is on. There's energy, excitement, mystery—will the two connect? They may, and the cycle begins anew. Or they won't, and the sought, energized only by the chase, runs out of steam.

If the quest ceases and the seeker stops seeking, the sought loses power, is unplugged, and must do something to restart the course. Now the seeker has the lead. The sought will, uncharacteristically, extend a come-hither message in order to resume her role. The seeker, intrigued, hungry, or delighted, accepts the bait, and they begin anew.

Ultimately, in *The Two-Step* and in life, a healthy relationship works when it is interdependent: the roles of seeker and sought are interchangeable, based on circumstances and need, not dominance and control. Only in a fictional movie, like *Jerry Maguire*, can one human complete another.

What I heard repeatedly in the rooms of the Relationship Program was that other people are the substance we use to fill our spiritual emptiness—our God-sized hole. I've come to believe that only something unseen, a power greater than I, is needed to satisfy that yearning. For me, this is the essence and the work of twelve-step recovery.

I also had to give up the illusion that I was the strongest force in my life. Yes, you read that right. In some altered dimension (aka my brain), I made up that I was the master of my universe. I hear that belief described as ego (*easing God out*). I could take credit for the rain holding off at Shea Stadium so the Mets could play a game Ben had tickets for. That's how mighty my self-will was. I believed I had control of the weather.

"How do you let go and let God?" I would ask at meetings, quoting a popular slogan. Each person I questioned had a unique response.

"I lie in bed, close my eyes, and say the Serenity Prayer."

"I get on my knees in the morning and pray for help."

"I write what I want on a piece of paper and put it in my God box."

Your what? Turns out that empty Kleenex cartons, Band-Aid tins, and all manner of other receptacles can be used for depositing handwritten memos of people, places, and things that are beyond our control. "I can't, but God can" is an expression I sometimes heard.

Over time, and using these suggestions and hundreds more, I felt the infinite hole I harbored start to shrink, as an essence that I couldn't see or even describe, only felt, began to fill it. My obsession slowly lifted as I shed my director's role and came to believe that there was indeed something greater than I in the world.

Years into my going to meetings, a twelve-step counselor I hired had me hold a pillow in the crook of my arm, like a nurturing mother, and talk to it as though it were I. I was unhappy about a work-related issue, but the sentiments were similar. I wanted recognition for what I was doing and who I was being. Whose job is it to provide that? This gentle man offered me a solution. You can give it to yourself, he advised.

Here's what it might have looked like if I applied that technique during my younger parenting days.

"Jane, I'm so proud of you," I would say, clutching the pillow. "You have worked really hard, and your baby is beautiful. You're doing such a good job. I love you, and I love how much you care about your children. They are lucky to have you as a mother."

I broke down and sobbed as I delivered those words. It was exactly what I needed to hear, spoken by me to me in a loving tone. This skill has served me. But I didn't learn it until I'd reached my lowest point. That's when I'm most teachable anyway. Foxhole religion.

That brings us back to my relationship with Fran. Upon the birth of Lily, I had exceeded my capacity to give and couldn't see that my spirit was fading. Tensions at home ran even higher, now that there were three children to care for. Ben was out several nights a week. We were both exhausted, and neither of us did much to make the other feel loved or supported. I had to look elsewhere to get my fix.

I became more dependent on having Fran's light shine on me individually. Showing up to volunteer at school was a means of getting a quick hit, but I also needed my own one-on-one time. I didn't want to share her attention, though I would if it were all I could get.

Taking walks together served us well, since we both loved to keep up a brisk pace for forty-five minutes and use the time to talk about real stuff. It was something I could arrange to do with her and not have to find care for my infant daughter. I'd secure Lily in the Snugli and strap her across my chest. Whether we followed a three-mile route in Fran's neighborhood or mine, I was guaranteed enough time to cover what was most pressing—a misunderstanding with Ben or a resentment against my mother. I valued my friend's perspective, wisdom, and nonjudgmental listening. I would have loved a daily slot on Fran's schedule, but, as Silvie pointed out, even though I may have been top of Fran's friends list, she put other priorities first: work, church, family.

I didn't understand that concept. I had to put family first, but right after that, friends was my next priority. For me, it was a requirement.

Still, Fran sought to please me and said yes when she might have better said no. "Yes, I'd love to go for a walk with you tomorrow afternoon."

I'd have Lily breastfed and strapped into the carrier at three thirty in anticipation of Fran's arrival at four o'clock. Then the phone would ring at 3:50 p.m.

"Jane, it's Fran. I'm sorry. I'm not going to be able to walk today. There's a committee meeting at church tonight, and I'd forgotten to check my calendar when I said yes to you earlier this week."

The first few times this happened, I was the understanding seeker. "That's okay! I know how that can happen. We'll do it another time," I'd say, hoping Fran would come up with an immediate offer of her next free afternoon.

Over time, I detected a pattern. I'd set up an attractive scenario—a walk to Calf Pasture Beach, a visit to a crafts fair or a
quilt show—and an hour or less before our departure time, the
phone would ring.

"Jane, I'm so sorry. I can't make it. I feel terrible. I have to
stop by the hospital. I found out that one of our students'
mothers had a fall, and I promised to stop over there to see
how she's doing."

Who could argue with such virtue?

"Of course I understand," I lied. "It's so good of you to do
that."

I wanted to be the one in the hospital. I wanted Fran's undivided attention.

The issue for me was that when I wrote our date on the
calendar, it was in permanent marker. Fran's notation was
more likely penciled in. The problem was mine. Entirely mine.
This woman was being who she was.

Sadly, my unhealthy thinking told me, *Jane, if you were
funnier, kinder, more authentic, creative, generous, she would have
come today.*

Besides blaming myself for not being enough to attract this
person to me, the other regret I have is that I allowed myself to
be disappointed over and over again.

Part of my insanity was doing the same thing over and
over and expecting a different result. *Next time, the invitation
will be too delicious for her not to ink it in.* Often she *would* show
up. Almost as frequently, she'd cancel. She never said no, and I
kept seeking.

After several disappointments, I'd pull back and not pursue
her. Just as *The Two-Step* depicts, inevitably, she—the sought—
would come forward. She'd start a conversation, and I'd find
myself lured in.

"I've missed seeing you at school," she'd say. "How's Lily doing? Are you still walking with her at the beach every day? I miss our walks; without you, I never take the time to exercise like that. You're so good about getting what you need."

I'd take the bait, invite her for a walk, have the time honored, and enjoy a conversation-packed hour or two of Fran's generous spirit. This is where the addictive nature of the relationship kicked in. I'd gotten my hit. I was high, exuberant. I felt loved, seen. It was all worth it. I'd forgotten the pain and disappointment of the previous broken dates, the withdrawal I experienced waiting for the next time. The insanity of not simply stepping away from what was hurting me.

The cycle of invitation, acceptance, phone call, disappointment played out over and over again. For years. I kept going back to a well I knew couldn't sustain me, hoping each time that my bucket would come out full.

IT WASN'T UNTIL my mid-forties that I fully understood that eating foods I craved was the second-place alternative I substituted for getting what I wanted from relationships. "I'm putting this into my mouth now so that I don't have to feel the pain of what's missing in my marriage/friendship" were words that at no time entered my mind nor crossed my lips.

I'd concede to having a sweet tooth—who didn't?—but not that I was addicted. Back in my high school days, I always carried a roll of LifeSavers (interesting choice of names) in my pocketbook. As soon as one Choc-o-mint had dissolved in my mouth, I'd slip another one into my cheek to take its place. Since I had a constant feed of sweetness, I didn't even notice I was lying to myself. If I got down to the last one in the roll and there were a few classes left before the end of the day, my mind began calculating when I might stop by the school store, if it was open between periods eight and nine, or see who else was carrying a sweet treat and could share theirs with me.

I'd been brought up on desserts at every meal, including powdered doughnuts or other pastries at breakfast. Sugar was a God-given right, and I had a hard time blaming it for my mood swings. Since I rarely had it out of my system, my mood stayed heightened.

Though always delicious and satisfying, sugar eventually began to have a negative effect on my body and mind. At eighteen, I felt invulnerable and ate as much as I wanted with abandon, but my body's tolerance changed as I got older. By the time I reached my thirties, I noticed that, after treating myself and the kids to ice cream cones at Friendly's one night, I'd wake up the next day with a sense of gloom. My children, whom I'd adored the night before, were now monsters draining every bit of my energy. Ben's neglect magnified. Why was I bothering to create art objects? No one would want them. The only thing that was different between yesterday and today was my consumption of sugar. But still I wanted more. For the fifteen minutes after I indulged that desire, all my cares went away.

My relationship with Fran, like any obsession, had similar highs and lows. Navigating that terrain took up space in my head that could have been used more fruitfully in other spheres of my life.

FRAN AND I went on this way for eight years, but I'll spare you more details. The ecstatic highs included our designing her daughter's wedding gown together with a friend of mine, celebrating the success of the Holiday Fair, and sharing birthday treats with tickets to off-Broadway shows. Great lows—crumbled promises, professional neglect, and days or weeks of longing—accompanied the highs. One episode felt worse than the next, yet I continued to go back for more. I thought victimhood was like a merit badge in the Girl Scouts and wore mine with pride.

Eventually, with my therapist's help, I was ready to take a decisive step. I'd always believed that you could work things out in a relationship. No matter how upset I'd become with my mother, she was still my mother, and that was that. But in a friendship, according to Silvie, you didn't have to work it out. You could walk away. This was news to me, but it finally felt right.

As I swallowed years of disappointment in my marriage and absorbed the pain of my struggles around Fran and other mortals I'd elevated above me, my body reacted with its own set of ills. In my mid-thirties I developed a hiatal hernia, a year or two later a slipped disc, and eventually rheumatoid arthritis. This was all before I'd heard of Louise Hay, author of *Heal Your Body*, who explained how our symptoms often tell a larger truth. I was in constant pain, and I couldn't see that by compromising my spirit over and over again, I was injuring my immune system. My body got my attention in a way that my soul hadn't.

Eventually my therapist said, "You need to say no to this relationship, Jane." My ambivalent feelings over a recent correspondence made this abundantly clear.

Fran had sent me a greeting card with a message that she looked forward to seeing me after she'd completed her final paper for the MSW degree she'd been working toward. It had been weeks since we'd spoken, and she mentioned that going for a walk with me would be her reward. I'd been withdrawing from the touch of sweetness our friendship permitted and chose not to respond when I received her note. In the past, it would have been exactly the right message to reel me back in. No more. Where once she might have waited for my call, she phoned me. I announced to her then, "I can't do this anymore."

That was May 1989.

"I thought you might say that," Fran responded. We spoke briefly, but it was done.

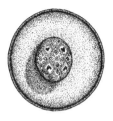

Chapter Twelve

*T*he thin veneer of my life depicted someone who was thriving. At extended family events, Ben, the kids, and I showed up bright and shiny. Appearing on a professional panel, my bio included impressive personal details. The kids' bar and bat mitzvahs promoted the storyline of our model existence. We were living out our roles and checking off the boxes. It all looked just fine.

I occasionally complained to friends, but never in depth because I couldn't see then the steadily widening gap between Ben and me. It grew slowly and wouldn't show up on an X-ray of our marriage for many more years.

One of the ways I maintained my sense of self and was able to accept Ben's devotion to his work was through my own developing career path. While emotionally I was frustrated by our diminishing connection, I still managed to build my own thriving and successful business through an uncommon art form: decorated eggs. It began in 1973, when I learned the craft of Ukrainian Easter eggs—*pysanky*—from my colleague at West Hill High School. When she told me, "One of the things we do with our art classes is Ukrainian Easter eggs," I thought I was in the wrong job. *Easter eggs in high school? How juvenile!*

Contempt prior to investigation—this was how I always addressed concepts that were new to me and that I couldn't grasp. I mentally ridiculed the idea. I've since learned to be in wonder, not judgment. But at the time, I thought I already knew best.

That day, the art teacher whose aunt had handed down this tradition to her slipped through the door leading to the supply room and emerged with two egg cartons. When she opened the first one, exposing a dozen brightly colored, intricately patterned eggshells, my mouth opened and a noise emerged that was part whistle, part gasp. "How do you do that?" I almost shouted. Here were the most beautiful objects I'd ever seen.

"I'll show you!" she offered, and conducted a mini-demonstration in her classroom.

"I have to do this!" I exclaimed. "Tonight!"

My colleague packed up a kit for me so that I could get started right away at home. I stopped by the grocery store to get a dozen eggs and a box of McCormick's food coloring and dashed back to my apartment. By the time Ben got home, I was deeply engrossed in decorating my first egg.

"What are you doing?" he asked, seeing his wife's new posture, head bent over an egg held in her left hand, a *kistka*—the stylus used for drawing on the egg's surface—in her right, and a candle burning on the dining room table, the smell of melted beeswax in the air.

"Wait till you see this!" I replied, nearing the end of the process. "Come, watch!"

"You finish," Ben replied. "I'll be there in a few minutes." He headed into his office in the spare bedroom and deposited his briefcase full of student papers, changed out of his jacket and tie, and switched on the TV in our bedroom. That night, his preference for the television didn't bother me at all. I'd found something so absorbing that his actions were less important than my own.

Ben returned to watch as I was melting the wax off my two-toned egg. "Pretty," he said.

"I can't wait to do my next one, but it'll have to be tomorrow. I'm pooped," I said, exhilarated by this new medium, my husband's affirmation, and my own creativity.

A large photo of that first egg took up a full page in my book *Decorating Eggs: Exquisite Designs with Wax and Dye*, published in 1996. I had no idea on that winter's night in 1973 that I had, as they say, found my métier, as well as a therapeutic diversion from future troubles.

The act of creating *pysanky*, the Ukrainian word for "eggs which have been written on," became addictive in a healthy way. As soon as I completed one, I couldn't wait to make the next. But I didn't feel bereft if something interfered. There was no withdrawal, no urgency. The process was available to me whenever I had the time to sit down and create. Being enthralled and joyful upon the completion of each egg felt like enough.

While I was waxing and dyeing an egg, I was completely centered, in flow, and at peace. I wasn't hungry, and I didn't brood about what was missing in my life. I never tired of the process. The only withdrawal I suffered was running out of time, frustration over when I could next apply patterns and color combinations, and not being able to get back to my table to work because of competing obligations. There was no harm being done while I was creating my designs.

The end products were beautiful objets d'art that I could enjoy and eventually sell.

FRIENDS WHO SAW my earliest designs said I should enter them in a local craft show, the Pink Tent Festival, in Stamford that summer. Their interest in me and my art was exciting and motivating. Craft shows in 1973 were a relatively new phenomenon. The one coming up on the large green near the Mill River was in its second or third year. Other than displaying and selling some of my pen-and-ink drawings in college, I had never put my artwork up for sale. But I went through the motions to apply, carrying a dozen of my eggs to show a jury member a few months before the event, being accepted, and then creating inventory, a booth, and a logo.

I named my company An Egg by Jane and became a small-business owner.

Two things happened at that show in July that began the arc of a thirty-plus-year career. My booth consisted of a card table and tablecloth, with my work displayed in a variety of holders. I priced each egg at $8. Strangers approached my booth, took out their wallets, and paid me money for my art. Not friends, not relatives, but complete strangers, who weren't there to make me feel good, actually parted with their own hard-earned cash to purchase an object I had created.

More surprisingly, an older woman with white hair and formal posture extended her hand to me, admired my work, and introduced herself as the special-events director from Bloomingdale's. She asked if I'd be willing to conduct a Ukrainian Easter egg–decorating workshop at the Stamford store the following spring.

My first thought while packing up my booth after that show was, *It's so easy to make money selling your art.*

This initial experience with commerce was an example of beginner's luck. I didn't continuously have magical opportunities like that at shows, but a career was born, and I followed its trajectory for the next three decades. I went from decorating eggs at a kitchen counter to renovating our family room into a designer's space where I could invite customers in for studio sales and hire assistants to help me with production. I had my own area to design, create, and conduct the business of my art.

I envied my crafts colleagues whose husbands built their booths or who took an active interest in their work. Ben seemed happy that I had something that made me happy. I wanted more than that but didn't know exactly what or how to ask. I tucked away those desires, substituting mothering and egg decorating for my fulfillment, appropriate cover stories that worked for a long time.

Of course, I also wanted to be taken seriously in my field, which is tricky when your art form is not easily recognized or appreciated. I sensed a touch of sympathy or pity when I revealed what I did to strangers. "Oh, that's nice," they would say, eyeing the room for an escape. If I had a photo of my work with me, which I quickly learned to do, the story was different. "Wow!" they'd respond. "How do you do that?"

But in 1985 I got a credential that changed my career. Because exhibiting my work regularly at shows required more time than I had, I'd been teaching after-school art classes in our family room for extra cash. Two afternoons a week, I'd convert our playroom into a creative space for children. I laid a large, oilcloth-covered, square plywood tabletop over two sawhorses, which then became painting surfaces for a flock of elementary school students. They'd arrive at my back door by 4:00 p.m. and have a lesson with me for an hour a week. One afternoon, when they were busy painting a still life I'd set up, the phone rang.

"Jane Pollak, please," I heard, as I glanced around my small classroom to make sure my students had enough pigment in their tempera trays.

"I'm Jane," I replied, holding the receiver to my ear.

"I'm calling on behalf of the White House. Are you the person who decorates eggs?"

"Yes." On hearing the phrase "the White House," I quit looking at the young painters and ran my fingers through my hair.

"Would you consider decorating an egg for the Easter egg roll at the White House next spring?"

Holding the phone to my chest, I took in a breath. I considered briefly. After a pause, I said, "Yes, I'd be happy to."

"Wonderful. I'll send you the details. You will be invited to attend the event in Washington with your family. Plus, your egg will become part of the Smithsonian Collection."

I'm sure the children completed their pictures, and I cleaned up the paints and upended the wooden board against the wall where it lived between sessions. But I remember none of that, only the feeling that someone—the White House, in this case—was seeking me out.

My first important credential was acquired, and it followed me throughout my career. "She did an egg for the White House!" a friend would brag about me to a new acquaintance. "Her eggs are in the Smithsonian" had a cachet that required no further questions about the validity of my work. I was recognized.

My participation in craft shows started with the Pink Tent Festival in 1973 and lasted until the late '90s, with varying degrees of success. Some weekends I'd earn $2,500, and some less than $1,000. Craft artists vied for entry into the most selective shows. I learned how to have my eggs photographed for jury competitions, how to design a booth to attract customers and sales, and how to define and market to my audience.

The highest-earning show I was ever accepted into was held in Boston. It was called Crafts at the Castle. I was thrilled to be invited, even though it meant spending three nights in a hotel on my own dime and hiring someone from that area to help me with sales.

Still, I sold nearly $10,000 worth of inventory at that venue one November weekend and did equally well there the next two years, only to be rejected by a jury after that. Such was the nature of the craft movement. You could create your goals and apply to shows, but there was no guarantee that you'd be invited back.

Once my book came out, in 1996, I took my business in another direction, combining my growing speaking business—giving a keynote talk on how to turn a passion into a successful business—and carrying my art with me in a portfolio I could sling over my shoulder. I earned a speaking fee in addition to the profits from the sale of my art after I'd spoken.

Over the course of my business, my eggs went from $8 each in 1973, to $480 each in the early 2000s. I received coverage in the *New York Times*, multiple magazines, and catalogs, and ultimately landed a spot on *The Today Show* on Good Friday 1997, when network TV still ruled the media. My book soared to number 12 on Amazon.com. That may have been the high point of my career.

By the early 2000s, I'd been decorating eggs for more than thirty years. I had said everything in eggs I needed to say. I advertised a final studio sale to my client list and, with Ben's help, got rid of my entire inventory of artwork, supplies, and all the decorating gear I'd accumulated, taking in over $10,000 in the process.

You can't leap a chasm in two bounds, I was told. Let go and let God. After that sale, I had an organizer come in and help me pack up my art supplies and books and set me up as a speaker and a coach.

Since 2005, when I made an egg as a gift to my son and his fiancée, I have not touched an egg or piece of wax in that way again.

All of this is to tell you that I was not curled up on a couch, suffering the neglect of my primary relationships. I showed up for everything in my life while this hole in my soul slowly grew.

BEN RARELY COMMENTED on my art career. It was simply what I did. I relied on Fran's feedback for validation.

"Your work is so beautiful, Jane, and your display is inviting and inspiring. I'm bringing my sister-in-law to the show. I want her to meet you," she had said.

The most important thing about spending time with Fran was her ability to reflect my world back to me. She saw me and acknowledged who I was. If anyone had said anything like that to me before, I hadn't heard it. I felt special in Fran's eyes.

My business success felt secondary to this personal recognition. Without my own strong inner voice, the one that got louder and louder with my recovery, I was dependent on another person to make me happy.

How many of us walk around, appearing successful to the world, but inside struggle with a secret?

When I let go of that one relationship, my world opened up exponentially. Where once all I cared about was the attention of a single human being, I became able to allow in and value the thoughts and affection of everyone I had blocked out of existence.

This didn't happen overnight, but it began the two-decade journey to the demise of my marriage. Saying no to Fran was the first step toward declaring my own worth—not as a woman, a mother, or even a friend, but as me.

I had never said no to anyone before, especially not Ben.

Chapter Thirteen

ooking through old journals, especially those written on the days when I felt the worst about my relationship with Fran, I wish I could've swooped down with today's knowledge and cared for that young woman I was then. Journaling was an outlet, a place to tuck away my darker side. Writing letters helped, too, especially ones I'd never mail.

Not long after I'd said goodbye to Fran, I sat down and wrote a letter to God. I'm not sure I'd ever done that before, if Silvie had instructed me to do it, or where the idea came from. Maybe I actually wrote it to Fran but God read it anyway. Mostly, I remember what the message said and what happened after I'd written it.

*Dear God,*

*I wish that there was someplace I could go on a regular basis and share my innermost thoughts that I always saved for Fran. Someplace safe, where other people also want to talk about their deepest thoughts. That would take the burden off her, allow me to share my worries, and lighten future communication, instead of it always being intense.*

*If I had someplace else to go with all that crap* [I'm not sure I used that word to God, but it's what I thought], *I wouldn't have to be so dependent on Fran to always be the one to hear me. We could just have fun together. Please, God!*

*Love, Jane*

A FEW MONTHS later, in mid-August 1989, while former hippies and others were celebrating the twentieth anniversary of Woodstock, my brother's next-door neighbors invited Ben and me to a party, their tribute to that quintessential baby-boomer event. The atmosphere was casual and friendly as music from the '60s was piped outside from speakers suspended in the branches of a dogwood tree. I found myself drawn to a small group of women seated on the lawn near the back of the house. I joined them there, sat next to Andy's neighbor, and leaned up against the red clapboard shingles.

Two of the women were angled toward each other, heads close together. When I sat down, the woman with wavy brown hair and horn-rimmed glasses turned to me and said, "I was just telling Rebecca"—she pointed to our hostess—"about this great women's group I've been going to in Westport. It meets every Wednesday night, and all we talk about is relationships. It's quite intimate. I've been going for a few months now."

"Really?" I said, immediately interested in the demographics and subject matter. "How would I join?"

"You don't have to join. Just come. It's at the dance studio behind CoCo Spa—you know, on the Post Road near Southport?"

"Will you be there this coming Wednesday? I'd love to meet and walk in with you."

"Definitely!"

I arrived at 5:15 p.m. and spotted my new friend as she came in the door at 5:28 p.m. There were at least a dozen women already gathered and waiting outside the studio as an exercise class inside finished up. When the adjoining door opened, heat and sweat filled the vestibule where we stood, and we quickly traded places.

We walked into a large, mirrored studio space with blond wood floors, a hip-height ballet barre on three walls, and mats for us to sit on. We arranged ourselves in an irregular line around the perimeter of the space. At 5:30 p.m., a woman with long blond hair parted in the middle announced, "Service!" and read from the pages of a notebook, thus calling the meeting to order. Everyone there seemed aware of the format of the meeting, so I pretended like I was, too. They all joined in saying aloud the Serenity Prayer, which is said at most twelve-step meetings. I didn't even know it was called the Serenity Prayer until I'd come a few more times. I wondered how on earth people could memorize all those words.

After the formal reading from the binder, the leader asked someone to tell her story—to qualify—and share what had brought her to this group and what experience, strength, and hope she'd received since she'd been coming. As the woman giving the qualification spoke, I found myself nodding, even though our circumstances were vastly different. It had been three months since I'd ended the relationship with Fran. I still thought about her every day and resisted taking any action toward getting together. It felt like a struggle to rid my mind of those coils of memory. I had been crushed but ultimately had managed to crawl out from under the weight of my dependency. Here was a solution being offered to me.

At first I noticed my brain thinking, *What would Ben say about this group? What would his reaction be? Would he have fled during the prayer? Would the personal sharing be too intimate for him?*

After just a few minutes of being there, though, I let go of his hold on my thoughts and noticed that I became present to these women and what their personal stories stimulated in me. I was temporarily freed of the committee in my head, chaired by my husband—my mother by his side: *You shouldn't feel that way! Why are you so needy?*

In that meeting, I was relieved of the "bondage of self" I'd later hear mentioned in the Third Step prayer. I had been a prisoner of my own making in my tie to Fran.

Here was a group openly discussing the feelings—that God-size hole—that created such an attraction, and methods for extracting oneself from its grip. None of the suggestions was about how to make the person like you more or pay attention. That was disappointing at first, but I learned the wisdom of its message.

While listening to the qualification—the speaker's story—I felt her embarrassment, appreciated her self-knowledge, and identified with her compulsion to repeat a behavior she knew wasn't good for her. I wanted to hear more about how meetings helped her stay away from that toxic relationship. That someone could be that open and honest in a roomful of strangers made me sit up straight.

I couldn't wait until the following Wednesday, when the group would meet again. On the way out of the gymnasium-studio, I caught up with another woman I'd heard share. "I appreciated what you said," I ventured.

"I'm Diane." She smiled, turning toward me, extending her arms for a hug. *Boy, these people are really friendly and trusting.*

"Do you come every week?" I asked.

"Oh, I go to a Relationship Program meeting every *day* at seven thirty in the morning, plus this one, which is my home group." I had no idea what a home group was, but if she had one, I wanted one, too.

The Relationship Program had meetings every day of the week? How had I not heard about this before? Where did they meet? How did *she* know all this? Where was my copy of the memo?

"This is my first time, but I can't wait to come back. I feel so much better than I did when I arrived! But my kids are all in school, so I couldn't come to an early meeting every day. I wish I could."

"Once a week is perfect for where you are. God only gives you what you can handle. That must be exactly the right amount."

Her offering that nugget of wisdom felt good.

I began to attend that woman's meeting of the Relationship Program every Wednesday. After going to several sessions, I heard about similar groups in the area. Each had a particular focus, and the other two were coed. I ventured out beyond the Wednesday meetings and soon became a regular.

"I can't believe I never heard of this whole thing before," I told Phyllis, the first person whose phone number I asked for. Group members encourage calls between meetings, even naming the telephone as a tool of the program. "I wished I'd had something like this years ago."

"You know the saying about when the student is ready," she reminded me. God knew and gave me exactly what I had described in my letter.

I came home from that first Wednesday night meeting elated. It had been months since Ben had seen me so happy. "This group is amazing," I exuded. "They're so open and honest, and they all have stories similar to mine." It didn't dawn on me then that what I found in the meetings was what was missing in my marriage: intimacy, connection, and acknowledgment.

He continued watching the ball game on TV, nodded, and clicked the remote to another channel. "Great!"

Several weeks into my attending these meetings, Ben met me on our front walk one night as he was coming in from school and I was heading out to my group. "Dinner's on the stove for the kids, hon. Remember, I told you? Can you take over from here?"

"Where are you in such a hurry to?" he asked, as I descended the stairs to the driveway.

"My Relationship Group meeting. Remember? I mentioned it this morning as you were leaving."

"Boy, I think you're becoming addicted to those meetings. Are you sure they're helping you? That you're not just substituting going there for seeing Fran?"

His words stung, but I knew that I was getting better. Spiritual recovery is, by its nature, unquantifiable. I couldn't show him evidence on a chart or graph how I had progressed from point A to point B. Prior to my attending meetings, my mind had fixated on feelings about my friend. In recovery parlance, she had been taking up rent-free space in my head. Every thought in a new direction had been preceded by an involuntary, knee-jerk thought about my relationship and its needs.

I was learning, one day at a time, to change my thinking. To say the Serenity Prayer, which I had now memorized, instead of obsessing.

After a few months in a twelve-step program, I was becoming programmed. There was a new vocabulary to adopt, a set of principles to live by, and guidelines for my behavior. By the time I learned about recovery, in 1989, the movement had expanded beyond the early secrecy of 1930s-era AA. With multiple anonymous fellowships worldwide, it had become a more visible part of our culture.

*Saturday Night Live* featured sketches and characters that satirized what I was now a part of. I could nod in recognition at its mock self-help show, called *Daily Affirmations with Stuart Smalley*, which began airing in 1991. Under the widening umbrella of recovery programs, you didn't have to personally know an alcoholic to be aware of the disease's existence.

I was still sensitive to the stigmas, though. Even though I was benefiting enormously from what popular culture was parodying, laughing with Ben at the depiction, I wished there were a more respectful portrayal of the soul-healing work I had engaged in.

Gandhi's words rang true: "First they ignore you, then they ridicule you, then they fight you, and then you win."

Ridicule and opposition were both prevalent with Ben. He balked when jargon slipped into our conversation. After we bumped into some of my new friends at the movies on a Saturday night, he asked me how I knew the people I'd introduced him to without mentioning how we'd met. "Program," I explained later, even though there was a guideline about maintaining other members' anonymity. I thought it was vague enough not to violate that tradition.

"Why don't you say '*the* program'?" he complained. "It sounds like how the British say they are 'going to hospital,' instead of 'going to *the* hospital.' We're not British. Why do you call it 'program,' instead of 'the program'?"

I felt interrogated, as if I had to defend myself. With the perspective of time, I can appreciate how hard it must have been for him to watch me dive into a world that felt inaccessible, even as it drew me in. I was speaking as though he had full knowledge of recovery, and he was simply questioning my lexicon. Ben had no desire to be involved in what I was doing but stood by and witnessed my increasing attraction to it.

I wonder if things would have been different if I'd shared some of the concepts with him as I was learning them. If there'd been a Google back then, so I could point and say, "See, this is what I'm doing: 'A twelve-step program is a set of guiding principles outlining a course of action for recovery from addiction, compulsion, or other behavioral problems.'"

Since that first meeting in the studio-gymnasium in Westport, I've sat on folding chairs in church basements, synagogue social halls, YMCA meeting rooms, and occasionally freestanding buildings that are completely devoted to recovery. Before I eliminated ice cream from my diet, aka my food plan, I even met people from "the rooms" at Friendly's and held an impromptu meeting there, where we started with the Serenity Prayer and took turns sharing.

It took my attending several meetings before I was willing to raise my hand to speak. In fact, the first time I decided that I would take that risk, I typed up what I wanted to say beforehand and read it out loud. I no longer have the printed sheet I had brought with me, but I'm sure it read something like, *I'm here because for eight years I couldn't stop thinking about my relationship with a friend. I didn't know whom to talk to about it. I tried therapy, but the therapist didn't touch on the nature of the feelings you share in here. I was hooked on this woman. It felt like a sickness, which I was too ashamed to admit. You're helping me understand that it is a sickness—a disease, in fact—that can be arrested, not cured, and that there is something even better for me when I let go of my desperate need for one person's attention. It feels a lot like how I used to feel about my mother. I knew she loved me—or thought I knew—but sometimes it felt like I didn't exist for her. I didn't know how to live my life thinking that I might not exist for the most important person in my life. Just writing this and sharing it with you helps me. Thank you for listening.*

I was so afraid of others' judgments of me that I actually

included the signoff *thank you* line, for fear that I might forget the protocol for the end of most shares. I needn't have worried.

Everyone was respectfully quiet and after I'd finished said, in unison, "Thank you, Jane." Blood rushed to my face as I wondered if what I'd said had been worthy.

After that meeting, a younger woman came up to me and thanked me by name. Goose bumps dotted my arms. She introduced herself.

"I'm pretty new to this whole thing. Would it be okay if I called you?" I was flattered by her request, dipped into my pocketbook for a notepad and pen, tore a piece of paper out, and scribbled my number on it.

As I spoke to this new program friend, I sensed her regard for my expressed thoughts. That was not exclusive to this particular conversation or specifically to me. What Fran had brought, I thought uniquely, to our friendship—consideration and recognition—I began to find in limitless supply from the women in this room. There seemed to be a code to live by. Prior to my coming to meetings, I may have occasionally been treated this way. Once I began attending them regularly, I coveted this atmosphere of love and acceptance, which was so different from how I'd grown up.

In my family home, this quality of attention was the exception, and I craved it. In my new life, it was a given, and I got my fill. No longer was I on a quest for the one individual who could bestow it on me. It was offered in abundance whenever and wherever I availed myself of the rooms. I did not go into withdrawal after a meeting. I was full. I had energy, attention, and love to spare. Getting more didn't cost me anything, unless you count the dollar contributed to the basket passed around for rent.

Because meetings occurred multiple times a week in differing locations, I didn't have to identify one person to call up and arrange a date on the calendar to capture the experience again. In the past, I had repeatedly tried to enlist another human as my higher power, or whatever term you choose for that entity that you put first in your life. Now all I had to do was show up and be present.

Letting go of the belief that I was such an entity, my own higher power, began a long, slow transformation in me. I once had the notion that my mother's happiness, and then Ben's and ultimately my kids', depended on me. Humbly accepting that that job was too large was a first step in owning my powerlessness. Putting it into practice was another story.

Knowing the solution and applying it are separate issues. We've all heard that eating less and exercising more is the answer to weight loss, but who can conjure that up when served a bubbling cheese pizza straight out of a brick oven? Similarly, when faced with Ben's stooped posture carrying an armload of papers to be graded over the weekend, I felt a familiar pull toward fixing his life and making sure he was happy and cared for. When I began turning his happiness over to something outside me, I believe that's when he began searching for another source to draw that comfort from.

I practiced my newly acquired skills on my mother who lived a safe distance from me, i.e., not in my house. I repeated the mantra "Mom's happiness is her responsibility." This freed me up to accept that when she was being negative, it was not up to me to dance her into joy. The result of my letting go of that behavior was that she turned to others to perform the task. This new pattern was never mentioned, but I knew, in the recesses of my heart, that I couldn't cure her pain, no matter what designer label I wore, how many books I wrote, or how well my children did in school.

What I continue to love about program is that there is no graduation, which is why I've been attending meetings for almost thirty years as of 2018. Remember? I graduated from each of my other tribes prior to finding "the rooms."

I was relieved when I heard that there would be no expiration date on showing up at meetings, and that there are rooms all over the world. I've found recovery in Melbourne, Australia, in Dublin, Ireland, and on the high seas during a three-month journey by ship. There are also international phone meetings and online meetings. All I have to do is plug in. My lifeline is there when I need it.

Wayne Dyer said, "When you believe it, you'll see it." Today I see miracles, answered prayers, and solutions manifesting everywhere I look.

In 1989, my world had shrunk down to my feeling alive only during moments in Fran's presence. Once I got into program, that shifted. I looked forward to every meeting and had numbers to call in between and a sponsor—the person I asked to be my guide—to check in with regularly.

"You're much softer," a fellow said to me one day. I couldn't see it myself, but I knew that I was different. Life was becoming easier, and I felt lighter, less intense. I could see it in others, and my growth is reflected back to me. It's become a more reliable mirror than the one I used to get my information from.

The twelve-step rooms are so rich and so deep after having existed for more than eighty years that, as with the tech-world expression "there's an app for that," in recovery "there's a room for that."

I believe that everyone would benefit from being in the rooms, but a tradition of ours states that this is a program of attraction, not promotion. I rarely mention my recovery in my daily life. I hope that occasionally someone will want what I have and ask. That has happened, but almost exclusively with men and women already in the rooms who have recognized that one of my other programs would be beneficial to them as well.

Ben didn't share this belief, nor did my recovery rub off on him.

Chapter  Fourteen

etween my La Leche League guides (circa 1974) and discovering "the rooms" (1989), I filled the empty spaces in my soul with a variety of self-help gurus and workshops. Though this time included my becoming a mother and developing my art career, there were periods of loneliness and isolation that leached the joy from my primary occupations. Note that being a wife was not on that list. I didn't realize it could be.

My first chiropractor, Brenda Kornreich, was the person who lent me her copy of Wayne Dyer's six-cassette album called *Choosing Your Own Greatness*. Dyer and other motivational speakers helped me further dismantle old beliefs and open new worlds for me.

"I want you to hear this," she instructed. "It will change how you think." I was so closed to foreign concepts at the time that I suspected she was handing me voodoo. How could a plastic clamshell of recordings change my thoughts?

I did not believe then what I could not see.

But my intuition led me to good people. Though younger than I and a new mother at the time, Brenda also became a mentor. She'd been referred to me by a friend from CCNS, my kids' nursery school. I'd been to my internist a week before. After listening to my symptoms—can't lift my arm above my head, unable to roll up the car window—he diagnosed tendonitis and recommended cortisone shots. As a natural-childbirth kind of woman, I wasn't anxious to have a pharmaceutical remedy before seeking out something more hands-on first. I made the chiropractic appointment following my friend's advice.

Before I met face-to-face with Brenda in the examination room, her assistant conducted a thorough intake, including questions no one in the medical community had ever asked me: What do you do for a living? What are your daily physical habits?

"Show me how you decorate your eggs," directed Brenda, after she'd reviewed my forms. I demonstrated the posture I assumed when applying wax to the surface of the shell, my head bent down and forward, my arms resting on the table below my head as I pretended to hold an egg in my left hand and a *kistka* in my right.

Consulting my X-rays and witnessing my pose, she made her diagnosis. "You've lost the cervical curve in your neck. The referred pain you're experiencing is in your shoulder. I can treat this by adjusting your spine. You'll notice a difference within six weeks. I'll show you how to change the way you work so you don't reinjure yourself. I'll suggest another kind of chair, which will alter how you sit."———

I added thrice-weekly appointments with Brenda to my calendar. In addition to the adjustments, she imparted her philosophy of wellness during every visit. A tall, slim, vibrant woman, Brenda exuded power and energy even in the confines of her small examination rooms. Her skin was clear and bright, her teeth white and straight. She had a short, no-nonsense haircut. Her eyes penetrated you when cast in your direction.

Brenda talked to me about positive thinking, how our thoughts impact our minds and our physical health. She mentioned vibrational frequency. I nodded, again agreeing, even though I didn't understand. I did that so people would like me.

She also had strong opinions about food, how what we eat makes us into who we are. I could digest only one tiny morsel of this at a time. I was a willing learner, but at my own pace.

She viewed her patients as divine beings hidden beneath layers of old beliefs and disciplines. "Horseshit," Ben responded when I came home with Brenda's advice. He toned down his distrust over time as he saw my improvement.

She offered her own example of what life might look like if I wanted to work on myself.

I did, but the judging, lurking side of me questioned everything. *Do I really want what Brenda has? If I accept some of her ideas, must I accept them all? She's got a baby at home, but she's in here, caring for me.* Parenting was often a benchmark for my verdicts.

Our values were not 100 percent aligned. I had made different choices about motherhood, working part-time hours from home around my kids' schedules. Even before I knew the program slogan "take what you like and leave the rest," I put it into practice. I admired many of Brenda's ideas and began to explore the leaders she followed, like Wayne Dyer and Anthony Robbins. Loved Wayne, never got keen on Tony, though I tried.

As my treatments progressed, my shoulder improved and the pain went away entirely. I bought a kneeling stool for my studio and looked at other ways to better perform my activities of daily living.

By this time, I trusted Brenda enough to insert the first cassette tape into my car's player.

Supporting Brenda's message and expressing similar beliefs

in his own way, Wayne Dyer's voice slipped into my consciousness. Once I began listening repeatedly to his tapes, his words became my mantras.

Dyer's storytelling captured me immediately. He didn't lecture or regurgitate talking points. Rather, he told a series of long, elaborate, spellbinding tales that concluded with a remarkable coincidence illustrating his point. There was a specific lesson imparted: an example of why it's important to use your intuition, trust in something greater than you, or live by universal laws. It was a whole new world with attitudes and behaviors I wished to imitate.

It became public knowledge that Wayne Dyer was an ardent member of AA, but I didn't know then that his stories were reflective of recovery. I just loved hearing them.

I replayed the borrowed tapes repeatedly, bought albums of my own from the mail-order company Nightingale-Conant, borrowed copies by other motivational speakers from the library, and exchanged sets with a friend who was equally intrigued by learning a new way to live.

Ben never directly criticized my growing interest in things unseen, but I feared becoming one of the woo-woo types he made fun of. "Oh, like it's been sooo helpful to my father." Dr. Pollak had read Wayne Dyer's hardcover best seller, *Your Erroneous Zones*, when it came out in 1976. He claimed to adhere to Dyer's philosophy of living in the day with no regrets. But Ben was dubious. Nothing noticeable changed about his father's behavior, other than his proclamation not to worry about yesterday or tomorrow. He still drank too much and was sloppy and mushy whenever the two spoke. My choice was to either ignore my gut reaction that listening to Wayne Dyer was helping me or restrict my expectation that I could convert or convince my husband of its merits. I spoke less and less about these discoveries with Ben and found more receptive ears elsewhere.

The tapes Brenda lent me introduced me to the concept of taking charge of my own life. I had followed the traditional path of the good girl and rule follower well into my twenties—the trail blazed by the women of the '50s and popularized in *Better Homes and Gardens, Woman's Day,* and *Good Housekeeping* magazines.

During the late '60s and early '70s, anti-Vietnam protests, women's lib, and the Watergate scandal changed all that. Leaders were violating many of the rules I'd grown up with. College students took over buildings on campuses. President Johnson chose not to run after his term ended. Richard Nixon left the presidency. Jane Fonda opposed the war. Gloria Steinem demonstrated how women could stand up politically. And Helen Reddy's song "I Am Woman" blared from my car radio. But I needed someone who spoke to me on a personal front. Even though male, Wayne became that person and opened up the world of audio learning, which was becoming popular and available. I followed his lead.

*How to Be a No-Limit Person* was my favorite Dyer album. There was one tape in the series that I couldn't hear often enough. The album cover promised, "Enter relationships based on choice, freedom, and love."

His stories gave examples of acceptance, forgiveness, and setting boundaries. I could not recall having witnessed healthy examples of these behaviors growing up. Although my parents were well-intentioned, their rule of law was "because I said so."

It was through listening to Wayne Dyer that I learned about the importance of saying no. It sounded so simple, but the power of that two-letter word had not registered with me prior to my hearing it illustrated in this way.

"If you can't say no to the person, you have to say no to the relationship," Dyer intoned on an audiocassette I listened to in the early '80s.

When it came to my mother, no was not an acceptable response. I learned from that relationship how to deposit my own desires, hoping for future withdrawals. I would enrich those closest to me with my time and attention before spending that natural resource on myself. The vault containing my desires grew further away and harder to reach every time I said yes when I wanted to say no. I carried this way of being into my marriage and friendships. For a period of time, I received more back from Ben than I did from my mother, but eventually the pattern of love and neglect reemerged.

Mom was relentless about getting what she wanted. Whether it was nagging my brother about going to law school (he didn't), her daughter to lose weight (she did), or my other sister to stop dating non-Jews (she got married in a church), whatever was top of her agenda, Mom was unable to contain her thoughts on the subject.

It typically happened by phone.

"Are you bringing the kids down to visit this weekend?" she'd ask.

"Sorry, Mom, we're going in three different directions with all their activities on Saturday and Sunday. Next weekend is better."

"I don't want to wait a whole week to see them. What about Sunday night? Can you come here for dinner?" she countered.

"Lucy has a rehearsal until five that day," I said, hoping she'd understand that assembling everyone for yet another activity would be too hard for me.

"Why can't you come after that? What's so important that you can't make time for us?"

Eventually she would wear me down and I would resentfully agree to something I didn't want to do. I tried to say no, in my indirect way, but she wouldn't hear it.

What Wayne Dyer was teaching sounded a lot like a message I had heard a few years earlier, in 1976, when I'd signed up for an Assertiveness Training class. My initial entry into the self-help movement began when my oldest child was two. It was offered at Anne Marie's Figure Forum, the women's gym I had joined when we moved to Norwalk.

Having experienced success telling doctors how I wanted to give birth and nurture my baby, I now wanted to continue to be bolder in my daily life. The instructor gave us techniques for handling conflict that she said would make us more confident—approaches like "broken record," where you echo your adversary's words in a neutral tone, or "reflective listening," which taught us how to rephrase the other's words but not escalate the emotional field. I thought I needed these skills for dealing with department store clerks and bank tellers. I actually needed them to help me relate to my mother and my husband.

I wanted to be able to stay in a conversation with Mom and hold my own. I'd been a "yes, Mommy" kind of girl, and it had kept me out of trouble. As I grew and matured to become a parent of my own children, I became more confident in my abilities but still felt criticized and judged in her presence.

It wasn't long after I enrolled in the Assertiveness Training class that I had the chance to test out my new skill set at a family dinner at my parents' house in White Plains. We were gathered around the dining room table. Ben and I sat on the side of the table closer to the credenza and wallpapered storage closets. Lucy was to my right, in a high chair between me and Mom, who was in her usual seat, Dad was at the other end of the table to my left, and whichever other siblings and mates were there sat on the other side, closer to the hallway.

"How much longer are you going to be nursing Lucy?" Mom asked, before the dessert course was served and after more current topics had been addressed. She added a helping of broiled chicken to Ben's plate and handed it to me to pass on.

*Here it comes*, I thought. She frequently questioned this aspect of my mothering, particularly now that Lucy was a toddler. My La Leche friends continually reminded me of the value of long-term breastfeeding and made me proud of its duration. Not only were there numerous health benefits, but this practice was also noted for meeting the dependency needs of the child, something I was acutely aware that I wanted to provide.

My self-esteem had grown as I had watched my daughter thrive on the custom-made nutrition my body provided her. So many intimate experiences between my toddler and me ensured I was deeply tied in to her emotions and needs.

Mom had questioned how long I was going to breastfeed my daughter almost from the start—when Lucy was six weeks, six months, a year old, and every other time we got together and I nursed her. Each time my mother asked, I'd reply, "The wisdom is to let the child wean when she's ready."

This was met with judgmental statements, arguments, and condescension. My mother never acknowledged my study of the subject, nor my maternal instinct to do what was best for Lucy. When I first read the AA Big Book, a line that screamed at me, attributed to Herbert Spencer, summed up my parents' skepticism: "The highest form of ignorance is contempt prior to investigation." As smart and well-read as my parents were, there was some information they were not open to hearing about. I suspected there might be a deeper question or concern behind Mom's interrogation, since my unaltered response never appeared to satisfy her.

Taking on this topic seemed to be the perfect opportunity

to try out my new tools. I would apply the strategies and techniques from the Assertiveness Training instructor to tackle this subject with my non advocate.

"You're wondering about how long I'm going to keep nursing," I echoed, as taught, using the active listening tactic. I felt more secure with these mental notes in mind as I ventured into the unfamiliar neighborhood of verbal combat.

I'd never decidedly not answered my mother before. Here was a subject I felt most strongly about. I would duke it out because I was passionate to be heard and understood. Besides, she'd rejected every answer I'd given in the past.

"Yes! That's what I asked. I think it's ridiculous to still nurse a child who can drink from a cup."

"You find it ridiculous," I volleyed back.

The purpose of playing back her words to her was to allow her, even force her, to rephrase the question, perhaps to expose the underlying inquiry that formed a deeper agenda.

*How much longer am I going to have to vie for your attention?* I suspected she wanted to know. As a child in Mom's household and until my marriage and Lucy's birth, I had performed my father's role with her. She had looked to me for the love and attention that her husband would more appropriately have provided. Since that wasn't forthcoming, I supplied it. In return, I'd gotten her affection, approval, and the sense that I was most important to her, which I craved. This pattern would get repeated in the home I created with Ben, even after I became aware of its potential for harm.

In the early years of my new marriage, I had surplus energy and attention to offer. As a new mother, though, I was completely engaged in raising my daughter. Had Mom supported me emotionally, I might have had more to give back to her. But her constant doubting of my parenting capabilities depleted me. I was done placating her and needed to stand up for myself on this issue.

My unmothered mother could not escape the trauma of her past. I can understand why she would have wanted to be nurtured by me, her first daughter to become a mother. Sadly, Mom's unmet needs were so overwhelming that she was compelled to create a scene just to be in the spotlight. A theme I heard later from a therapist but didn't yet appreciate was, "Your mother will stop at nothing to get what she needs." She didn't even care if she looked foolish in the process.

She came back at me: "Yes, I find it ridiculous! How long are you going to keep it up?"

A foal lifting herself up onto a wobbly set of legs, I tried a new maneuver I'd been given—"You sound really upset by this"—making an observation, not a judgment, of my mother's temperament. I was still speaking calmly, although I could feel the cords in my neck tightening and the imprint of my fingernails in the palms of my fists.

"Goddammit, Jane! Will you give me an answer to my question? When the hell are you going to wean this child?"

"You sound really angry, Mom," I said, my last effort, voice shaking. I knew I had run out of gambits. I was done.

"Ehhh! Blow it out your ass!" was her final thrust.

I had been unaware of anything else in the room during our word-to-word fray but now noted the utter silence, save for the light tinkling of metal as Lucy trailed her child-size fork across the tray of her high chair.

Then she, too, stopped and a moment passed before someone got up to clear the dishes.

Later, Ben and I rehashed the conversation.

"I feel so stupid," I told him. "I tried it the way I'd practiced in my class, but my mother didn't follow the script. That was awful."

Ben, who had remained silent throughout my interchange with Mom, suppressed a laugh. From everyone else's vantage point, it had been quite the show.

"Jane," he said, "*you* won that. She made a complete fool of herself."

I wanted more from Ben than an assessment of the combat. I wanted praise and validation. I wanted him to pick up the shield and defend me in my time of need: "Jane knows best. I'm 100 percent behind her, and you should be, too!"

Although he spoke positively about my victory, I never *felt* that he was on my side. Throughout Lucy's infancy, he questioned my decisions about nursing and seemed nervous about how attached we two were. I didn't expect a daily thank-you, but some expression of appreciation along the way would have helped. I was left wanting more than I got. Isn't that the definition of addiction—needing to do it again to get it right? Ben's frequent questioning of my early mothering practices negated my enjoyment of his cheering for me after it was over. My picture of loving support was different than the one he delivered.

My scenario had an appreciative spouse saying, "I trust you. I see how hard you're working to take care of our child. You're reading all the books and meeting with other mothers to get the education and support you need. I'm so grateful and feel so lucky that Lucy has someone as passionate about mothering as you are."

If I'd heard anything like that, I would have been able to laugh off my mother's interrogation. I could have admitted my own doubts out loud. That recognition would have freed up some of my maternal fierceness and allowed me to relax and accept the help I craved. Instead, I became militant and judgmental of anyone who disagreed with me. La Leche League became my fortress as I took up arms against the skeptics.

The exchange with my mother was the first time I hadn't betrayed what I believed in or bowed to her authority. I had stayed in an impasse with the woman who birthed me. No jury would declare me the winner, but the judge inside me said, *Good fight*!

Writing about this story has forced me to analyze what might appear to the reader as support from Ben. Like a time late in our marriage when he thanked me for getting tickets to a Broadway show we wanted to see. Maybe this will be a better example of how his seeming support eluded me.

We'd read a rave review of Brian Dennehy's portrayal of Willy Loman in a revival of *Death of a Salesman*. I'd gotten the tickets and phoned in a dinner reservation at a nearby restaurant. We left our home in Norwalk around 4:00 p.m., allowing two hours to make the fifty-mile drive and park the car before eating.

"What time is our reservation?" Ben asked, as we hit a standstill on the Merritt Parkway. His jaw tightened, and he adjusted the volume on the radio.

"Six," I said, breathing in his nervous energy.

"Where exactly is the theater? Is there parking nearby?"

I read the address off the tickets and told him about a park-and-lock on Forty-Second Street that always had spots. His fingers gripped the steering wheel, going from pink to white as they tightened their hold.

"Do we have time to make it there?" This interrogation and his placing the responsibility on me—or my assuming responsibility, as I always did—was draining my desire to continue this expedition.

We were a few minutes late for our dinner reservation and ate in near silence during the meal. Ben kept glancing at his watch and rubbing his hand over his head, patting down stray hairs. He paid the check and walked ahead of me along the few blocks to the theater. The show was riveting, and the well-reviewed performance delivered as promised. As we left the theater afterward and headed back to the car, Ben patted my shoulder and said, "That was great. We should do this more often."

To which I responded, "Fuck you!"

I had allowed him to take all my joy out of the evening by assuming the role of pleasure provider. That was not my job. Throughout our marriage, including the argument with my mother, I put Ben's peace of mind ahead of mine. It was a blind spot the size of a continent. I was in recovery at this time and still couldn't see it. My reaction thoroughly confused Ben again.

I had been trying to do it all by myself—the early parenting, the art career, the happy homemaker. *Get it right, and he'll be happy*, I thought in error.

This pattern was older than our union. I was born into trying to make my mother happy. I'd carried that role again in my marriage, until it eventually collapsed. The main premise was wrong. Even when I thought I'd gotten it right, it felt wrong, first with Mom and now with Ben. Because my marriage lasted longer than my time in my nuclear household, this was my shot to correct the delusion.

Lucy was tied to me for as long as I was breastfeeding her. My mother must have wanted her untied and was unremitting in that quest. If my mother had understood her own upset, I might have had the capacity to hug her and offer her my compassion for what she'd missed as a young child. Because she came at me with anger and jealousy, all I could do at the time was cross my arms in front of me in defense.

Perhaps the deeper, sadder question she'd been asking was, *When will you return to being* my *mother?* That was never spoken, but writing this makes me pause and interpret her desperation. Why else would she fight so hard to stop me from nurturing her own grandchild? No one had ever advocated for her. When needs are not met in early childhood, they continue to come up until they are met, however that plays out.

I continued to nurse my firstborn until she was three. I can't remember if my mother ever asked me "how long" again.

When Lucy won a prestigious scholarship her senior year in high school, the press interviewed me, and Ben at the awards function.

"To what do you attribute Lucy's success?" the reporter asked us.

Ben provided the journalist with a standard list of attributes: family mealtimes, bedtime reading, and a house full of books, but in my heart the more fundamental answer was breastfeeding.


I HAD BEGUN to practice asserting myself in my marriage, with Silvie's help. In one session I told her about Ben's interrupting me frequently when we talked. She assigned me a task: ask Ben to allow you to finish your sentences during conversations.

That simple request felt daunting, confrontational, and scary, but I knew I had to accept her challenge.

As a newlywed, I had been unaware of being interrupted, because it was customary in my family of origin to talk over one another, not respond to what someone else said, and move on to the next area of conversation. Like the night our family ate dinner at my parents' club and my sister threw out the gambit "My landlord plans to raise my rent by ten percent this year. It's outrageous. The building is rent-stabilized."

Rather than acknowledge that his daughter had an issue she was bringing to the table for attention and feedback, my father glanced at her, then at me, and said, "Jane, will you pass me the dinner rolls, please? And the butter." And that was that.

I looked at my sister, exchanged a quick eye roll, and reached for the bread basket. I'm sure my father didn't ignore her intentionally—he simply moved on. Discussion was rare. It's how we communicated, and as a child I accepted it as normal.

But as I was coming into an emerging self-awareness, this out-of-balance dynamic became more obvious, and I needed to say something. It was scary to confront Ben. We were not in the habit of assessing our relationship. We seldom fought. We just went along. But the interrupting thing was weighing on me.

While we were talking in our bedroom one afternoon, I was relating something that had come up in a therapy session. "Silvie is helping me to ask for what I need. She said I should try—"

"Being more assertive? We saw how that worked! Do you think your meetings with her are helping?" he asked, demonstrating exactly the behavior I needed to address. "You still seem really anxious when you're with your mother."

This wasn't a case of his lovingly finishing my thoughts. It felt more like, *I'm going to tell you what you're thinking before you get to say it.*

I could feel my throat tightening. Being conscious and present in the moment of conflict was new to me.

"You interrupt me and talk over me. I can't say everything I want to say without you cutting me off."

My instinct was to take back my words and not put him in a position of having to worry about how we might converse after this. But I didn't.

Silvie named his tactic "bluster." When the person to whom you're making the request rants and rails but ultimately does what you've asked, they're simply blowing off hot air. The important thing is that he honored my wish.

Our conversations grew more balanced. Again, it didn't feel like much of an achievement, but our fights became fairer, and I knew that I'd been heard.

As small triumphs like this racked up, my inner self began to expand.

I KNEW THERE was a larger boundary to be set with my mother. I'd been in program for a few years when my sponsor at the time—I'll call her Ellen for the sake of anonymity—shared her story of setting a limit with her own mother.

Over lunch one afternoon, she told me about her break-through experience.

"I was at a point where her drinking was really bothering me," Ellen began. "Her denial was so strong that every time I'd say, 'You're drunk,' she'd say, 'No, I'm not.'"

The hairs on my arms stood up. I knew the feeling of speaking my truth and having it dismissed. The first time, pre-recovery, I suggested to my mother that her actions made me unhappy, she said, "I'm not changing!" When I listed a couple of incidents when I'd felt victimized—I used to memorize her injustices—she took another tack.

"I've been a terrible mother. You must hate me."

Ever the caretaker, I retracted my statement. I'd rather stomach her negativity than see my mother suffer. Now I knew there was a better way, and that Ellen could help me.

"I gave my mother an ultimatum," Ellen continued. "I said that I was going to cut off any communication with her until she stopped drinking. When she was ready, she could meet me in my therapist's office for a joint session. She didn't speak to me for over a year."

I was stunned. My mind was having a hard time grasping

the concept of setting that kind of limit with a parent. I was learning so much about life from my gurus on tape, plus the men and women in the rooms.

A few months earlier, a fellow had shared during a meeting that he was unhappy with his current dentist and asked to have his X-rays and records sent to a competitor in town. This recalled my innocence in my Lamaze and La Leche League days. *You can do that?* I marveled. *You can make a new choice? You're not stuck for the rest of your life?* I immediately changed dentists, too, from the one who gave me too much gas to a gentler, more humanitarian practitioner I'd heard about.

Ellen was telling me her story, and I began to imagine what it might be like to be free of a mother's relentless negativity. Wayne Dyer described a person tightly gripping the bars of a jail cell, crying, "Let me out!" then noticing that to his left and right and behind him there was no enclosure. He had to simply let go of his own mental imprisonment. What might happen, I wondered, if I turned around or, in this case, told my mother I couldn't allow her to treat me this way? I wanted to know more.

"What happened after that?" I asked Ellen.

"She never stopped drinking entirely, but she did hear me and didn't partake of her cherished vino in my presence. It was definitely an improvement. The most important part was that I set the boundary with her. I'd never spoken up for myself before. It's almost like she saw me for the first time. Funny to say that about your mother, but it was kinda true."

The clatter of plates and the hum of others' voices in the restaurant filled my head as I took this in. Ellen's story sounded as powerful as it was unfathomable for me. I felt like Dorothy must have before Toto pulled back the curtain on the Wizard of Oz. My mother was simply a woman who had grown larger than life in my head. If I could mentally shrink her down, as one therapist had suggested, to just a tiny figure, perhaps I would feel less intimidated.

I understand how odd this must sound to anyone who has a normal relationship with their mother—about as odd as having a loving mother sounds to me. I can't fathom what that might have been like.

In Ellen, I had my role model. The next step would be to tell my mother that her behavior—her constant judgment and criticism of my appearance, my mothering skills, and my lifestyle—was no longer acceptable. Our interactions had continued to devolve as my recovery had taken hold.

Week after week in phone calls or visits, her belittling words depleted my resources. To have anything left to give my family, I needed a break in our relationship.

"You don't need her permission," a friend in the rooms reminded me.

I had begun formally working the steps with a counselor in town, an older AA gentleman in his seventies, who had hung his shingle in the middle of Westport to help suffering alcoholics and others move through their recovery. Harry Wilcox was a slight, white-haired man with a calm presence and a firm handshake.

When we began working together, he repeatedly asked me, "Can you accept your mother as she is?" There's an entire pamphlet entitled "Acceptance" that's part of AA recovery literature. I knew that concept was key to my healing. But at that point, I was unable to manage acceptance. I wish I had been more enlightened, more Zen, or in possession of a greater magnanimous spirit. I wasn't.

Instead, I tried the next part of the Serenity Prayer. I mustered up the courage to change what I could.

Because my parents wintered in Florida every year, there

was an annual time-out in expected family visits while they were away. During the rest of the year, if two weeks had gone by without my mother seeing her grandchildren, she'd demand a visit, like that Sunday-night dinner appeal. When my parents were down South and socializing with friends on a daily basis, tennis, cocktail parties, and dining out slaked my mother's insatiability.

There wasn't a last straw that precipitated my desire for space; rather, it was an accumulation of emotional assaults over the years. Mind you, there was very little positive balancing the criticism: "Have you gained weight again, Jane? Those pants look tight on you." "Don't you think Lily needs orthodontia?" "Ben shouldn't be running that much. I read that it causes a lot of problems for men over thirty-five. Tell him I said that."

What I'm illustrating here is how much evidence there was for me to see the harsh reality of my relationship with my mother and still try to defend to you why I made the choice I did. You no doubt saw it a hundred pages ago, after only one incident. *Fool me again*, I kept begging.

I should have walked away from my marriage before the thousandth cut. But, as with the hurts I withstood from my mother, I was unable to see it for myself. Like Wayne Dyer said, when you believe it, you'll see it.

But I never came to believe that a marriage contract was anything but a sacred vow or that a mother could be anything less than loving.

I chose to formalize a separation from my mother by writing a letter stating my need for space. I couched it as my desire to stay focused on the personal-development work I was engaged in, which was true. Would Mom please not contact me by letter or phone until I expressed readiness to hear from her?

I ran it by my sponsor, as well as Harry and close friends in the fellowship. I did not seek counsel from Ben or my siblings. I had no evidence that they would support my decision.

"You are really courageous," one fellow said supportively.

"It's going to change everything," offered another.

"I wish I could do this. You're very brave," I also heard.

I mailed the letter.

During those four months, I no longer feared a ringing telephone. I felt free on Sunday nights when I used to have to muster up all my positive juju to make the dreaded weekly call home. There was a lightness in my body. Anticipating my mother's critical remarks was a thing of the past.

"You will know a new freedom and a new happiness" is one of the promises of recovery. I was experiencing exactly that.

My father was not a letter writer, nor one to express emotions of any sort, although we knew that he loved us in his way. So it was with some trepidation that I opened a letter I received from him during the break from Mom. His words started off sweetly, chattily, complimenting me on the new brochure for my business that I'd sent him.

*The only fly in the ointment, to use an old cliché, is a certain lack of relationship between my wife and her daughter. Your co-dependency course [sic] may have helped you in many ways, but, judging by the evidence of what is now going on, I think it has had an effect that is not fortuitous.*

*Life is too short and your parents' love (and I mean both parents) is too important to allow anything to interfere with that relationship. You, Ben, and the children are very dear to us, and our mutual respect and love should not be put aside.*

*All my love, Dad*

TO MY CLOUD of witnesses in recovery, I shared my father's letter and asked for support. It was thoughtfully written and expressed sentiment. What it ignored were any feelings I might have about the relationship and how my mother continued to behave once I reached adulthood and independence.

The best suggestion was still Ellen's. I agreed to meet my mother, escorted by Dad, in my twelve-step counselor's office when they returned north in April. The purpose of these sessions would be to improve our bond.

Mom and I had a few sessions together; Harry led the conversation. Dad waited at a nearby coffee shop,

"All Jane wants from you, Anita, is for you to acknowledge that some things you've said have hurt her. Will you do that? Can you tell her you're sorry?"

"But I'm not sorry. Jane is stubborn, and I needed to tell her that she wasn't right about everything," she insisted, her comments directed toward Harry, as though I weren't seated a foot away from her.

"I know that," he said gently. "Jane simply wants you to hear that your words have been hurtful to her."

"That's her perception. I wasn't saying them to be hurtful."

"Yes, Anita, we understand that. Just for today, can you say that you're sorry that she felt hurt?" he coached.

"That's ridiculous. It wouldn't mean anything to say those words, just because you're asking me to."

"Actually, it would be very meaningful. Wouldn't it, Jane?" he said, glancing toward me. He was getting a full dose of what I'd been up against.

I looked at my mother, nodded, and said softly, "It would, Mom."

"All right, then," she said, then paused dramatically. "I'm sorry, Jane. Okay?"

Even though she had to be prompted, reminded, and encouraged, the fact that she finally said those words made me feel heard. I can't remember a previous time when she'd responded respectfully to any other request. I wonder, in the deepest recesses of her soul, how that moment was for her. I'd like to think that it was transformational. *I can apologize, acknowledge my daughter, and know that even though I did something wrong, I'm not wrong for being on the planet.*

But subsequent behavior indicated that she said what she needed to say so that she could go back to business as usual. It didn't matter that she didn't actually mean she was sorry. What mattered to me was that she said the words simply because she was told they would make me feel better.

I transformed in that interaction. Mom's evolution was less remarkable. That is, no one in the family said anything about the minuscule improvements I perceived.

There was a greeting card Ben and I had laughed over when we'd seen it at our local stationery shop. The outside said, "What are the three little words you most long to hear?" Inside, instead of the predictable "I love you," were these instead: "I was wrong."

Why is it so hard to admit that? Self-righteousness, I knew, topped my own list of personality flaws. It felt like it was in my genetic code. Justifying my every behavior came naturally to me. Did my mother suffer from the same malady? Had I inherited my defensiveness from her? Without the benefit of the rooms and unconditionally loving support, she must have found it excruciating to allow any frailty to be exposed. If she said she was sorry about the way she criticized me, what else might she need to atone for? It was a chasm she had rigorously avoided. Saying "I'm sorry" was not a familiar sentence in my household.

Mom and I resumed our communications, albeit with a shaky new foundation. She was more solicitous of me, less critical, and just a little bit frightened by our shifted dynamic, and that I might say no again.

Saying no to the relationship for those four months was the single most significant act I'd taken with Mom. After that, it was easier to assert myself more frequently when I needed to. Not always, but better. Progress, not perfection.

After those joint sessions, I asked Harry what he thought. As a lay therapist, he was not bound by the code of ethics professional therapists commit to. He did not withhold his opinion. "Your mother doesn't have a clue about who she is. She's like a street rat, grabbing at whatever morsel she can find."

My mother compared to a street rat. My heart collapsed as that image took its place in my mind.

Rather than feeling vindicated by his assessment, oddly, I felt compassion well up in me. This man had witnessed my mother in action. His validation of my experiences over a lifetime gave me a helicopter view of the most powerful figure in my life—a desperate woman trying to survive using outrageous behaviors. His depiction of my mother, this woman who survived the loss of a mother before she was two and continued to do whatever she had to do to get by, was accurate and sad.

The respectful distance that came out of this incident between my mother and me lasted a year or two, until my father's illness triggered a reversion to her old ways.

During this time, I wondered whether Ben might be worried that I'd take a similar stand with him. I was growing stronger spiritually but still held on to a bucket of resentments toward him that I'd been depositing throughout the years.

I never thought that he'd be the one to walk out on me.

Chapter Fifteen

$\mathcal{M}$ y chiropractor's lifestyle and philosophy raised my consciousness about foods that weren't serving me, as she put it. Like sugar. I frequently nagged Ben about his Diet Coke drinking. Perhaps I should have looked at my own habits before criticizing his.

She was giving a lecture one night that a group of us from CCNS, my kids' preschool, were attending. Brenda joined us for dinner before she spoke. Since it was a school night and we all had young children, no one had wine. But each of us ordered a diet soda with our meal, except Brenda, who ordered sparkling water.

I realize that doesn't sound unusual in our twenty-first-century world, but it would be the equivalent of someone asking for wheatgrass juice today. It may be on the menu, and you know it's better for you, but you wouldn't opt for it. What I'm trying to say is that she was walking her talk. I couldn't *not* order a sweetened (albeit artificially) beverage at the time.

As the years passed and I became more committed to living without addictive substances or behaviors, I made the decision, in May 1993, to refrain from eating between meals and not to eat any processed foods in which sugar was the first or second ingredient. No candy, gum, ice cream, cake, or cookies.

I'm hesitating to tell you that I declared this abstinence the day I walked into the Food Program, for fear you'll agree with Ben that I was becoming addicted to meetings. While I never called myself a compulsive overeater, which is how many members identify, I knew that I was addicted to sugar and that I had a problem. A friend once said that a pint of Häagen-Dazs never spent a night in his house. That was true for me as well. If ice cream was in the freezer, I had to have it.

This is what obsession and addiction have at their center: the compulsion to partake in something—drugs, alcohol, sex, shopping, gambling, sugar, etc.—that will bring momentary pleasure, relief, and escape. Until my late thirties, sugar allowed me to suppress my feelings. A slight by my mother, a sarcastic remark from Ben, or a canceled date with Fran was easily erased with a frozen confection. The drawback of this false cure-all is that eventually the elixir loses its effectiveness and actually creates more problems than it solves—in my case, depression and weight gain.

When I tell my story in the Food Program, my bottom—the day I knew for sure I was compulsive with food—came in my late thirties, still a few years before I stepped into any recovery. Ben and I were attending a relative's bat mitzvah in New Jersey. I had a couple of glasses of wine, my limit, during the cocktail hour. Seated at a table of ten for the luncheon, I ate normally during the salad and entrée courses. When dessert arrived, it was baked Alaska, not a favorite. Yet after I ate mine, I asked Ben if he wanted his. He slid his plate in my direction, and I finished it off. I turned to the man on my left, whom I didn't know, other than having exchanged introductions and pleasantries when we'd sat down. Noticing his dessert sitting untouched, I gestured, *Are you going to eat that?* and smiled to make it seem like a joke.

"Please, have it," he answered, and exchanged his full plate for my empty one. When I put the first forkful into my mouth, he let out a snort and said, "Now, there's a woman out of control."

I felt mortified, but it didn't stop me from finishing every crumb and drop of meringue.

Pride kept my weight reasonable. I was not obese, which is what I would have expected walking into the Food Program, a roomful of fat people. Surprisingly, only a small percentage of the members I saw in the rooms "wore" their issues with food. Bulimia and anorexia, severe eating disorders, caused a lot of people who came to appear thin.

But I knew I had a problem with food. I also knew that if I started going to those meetings, it would change my life in ways that scared me. Ben might complain again about having to be so careful with me.

I couldn't put words to it then, but I used food to cover feelings, not to mention filling the spiritual hole inside me. Without the buffer of a double scoop, how would I cope?

Though I'd heard of the Food Program, I dreaded the prospect of narrowing my food choices. But I'd begun to pay particular attention to one woman in the rooms. Her shares sounded like she had deeper recovery, if you could measure something like that. She had a confidence about her that I envied.

"What's your secret?" I asked after one meeting. She knew what differentiated her. "The Food Program. There's something powerful about saying no to foods that trigger me and get me craving more," she explained. "It makes other choices, besides food, easier and clearer, for some reason."

A member for several years already, she told me about her favorite meeting, two towns away. I met her there a few days later and made the decision to become "abstinent," the Food Program equivalent of sober, one day at a time.

As a result of defining what goes into my mouth and when, I began to receive that clarity. Acquaintances I'd have happily met at Friendly's in the past eventually lost their appeal when coffee (no sweetener, thank you) was the only thing between us. I could no longer swallow conversations that would have gone down more easily with hot fudge. Without numbing out on food, I began to say no to anyone I no longer wanted to hurt my body over.

This new choice forced me to pay attention to how I spent my time and energy. I started saying no to situations, not just around meals, that were wearing away my spirit. A childhood friend, whom I'd always cherished, was married to a man who demeaned and neglected her. Before they were even engaged, she would regularly phone me to cry, "He comes to the city to be with me every night of the week, but on the weekends, he goes off to the Cape with his father to play tennis, and I'm here alone."

Before recovery, I'd cluck and pat and offer soothing observations and suggestions to improve the situation.

But as I got healthier and time passed, her husband's behaviors got worse. I also noticed that she didn't really want my advice. It felt like she only wanted a witness. Her stories became alarming. Once, she reported to me, "He slammed the kitchen door so hard while I was feeding the kids, a framed photograph of our family fell off the wall and crashed to the floor."

I began to doubt that my listening was helpful. It was excruciating to me to hear over and over again how hard her life was. I realized that my allowing her to share her horror stories diffused and diluted her experience. Venting these stories allowed—or enabled, in recovery terms—her to go back into the ring with this man. That was the last thing I wanted to facilitate. I knew it would sound like tough love, but I believed that if I removed this soft place for her to land, she might feel closer to doing something about her situation.

"I know this is going to sound harsh, but if you're not willing to do something about this, like leave, then I can't keep listening. It's making me sick to hear how he's abusing you," I finally told my friend, hoping that eventually that still small voice within her would speak up.

Rather than taking any action on her own behalf, she stopped calling me with the horrific tales. My feelings were mixed. I missed our time together and those regular conversations but no longer had the heavy feeling those calls had given me. I'd like to think that my action of protecting myself hastened her eventual exit from the marriage, which ultimately happened. But she had many other friends who would fill the role I had occupied, and the suffering lasted for years. So often I wanted to give her the recovery I was experiencing, but it's not transferable. Each person has her own path.

So much of the process is about self-care, loving and nurturing our own souls. It may even look like selfishness to the mere observer. But if everyone on this planet fully loved and cared for herself, well, you know the rest.

A WORD ABOUT me and meetings. By the time I got to the Food Program, I'd been in recovery for four years. My programs overlapped. Between that fellowship and the one for adult children, I attended three or four meetings per week. I no longer felt the need for my first fellowship.

Prior to this new stage of my life, I preserved every detail of import for Fran's edification, hungering for the moment when I could be in her presence to unwrap the morsel I'd saved. Once I entered the rooms, I had witnesses whenever I chose to attend a meeting or make a phone call. Although I loved going to meetings and they became central to my social life, if I couldn't get to one, I didn't get edgy, plot other ways to get out of the house, or feel that familiar urgency cycling in my brain, blocking out other thoughts. Well, maybe a little bit, but nothing like my full-blown enslavement from before.

The person who most helped me maintain my abstinence was Pat. I called her every day to report what I'd consumed in the previous twenty-four hours. I know this must sound extreme, but if you've ever used food to hide feelings or gotten panicky when Friendly's was out of your favorite flavor, you may have an inkling about how much food occupied my mind. Talking to Pat and being honest about what I was spooning in daily forged a vital and unexpected relationship.

When I first saw her at a meeting, I thought, *What's a beautiful young woman like her doing in a place like this?* She wasn't obese, sat on the folding chair like a ballerina, had an every-hair-in-place coif, and shared her joy in abstinence every time she spoke in the circle. I never thought she would understand or relate to my love affair with sugar or be able to help me live without it.

Our paths would not have crossed in the world outside the rooms. She was a salesgirl who'd grown up in a blue-collar home in central Connecticut. A high school graduate, she'd gotten into alcohol and drugs in her teens and lived as a wealthy man's mistress for several years, jet-setting around the world and riding in limos, until a cocaine high and drinking fog could no longer cover up the pain she was masking. She'd sought therapy, on her keeper's dime, and gotten into recovery long before we met in the rooms in 1993. By then she was contentedly married to an insurance salesman and gave birth to two girls as our friendship grew.

After I'd become a regular at her meeting, Pat started calling me to check in. She had already embraced the phone as a tool of recovery.

"Hi, Jane, it's Pat. I'm making an outreach call. How was your day?"

I was flattered she picked me to call. Telling her about my comings and goings felt good. While I wouldn't ever have called someone to report my annoyance that my kids' bus had been late and thrown me off schedule, the constancy of our conversations permitted me the time and attention to tell another human being about little hurts and injustices I would previously have experienced and stuffed away or stuffed down with peanut M&M's. These conversations also allowed me to share the proud moments that otherwise could have been missed. They never felt important enough to rotate a dial ten times and hope someone would pick up.

A spouse was supposed to play this role, I'd hoped, believed, or a mother, a sister, or a best friend. I had never found someone to fill that spot. The relationships I formed in recovery and my attendance at meetings began to satisfy that cavernous need.

During my twelve-step counseling sessions with Harry, he asked me about prayer and my relationship with God. Often during someone's qualification, I'd hear, "And then I hit my knees." At first I imagined the person slapping those joints with both hands. Later I discovered that it meant getting into position to pray to God.

Growing up Jewish, one does not kneel to pray. It's regarded as a Christian ritual, something done in churches, where kneelers are attached to the pew in front of you and flipped down as needed. But Harry convinced me otherwise. Step 7 says, "Humbly ask God to remove our shortcomings." Could I assume a posture of humility? Harry inquired. It was more for me than for God. I said I'd try.

For weeks, after I completed my morning meditation in bed, I headed to the bathroom, where I'd double over the small area rug, drag it to the toilet, close the lid, and rest my elbows on it as I lowered myself to my knees and onto the padded surface. Although I believed that Harry had given me good advice, I thought bringing this practice into my bedroom would be too much for Ben to handle.

I'd whisper the prayers I'd chosen to say, flush the toilet so he wouldn't question my time in the loo, and unfold the rug, sliding it back next to the tub with my bare toe.

Reporting my successful new prayer ritual to Harry, I waited for his kudos. Instead, he asked, "Why are you going into the bathroom to pray? Why not get on your knees at your bedside?"

"I'm afraid to pray in front of Ben. He doesn't believe in God. He hates religion. He hates anyone being dependent on God. He'd freak out."

"How does that feel to you?" he asked.

"Shitty," I said, and paused. "I know what I have to do," I added, after a silence that allowed me to process my thoughts.

"What the hell is that?" Ben asked the next morning when he woke up and rolled over, only to see his Jewish wife kneeling next to her side of the bed, hands in prayer position.

"I'm praying," was the only answer I could come up with.

"What the hell?" he repeated.

"I know, I know. Looks crazy, I'm sure. But it's helping me.

And it's the step I'm working on. Can you handle my doing this? Or do I need to find another place?"

He made that back-of-the-throat noise I'd hear when his mood darkened.

More bluster, I guessed.

I found that getting on my knees did make me feel humble. Taking the time to situate myself physically on the floor, then reciting a series of prayers—I had memorized several more by this time—took me into another realm for a few minutes each morning. I felt better when I stood back up, as though something had been shed.

The routines that recovery added to my life (meetings, phone calls, prayer, and meditation) and the behaviors it removed (eating foods that made me feel hyped up and then depleted) narrowed the path of my days. My purpose was becoming clearer as the sugar fog and overeating subsided.

It also began to shine a light on what was missing from my marriage.

The regular calls with Pat and my meeting attendance created the ease and familiarity I'd always wished for. Knowing that Pat was going to call lightened everything else in my day. I'd have someone to talk to about the little stuff. There was no pressure, only a safety valve that allowed me to let off steam when life heated up.

When I selected her as my sponsor, I began doing the dialing.

No matter who called whom, there was no seeker or sought in our arrangement. If I didn't get to the phone to call at exactly five o'clock, Pat dialed me. The friendship didn't need to be tested. It just was.

Chapter Sixteen

*I*f you could choose," Ben once asked me with a tinge of sadistic humor, "in what order would you want our parents to die?"

"Easy," I replied. "My mother, your father, my father, your mother."

"Me, too," Ben agreed. It was good when we agreed.

In fact, our parents passed in almost the opposite order—his mother died first, in her early sixties, in 1979, and my mother lived the longest, dying at eighty-eight, in 2005. Ben's parents' deaths seemed to happen long-distance, since they lived in New Jersey. He went there often to see his mother during her hospitalization of merely weeks. I accompanied him half the time. I admired his attending to her, though I was surprised at how little mourning there was after her untimely death. His father's lengthier dementia and hospitalization required less from Ben, and less was given. I went only a few times to see Bob at the end of this life.

Losing my parents was a different story.

"Why is this happening to us?" my mother exhorted when

my father's remission from bladder cancer ended and he went back into treatment in the spring of 1993, after nearly a decade of fine health. He was now seventy-eight and had had a good life.

Dad's final days in White Plains Hospital were almost as sterile as the room itself. When I visited him for the last time, he was in his hospital gown, hooked up to an IV, seated, eyes half open. He may have known he was dying but gave no evidence to me. There was no goodbye from Dad, no epiphanies or expressions of love. We acted as if we'd see each other the next day or the one after that.

He died peacefully on August 7, 1993.

It's not infrequent to hear stories of long-married couples perishing within a short time of each other—the "widowhood effect." Not so for Mom and Dad. My parents had celebrated their fiftieth wedding anniversary on August 16, 1992, almost exactly one year before my father's death. My mother lived a dozen more years after that.

All hell broke out a few days after his funeral. Mom maintained a modicum of composure during the service and the shiva, though she still commanded us all.

"Goddammit! Where's Carolyn? How could she miss her flight?" she yelled when my brother's wife called from Denver to say she hadn't made her connection and would be arriving later than expected the day before the funeral.

"Have her call a car service, Andy. I need you here with me."

"Jane, tell Lucy I want her to speak about Grandpa."

"Meredith, you stay at the house with me. I can't be alone."

Each of these would have been more tolerable if they'd been requests, instead of commands. If there'd been a history of her politely asking to have her needs met throughout our lives. But that was never the case.

I believe she was so afraid she wouldn't get what she wanted that, instead of stating her needs, she made our potential lack of compliance unacceptable.

"Be at the house no later than nine a.m. tomorrow, so we can get in the limos together to go to temple," Mom announced. "Tell your friends not to send flowers. And don't have them bring food. We're not *schnorrers*," she reprimanded us, using a derogatory Yiddish word for "beggars." Before the perceived crime was even committed, we were already wrong.

It's a challenge to be in the presence of someone who has her shield up, her quiver of unhappiness loaded, and is so frightened of rejection that she is incapable of choosing any different behavior.

If she hadn't been so threatening and insulting, I might have felt compassion for her. I was so busy trying not to feel offended, my reserves were depleted and I had nothing left to give her.

She was a mentally ill woman who looked like my mother but was unskilled at delivering what all children seek: love and attention. She didn't behave this way on purpose. She didn't have the skill set to behave differently. She did the best she could. My younger self never accepted this truth.


ONCE WE KIDS went back to our lives and she was home alone, Mom could not cope. Dad had been her buffer for over fifty years. Even at his sickest, she still had the façade of their relationship to mask her own darkness. Now that was gone.

In the embrace of my fellowship, I felt carried during those early days of abstinence and mourning. I hardly cried about the loss of my father. My mother's neediness overshadowed any emotions of sadness. It was impossible for me to distance myself enough from her behavior to recognize that this outwardly powerful but inwardly anxious woman had just lost her partner of fifty years. If it had been anyone else—an aunt, another friend's mother, an elderly fellow in the program—I'm sure I would have found that compassion somewhere deep inside myself. But at that time, I had no reserve to share with my mother. I'm not proud to say this, but it's the truth.

I processed my emotions out loud in the rooms but otherwise tucked them away.

My father's burial instructions were for him to be cremated, his ashes placed alongside my mother in her coffin when the time came. Ironically, the funeral home lost track of the cardboard carton containing my father's remains, and they were never found. I feel oddly detached about this. I'm not one to visit cemeteries, so the symbolism or tangibility of it had no meaning for me. My memories of Dad are sufficient.

A few months after my father's death, my mother broke down completely. In Harry's words, my poor street rat of a mother was completely lost. In my soul, I wished I were the kind of daughter who could curl up next to her during her early widowhood, hold her in my arms, and soothe her tears. But her dramatic behavior, dismissal of me as anything other than an appendage to her pain, and constant nasty remarks drove me away.

Compassion and disgust stirred inside me. This Oz-like creature, so grandiose in her dis-ease, was actually a tortured, motherless child who was incapable of caring for herself. She manipulated us to do that job, causing resentment and anger until she got what she needed. Even the negative reinforcement, our yelling or annoyed responses, were better than being abandoned, as she had been as a baby. Any interaction would do. All she wanted was to connect.

Just like I did.

During this emotional time, I recall conversations, hugs, and visits with friends from the rooms. Though I'm sure he was there, I have little recollection of Ben's attention and care during my mother's deteriorating years.

On her birthday, October 12, 1993, I had the difficult task of packing her bag and taking her over to New York Hospital in White Plains, where we'd been told they could treat her. I'd never seen a nervous breakdown live, but her recent behaviors fit the description, especially finding her seated on the floor of her closet, her knees hugged to her chest, moaning.

She was admitted to New York Hospital and spent the next three months under their supervision. I think the prospect of being taken care of, albeit at a psychiatric hospital, appealed enough to my mother to commit herself. Her meals would be served, she'd be under the scrutiny of a team of professionals, and she would have no responsibility other than to get better. Although she balked later, the charm of that promised attention may have been the deciding factor.

I wanted to get her diagnosis from New York Hospital, to have her condition labeled, for my own curiosity. Was she bipolar? A borderline personality? Clinically depressed? I sought words to describe what untreated behaviors we'd been subjected to. Crazy as it sounds, it would have helped me understand that she didn't mean to be how she was.

But her hospitalization occurred before files were saved digitally. All records from that time have been destroyed. The therapist Mom had been seeing responded to my request for her analysis only after I'd mailed a self-addressed, stamped envelope. She did not return my calls. Ever protective of the psychologist-client relationship, she would not turn over the information I sought, only that it had been a pleasure working with Mom.

What carried me through Mom's hospitalization was not comfort from Ben—that wasn't his strong suit—but my regular calls with Pat, where I got to process the dailiness of it all and be heard.

THERE WERE THREE rounds of hospitalizations over the next decade as my mother's medicated state progressed. She stabilized after that first stay at New York Hospital, enough that we could move her into an assisted living facility, where she would reside for her remaining years.

It wasn't a smooth course, and her behaviors and defenses eventually returned full force.

Whenever I tried to make my mother happy, no matter how hard I worked at it, I failed.

Why am I spending so much time talking about my mother when the focus of this memoir is my own growth and transformation? Because it's taken me most of my lifetime to see the parallels between that relationship and the one with Ben. Unlike my mother, he came from a family of privilege and was prized by his parents. But I recognized a similar sadness in him that I longed to shift.

I recall a particular moment when we were graduate students living at Whittier Hall. I walked up the steps of the foyer and entered the social area beyond the reception desk. Ben was seated, not by the card table where we often shared lunch, but on a leatherette bench across the room. His head was down, his shoulders hunched, his chin resting on the palm of his right hand. He may have just been lost in thought, I'll never know, but my overwhelming and immediate thought, the one that snapped me into service and that I then summarily tucked away, was, *I can make him happy.*

Like my years with my mother, my occasional successes were tiny pebbles along an intricate path of attempts, disappointments, and falling short. No good girl would ever quit trying.

BECAUSE SHE WAS well enough at the time, Mom was scheduled to go her condo in Palm Beach in mid-December 2005. Our Thanksgiving gathering with extended family not two weeks earlier had gone particularly poorly. Mom had all but ignored me, except for a formal greeting: "I hope you're well, Jane." This sounded like something acquaintances say to one another, not mothers to daughters.

Monday morning, December 5, I received a call that she was in the emergency room of White Plains Hospital. Rather than feel frightened or upset that my mother was hospitalized, I thought, *Again? What for this time?* There had been many of these calls during my life. It felt more routine than dire.

I met my sisters in the ER and stood chatting with them at the foot of her bed as specialists examined her.

"Shut up!" she yelled at the three of us, raising her head from the pillow, straining the tendons in her neck. Even though she was in a johnny, lying on a gurney, she was still able to command center stage.

Barbara, Meredith, and I exchanged glances with each other, we three grown women who had just been censured by this powerful, horizontal, unwell woman.

"Shut up." Those were the last words she spoke to us.

Two days later, having suffered a stroke, Mom lay in a coma, attached to tubes and an oxygen mask. My brother flew in from California, and the four of us maintained a vigil for the next several days.

While my siblings were taking a break one late afternoon,

I was alone in the room with our mother. I took off my shoes and jacket and crawled into bed with her. I knew she would not respond to me, but there were things I had to say, that I'd been taught to say. The nurses had placed her on her right side, to prevent bedsores, I supposed.

Spooning her from behind, I put my left arm over her shoulder, my right arm bent against the part of her back that rested on the bed.

"I want to thank you for all you did for me, Mom," I whispered. "I forgive you, and I love you."

I hope that the theory of hearing being the last sense to go is true. That my mother left this earth with my expression of gratitude, compassion, and love. She had a hard go of it, losing her mother so young, being handed off to her elderly grandparents, marrying a man who was not demonstrative in what affection he had for her. Her happiest days were when we were small, loving, and dependent. Whatever her demons were, she tried valiantly to fight them. She was tenacious, lively—a oner, in crossword-puzzle parlance. My brother selected the word "indomitable" to describe Mom in her obituary.

Much of who I've become is a result of having had Anita Siegel Goodman as my mother.

We kept a vigil at her bedside. Meredith brought along a tote bag full of office work to manage while we sat there. I knitted and purled the sleeves of a sweater. Keeping my hands busy was a godsend during those long hours. Barbara and Andy kept the conversation going to help silence the whirring of oxygen entering and exiting the tubes in Mom's nostrils.

"I've got to get back home," Andy said in frustration sometime on Saturday afternoon, and began looking into flights to California. None of us got close enough to the nurses on duty to get any sense of when the end would come.

I arose early Sunday morning, the eleventh, and wrote in my journal, "I can't go in there today. This is too hard. I have nothing left to give."

I went downstairs to make breakfast, when the phone rang. It was someone from the hospital saying that Mom had passed.

Even though her death was imminent, I was devastated at the news of it. Telephoning her friends and our family members to relay the news was hard. I choked up each time I had to say, "I'm calling to let you know that my mother died."

The day of the funeral, our family gathered at my sister Barbara's house in Rye and rode in family units to the synagogue for Mom's service. I looked over at my husband, our children, and our daughter-in-law-to-be, all dressed in black, seated in that limousine.

"I know this sounds crazy," I said, "but everything I've ever wanted and loved is right here, right now."

After my mother died, there were no arguments about who would get what of her possessions. We quickly settled the estate and moved on with our lives.

Chapter Seventeen

*H*aving been with hundreds of people at school each week and running the SAT prep course evenings and weekends, Ben preferred a Friday night dinner for two, followed by watching TV from the couch. That beat putting on a face and being with yet more people.

I, on the other hand, spent most of my days in the solitary practice of my art, chauffeuring kids, grocery shopping, and preparing meals. I longed to leave the confines of the house for a public venue.

It was an argument we rehashed throughout our marriage. His words sounded flattering. "I just want to have dinner with you." But we often sat mute in the restaurant, Ben's mind elsewhere.

I enjoyed my husband most when we were with other couples. He was funnier, more engaged and animated in public. Often when it was just the two of us, he became sullen and withdrawn. I tried to describe to him what that felt like, but it never resolved.

When our marriage hit the rails, around 2008, and we

were grasping at Band-Aids to fix it, I hired a therapist friend in Massachusetts to use a technique called video mirroring to record us in conversation. She set up her camera in our living room and posed questions that intentionally aroused conflict. The digital images she recorded allowed us to see what we looked like when stressed. Whatever went on in his head and while processing, Ben got to view it with an outsider's perspective.

"I had no idea that my expression could be so mean-looking," he admitted. That felt good to me. I needed a witness that I wasn't crazy. How he acted and what he said he felt were not aligned. That self-knowledge didn't stick, though.

One couples' counselor caught a similar moment when we were in her office. She was recording our phone numbers at the end of a session. When I recited my office number, Ben's face contorted.

I read into the contortion: *He hates that I have my own phone number now. He doesn't want the therapist having this information. He doesn't like that I said "two, zero, one, three," instead of "two, oh, one, three."* He could be very critical of how I languaged things —like using language as a verb. I tiptoed around his sensitivities, which I had to guess at.

The therapist noted the change of expression, too, and said, "Ben, you look distraught. Can you tell Jane and me what just happened?"

It relieved me that she took the moment to challenge him. I needed a model for how to do that. My husband would simply dismiss my comment by saying, "I don't know what you're talking about." I realize that he didn't do this intentionally. It was a behavior he had learned to cope with whatever challenges he'd grown up with. Still, it was present.

"I was trying to figure out if those numbers were exactly

like our house line's. I was trying to see them in my mind." So benign, yet I had read into his expression a world of meaning, as I had as a young child, trying to make things right in the household. I was an expert.

WHILE I WAS becoming more embedded in my twelve-step communities, Ben created his own clan. His need for socializing was largely fulfilled in his daily work: after-school student visits in his chairman's office or evening phone calls with parents interested in enrolling their children in his SAT classes. He'd spend fifteen to twenty minutes engaging them, asking about their kids' scores, and eloquently describing how this course was different from other nationally known brands, like Kaplan or the Princeton Review. I was jealous of those parents, not because these were intimate conversations, but because any time Ben spent on the phone with them depleted whatever reserve I might then draw from.

I didn't realize the toll this was taking on me. Before I got my own telephone line for my work, I felt obligated to answer all the calls that came to our house line. Pre-cell phones, Ben refused to get a dedicated line for his business. For years, the family line rang with mothers asking to speak to Mr. Pollak.

My tone must've been a giveaway of my mood.

"Mrs. Pollak?" they'd ask when I picked up. "I'm so sorry to bother you! Is Mr. Pollak there?" Or some other kind apology to mollify me. I'm sure my "hello" spewed annoyance.

In addition to creating class lists and course outlines on his desktop computer, Ben also spent time online when search engines like Yahoo and Alta Vista came about, prior to Google. What most fueled his interest was finding people from his childhood. Every five years, he'd receive the Fair Lawn High

School Alumni Directory. There was something very special to Ben about his youth, something irreplaceable. He pored over those directories.

The amateur psychologist in me clung to one theory. During our first rough patch, when we were both in our mid-thirties, and I was feeling the worst about myself in the relationship, I asked Ben to please go see someone about his moodiness. I was still seeing Silvie. After the first visit with the psychiatrist he'd selected, Ben came back and shared a piece of what had gone on during the session.

"The guy asked me if I had had any traumatic experience as a teenager. But I told him no."

"Ben," I said, "what about Michael Nieman?" I was referring to his best friend, who was hit by a train and killed when they were nineteen.

"Oh," he responded quietly. "Oh, yeah. I forgot about that."

The doctor told Ben that he may have been "fixated in adolescence" and was delving for an early suffering that may have caused this disorder. That phrase helped me understand his deep connection to his past and his desire to go back to that time and find people from then. And how perfect to spend his entire career with a demographic that didn't age but stayed between ages fourteen and eighteen.

There we were, now in our mid-thirties, living a decidedly middle-class, suburban lifestyle with three children, a house, and two cars. Whatever had happened in his childhood that hadn't gotten worked out emotionally or psychologically seemed to be bubbling up to the surface now.

"Jane! I just found Harvey Milstein on Yahoo," Ben would report excitedly. "Boy, did he get fat! Listen to this: he's a trial lawyer. That's a surprise. He was always class clown. Who knew?"

It became an obsession. Exploring the past, Ben would en-

ter names, follow leads, and get suspended in a time zone before Ben + Jane existed as a couple. I was busy with the kids,
my craft business, and my fellowship. I went from feeling jealous that he was otherwise occupied to feeling grateful and then
indifferent.

This new behavior allowed me to come and go as I
pleased. If he was getting his social needs met online, I didn't
have to feel guilty or account for how I spent my time. If I'd
felt neglected before, I now bordered on feeling invisible. But
with that invisibility came freedom. He barely noticed where I
was or with whom.

If he wasn't grading papers or watching TV in the living
room, he was hunched over his computer in his office.

Occasionally, I'd find myself at Ben's desk in his study off
our bedroom. If I needed to look something up on the computer while I was upstairs, I'd log on to his Yahoo account,
enter his password, and then link to the site I was looking for.

I was mildly surprised one day when I'd inserted the usual
password and an "invalid" dialogue box appeared. *Hmm, that's
funny. I wonder if he changed his password.* Not giving it any further thought, I went downstairs to my own computer and resumed my search.

I wish I had made note of that date, because I now believe
that whatever he'd been looking for in his alumni directory
and in his Yahoo, Google, and Facebook searches, he'd found—
and was hiding. I'm not sure what I'd have done with that information, but it could fill in a missing timeline piece: when
his other relationship actually began.

OVER THE COURSE of our marriage Ben and I saw counselors
individually and as couples. Those men and women kept us

together for the thirty-eight years we were married. We'd see a professional for several sessions and work on the tools we were given, and things would improve. Then we'd reach a plateau and get comfortable again.

He and I began seeing a therapist in Westport whom a friend had recommended. What always amazed me about our sessions together was that Ben spoke eloquently in his understanding of me and my needs. During those one-hour sessions, I felt seen and understood by him. That didn't translate back at home, where I felt unseen again, walking by Ben watching TV in the living room as I went to my studio, or similarly when I passed his desk in his office on the way to our bedroom.

He was always at his best in public.

In my one-on-one sessions with this new therapist, she reinforced what a good husband Ben was. How he talked about me in her office showed him to be better than most spouses she counseled. "You have a good man there, Jane," she'd say. Since she saw mostly couples, I made her the expert and trusted her judgment of him over my own reality. She wasn't reinforcing what I felt, but maybe I was too harsh a critic. Again, my body was experiencing a different sensation than my head was understanding. I ignored the signal.

This advisor suggested a homework exercise in which we make a game of dating other people through role-playing. We were not to actually go out with men or women outside the marriage, but to infuse our marriage with the newness that dating brings—to make our romantic time together exciting again.

To comply one night, Ben and I drove in separate cars to a restaurant in Darien, where I pretended to be an admiring parent of one of his SAT students. I'm only just realizing that he played himself and got to portray the same adored role he'd always sought.

Over dinner we held hands, and it progressed from there. We were two A students conspiring to impress our therapist. The positive outcome of that rendezvous got Ben and me back on an even keel, and we continued more or less happily for another period.

But in November 2009, when Ben asked for the second time, "Should I move out?" I had no heart to try again. My spirit was flat.

Knowing that this time my answer was yes, I arranged to go for a walk with Pat the next morning. I needed to vent instead of chowing down on cookies—not an option—to avoid the pain. Pat knew how strong a program I worked, as well as the kind of life I was leading. Who else could I be completely honest with? She had had a ringside seat for the deterioration of my marriage over the last several months. Its denouement was surprising but not out of the blue.

We met at the running track of a neighboring middle school, where I told her the latest development. "He's moving out on Sunday," I informed her.

"Jane," she said, taking my arm and pausing our walk for a moment, "men don't leave unless they have someone else."

Ben was so cantankerous and disagreeable, the thought of his having an affair had never crossed my mind, and I dismissed her suggestion immediately. "Ha! Impossible! Couldn't be."

In the movies, when a man was having an affair, wasn't that when he brought flowers and jewelry home to his wife and acted sweeter than cream? I simply could not compute that possibility, which of course turned out to be exactly the case. While Pat's assertion is not documented statistically, it stayed with me.

Mulling it over, I likened it to the endless scenarios I had heard describing behavior in corporate America. Rather than firing an employee who's been at the same place for years, management makes the situation untenable, hoping she'll quit out of anger and frustration. Companies don't want to fire the worker because then they'll have to pay unemployment.

It felt like that. Life at home had become so unpleasant, with oceans of neglect and very little joy. Maybe Ben hoped that I would get fed up and kick him out. But I was in for the long run, no matter how awful it got. The rule said marriage is forever. When I showed no signs of departure, he offered to leave. Still, it came in the form of a question.

Ben arranged to move his things out the Sunday of Thanksgiving weekend. I chose to head to New York City to meet a friend so I wouldn't have to witness his departure. I came back to an empty house that evening and no idea where this man I'd been married to for close to four decades would now be living.

Ben, unbeknownst to me, had a secret. I didn't know there was another woman and thought that this was still about working out our issues.

After the news of his relationship had been revealed during a joint session, Ben made the decision to give our marriage another try. I honestly can't remember what provoked that choice on his part—my tears over the letter he'd read, or my conviction that infidelity was my bottom line and divorce was the only option—but we started dating again, which was awkward. He told the other woman that he was going to work on our marriage.

Even knowing the circumstances of his leaving six months earlier, his betrayal of me and our family, I capitulated to his request. I still wasn't willing to nullify our contract.

The most important developments for each of us during the separation, beyond the couples' work, were the individual experiences we had at a highly recommended facility in Pennsylvania. The institution, Caron, offered a five-day rehabilitation program for relationships, called Breakthrough at Caron.

I went early in January, Ben in June. The days there included group activities, lectures, individual counseling, and the main event, psychodrama, where each member gets the spotlight using this dynamic tool. As you create a tableau of your childhood world, your life reveals itself in its starkest, core reality, while other members of your cohort portray the important players: spouse, mother, father, siblings, etc. These sessions were led by seasoned therapists well-trained to handle emotions, conflict, and the antisocial behaviors humans exhibit when pushed to the limit.

Each of us got to cast our individual dramatization. We also got to be cast as the mother, child, friend, etc., in our peer's reenactments. There was meaningful learning, whether you were the one directing the action or a player acting out scenarios from someone else's background. In both instances, it was as healing as it was revealing to participate and witness real-life situations reflected through a therapeutic lens.

As a result of our separate stays at Caron, Ben and I each came away with a personal intention. Mine, in January, was that I would never betray my inner child again. Throughout my life, I had sacrificed my deepest desires and put other people's needs and wishes ahead of my own. "I can take it" was my mantra, until I couldn't, but had no skills to say those words.

I heard early on in the rooms, "It's better to give a resentment than to get one." I didn't put this into practice nearly enough. I allowed myself to be the victim in ways great and small. No more. My ultrasensitive gut now sends out a sonarlike warning signal that alerts me, *This doesn't feel good.* I take action. I turn down a request, excuse myself from a tense situation, or tell a person I'm uncomfortable with the conversation.

You've just read my explanation of how I would never betray myself again, yet allowing a dating relationship with Ben before his stint at Caron was a complete contradiction. The only defense that makes sense to me is the one Oprah offered when she met, years later, with the man who had raped her as a child. "I fixed him eggs," she told an interviewer, with no touch of irony. I can't explain or defend my decision to give the marriage another go. Even after all my recovery, therapy, and breakthrough experiences, I was unable to let go of my insane fantasy.

Having seen the Caron process in action, I was curious to find out how Ben would take to the group dynamic and support five months after my experience. I had guardedly high hopes that it could be a transformative experience for him as well. Given that he'd been seeing a shrink and was willing to try a program that advocated twelve-step recovery, I wanted this to be the miracle that would bring our family back together.

It turned out he loved Caron and detailed to me how close the members of his group had become. We met at a Chinese restaurant for dinner the Friday night of his return. Over sesame noodles and vegetable *moo shu*, Ben talked with animation about the process, how his cohort selected him to play their higher power, which he, as a nonbeliever, found hilarious, but he revealed nothing about his takeaway.

Even though his mood was light and he seemed happy, my heart felt leaden. He hadn't phoned me from the road on his long trip home to share his experience, nor offered to pick me up for our dinner date, the way someone anxious to share a happy epiphany may have.

"We'll talk at Elaine's," he promised.

My throat closed.

Our session that week necessarily began with talk of Ben's time at Caron. "I realize that I have never put myself first. I need to really give myself that and find out whether my relationship with this person in Maine will make me happy. I have to pursue it. I owe it to myself."

Whatever optimistic bubble I'd mentally inflated in my brain burst in that instant. I'd spent thirty years working on myself, trying to understand our relationship and build my own self-esteem. Not everybody is interested in that pursuit. To have expected a 360-degree turnaround was unrealistic on my part. Ben had pooh-poohed recovery and counseling throughout our marriage, but he had heard at Caron exactly what he wanted to hear.

I finally understood this as though for the first time. Our relationship was indisputably over. *You've always put yourself first*, I thought, and knew what I had to say.

It was as though the universe prompted my next line. Right then and there, these words left my mouth: "Then I want a divorce."

Elaine didn't openly congratulate me, but she did acknowledge that many couples continue to live together in spite of a situation like ours. My choice, I heard her say, was courageous and strong.

Something had finally clicked in my soul. Applying everything I'd learned from the rooms to an intimate relationship was the hardest thing I had ever had to do in my recovery.

After that, it was a matter of selecting a mediator to negotiate the terms of our divorce. On March 17, 2011, our marriage of thirty-eight years ended officially at the Stamford courthouse, two blocks from our first apartment.

ONCE THE LEGAL separation and divorce proceedings were officially underway, I didn't want to live in the family home anymore. It felt stained by the secrets that had been kept there. Less than a mile from that property, a brand-new luxury apartment complex had been built on the Post Road, across from a Whole Foods and within easy walking distance of my gym, bank, and a cinema multiplex. With the help of my recovery friends, I had determined exactly how much I needed to live on. Ben had no objection to the number I requested and began sending me checks for that amount even before we officially signed the divorce papers.

I moved out of the house in September 2010, leaving a few items in the basement. I ordered all new furniture, except for a set of handmade dining room chairs I'd picked out at a craft show years before and brought with me.

When shopping for housewares at Crate & Barrel right before my move, I felt a surge of sadness travel from my belly to my throat as the saleslady innocently said, "Looks like you're outfitting a new home."

*Buying silverware and glasses is something a newlywed does, not a sixty something woman.* I was ashamed and embarrassed that this would be my new status in life: divorcée.

Although I kept up a front professionally and never blogged about what was going on personally, I slogged through that first year, taking it only twenty-four hours at a time. Friends surrounded me—program and civilian (as we call those outside the rooms)—and gave me wise slogans to hold on to. One divorced friend treated me to lunch and shared what someone had told her when she was newly separated. "It gets better." I clung to that and attended my fellowships with greater frequency, mostly so I could hear my own voice. I had never lived entirely alone.

At one particular meeting I went to, they circulated what is called a "We Care" sheet, with columns for attendees to write down their first name, their phone number and what they're feeling. For one entire year, the only word that came to my mind was "sad."

IN 2010, HAVING been separated for nearly a year, I was settled into my new apartment. With divorce on the horizon, I considered the possibility of dating. Even though my life with Ben was over, I was optimistic that all the work I'd done on myself over the decades, from Assertiveness Training in 1976 until now, might have changed me.

There was a spark in me ready to ignite. Call it soul, spirit, or God, something internal longed for connection. I was ready to be my own advocate, with a gigantic assist from my fellows.

I was good at keeping myself busy, socializing with new friends in my complex, seeing movies at the theater across the street, and attending meetings during the week. Eventually, though, I realized that I preferred to be in a relationship. This may sound odd, given my thirty-some years of complaints about Ben, but at least there'd been a mirror in my life to reflect back to me what was or wasn't okay. I realized that I wanted to have a man, a partner, with whom to share my thoughts, time, and love.

There were days when it occurred to me that no one knew where I was, what I was doing, or what mattered to me. Ben and I had fulfilled that role for each other. You don't know what you're missing until it's removed.

After only a few months of living in my new quarters, I became lonely and yearned for a mate. In my twenties, the externals for selecting the right mate were all-important: looks, career aspirations, background. Forty years later, kindness ranked high on my list. I wasn't looking for someone to grow a life with; more simply, I wanted us to share what we'd each cultivated along the way.

I had created a vision board for romance while still married to Ben. I thought that if I dreamed up how I wanted our marriage to look using magazine photos, I could manifest it in real life. It had worked in other aspects of my life: a bathroom renovation, a trip to Japan, and career goals. But I hadn't gotten any traction on the love front back then. There were clipped photos of couples embracing atop a canopy bed; another, of a man and woman gazing at a globe together; and a third, of two lovers walking arm in arm in an exotic setting.

Nothing ever happened with Ben that looked like any of the pictures I'd chosen and pasted onto poster board. Still, when I moved to 597 Westport Avenue, my new home in Norwalk, I brought it with me.

"Your romance board?" my friend who helped me with my move asked, as she unrolled it to hang it up.

"Yeah." I shrugged. "Should I give it another go?"

She used pushpins to attach it to the wall opposite my desk in the room that would be my office. Standing back, she assessed the pictures in front of her. Then she laughed. "Ha! This was never going to be Ben," she said. "No wonder you had to get divorced."

How did she know? I had never considered that acquaintances might have seen something in my marriage, or the lack of it, long before I did. With enough distance from Ben's departure, I laughed, too.

"Go for it! You know what you're looking for," she urged.

I'D BEEN AWARE of online dating since the inception of Match.com in 1995 but had been relieved that it was not something I'd ever need to partake in. I'd watch my older daughter dabble in Jdate, the Jewish matchmaking site, and how challenging it had been for her, although she did meet her husband that way.

I couldn't imagine subjecting myself to that kind of scrutiny. Craft shows were hard enough, putting out all your goods for the public to walk by, handle, and choose to buy or not to buy. Now *I* would be the product up for grabs.

Plus, at sixty-two, I knew I wasn't in a popular demographic. Most men my age preferred women in their forties and fifties, I told myself. Lying about my age wasn't an option. At what point do you explain that to the person you've met? And how?

I hoped that I would find someone who appreciated a woman who'd traveled the same decades as he had, who also needed afternoon naps, and who was comfortable in his own skin.

While it sounds easy to get a profile up online, I was not your slapdash kind of person who'd rush something up there just to have it listed. Like everything else I did, I preferred to post a handcrafted, from-scratch portrait of myself. Fortunately, another friend of mine had begun coaching women over forty in the dating arena. I hired her to write my profile and consult with me about how to answer the questions. She interviewed me at length and wrote a touching, comprehensive, and real narrative that included humor and irony. The fact that I loved NPR and Howard Stern would make sense to the right guy.

"Cast a wide net," she advised. "Don't make specific income, education, or height a requirement. You might miss a great guy out there who has everything else you want. There are plenty of intellectuals and renaissance men who don't have a string of initials after their name."

I trusted her and forged ahead. I opted for the handle CompoWalker, referencing Compo Beach in Westport, the most soothing place I knew. I was hoping to attract someone for whom that rang a bell, as I did a three-mile circuit there several times a week and would love to share that with a mate. It's a cliché to say that you like walks at the beach, but I thought my name choice was better than that of another woman, who advertised herself as Weston Wench. She had to shoo guys away with that alias. Admittedly, she was younger and prettier than I but hardly concealed a not-so-tacit agreement that would benefit the men who contacted her.

I hired someone to take photos that conveyed that, although in my sixties, I looked younger than my years and had a shapely body. More than one potential match asked how recent my photos were.

My first date was with a man named Michael, a psychiatrist from New Haven. We met at a Starbucks in Westport. He was in his early seventies, handsome, tall, and Jewish. I couldn't help thinking, *This is what Mom always wanted*, though I couldn't complete the sentence, speculating about whether she would have wanted him for me or for herself.

He and I talked comfortably, standing at the counter, as I ordered a tall decaf with cold soy milk. "I'll have the same," he told the woman in the green apron, offering her a $10 bill. I liked his ease and command of the situation. I began comparing him with Ben in my mind. My ex would have been visibly nervous and might have asked, "Are you sure they have soy milk?" not wanting to create an embarrassment for me or by association.

Throughout my dating life (and still), I subconsciously made those comparisons.

After an hour of flowing conversation at a table in the middle of that coffee emporium, Michael asked me if I'd like to have dinner on Saturday night. As with the first experience I had selling my art in 1973, I thought I had this dating thing all figured out. That very first contact and date with Michael was going to be it. I'd found my next mate! *What's the fuss been about? I go online for a few weeks, meet an attractive guy, bingo! Why all the complaining?* I mentally flipped my hair with the fingers of my right hand and raised my chin triumphantly.

Not so fast . . .

That weekend, our dinner at my favorite vegetarian restaurant got off to a rough start. I'm usually accurate about appointments and write down dates quickly and precisely, but there was a communications glitch somewhere between our establishing our next get-together while at Starbucks and my arrival that night. As I was driving to Bridgeport, my cell phone rang at 6:35 p.m., with an irritated Michael on the other end. For date number two, this was inauspicious.

"I thought we said six thirty," he grumbled.

"I thought you said you were going to be fifteen minutes late because of your son's event, so I was aiming for six forty-five. I'm not far away," I calculated.

He stood to greet me when I arrived and kissed me on the cheek. He'd chosen a table behind the main desk where we would place our orders. The restaurant I'd selected, Bloodroot, was self-serve, was owned and run by a lesbian cooperative, and offered the most delicious, healthy food in the area.

Michael escorted me up to the front of the restaurant, where we studied the chalkboard menu that night, talked to Selma, a cofounder, and decided what to eat. I felt a little funny being there on a date because I'd been a regular patron there for ages, most recently with Ben, though not in the past year, since our separation. I had called Selma after making the date with Michael to let her know that I was getting divorced and would be arriving with another man. Mature as I thought I was, I still cared what others might think. I wanted to ward off any misconceptions before they might be uttered.

It was important that anyone I date like this food, because what I ate was important to me. If I was going to have only three meals a day and nothing in between, I didn't want to waste even one. Michael clearly appreciated having been introduced to Bloodroot—another plus in his column.

But during dinner he completely dominated the conversation. For nearly two hours, he held court. I had the opportunity to learn a lot about his two marriages, six children, and extracurricular activities, biking and rowing—enough to know that he wasn't a match for me. I wanted a two-way exchange and a man who was sensitive enough to notice if it wasn't.

Even though I knew it was happening, I was still not the kind of person who could easily fit into the discourse "It's my turn, please." I'd spent decades in the role of audience with Ben. If on our second date my suitor, and a professional listener, no less, didn't notice how one-sided the night was, I wouldn't be the one to educate him.

"This was great," he said, as we were getting up to leave. "Would you like to go for a walk?"

"No, thanks," I responded. "I'm ready to go home."

So much for beginner's luck. If I had been sixteen or twenty-two and had all the time in the world, I might have given it another try. But in my seventh decade, time was of the essence. The most important four-letter word I learned in dating was "next"!

I realized then that it would take time and practice. I wanted to be in a relationship and needed to do whatever it took, even beyond looking at my vision board daily, to make it happen. It seemed reasonable to find one man in a hundred who would be right for me. I would stay optimistic through the next ninety-nine. I was on a mission. So far, I had one notch on my dating belt.

I continued to go online daily to review prospects, buoyed by the support and love of my tribe, to respond to any overtures that arrived, and to continue corresponding with men who'd shown interest in my profile.

One practice I'd learned in the rooms was to create written visions for myself, in addition to the wall-mounted variety. A particular ritual was to dream up a list of one hundred things I wanted to be, do, and have. To actually put down on paper, in black-and-white, what my heart and soul wanted. Whoever gives you permission to do that? Annually!

We would read these lists out loud to each other and articulate our dreams and visions to the universe. Mine included a variety of wishes, including attending the Oscars, receiving an invitation to dinner at the White House (depending on who was in office), and having fresh flowers delivered weekly. One woman cried the first time she heard the lists being read. "I think so small," she shared through her tears. It takes courage to ask for what you want.

I took the concept of asking the universe for what I wanted and applied it to dating. To flesh it out, I created a spreadsheet of all the happy couples I knew and wrote down the male partners' names and everything I admired about them in their marriages. Great listener, likes to dance, respects his wife's work as much as his own, can stay in controversy, not afraid of his emotions, etc. After cherry-picking qualities from a dozen males I regarded highly, I had a list of thirty-nine characteristics of the man of my dreams.

I wrote another letter to God, asking for this person to show up in my life. I could imagine Ben balking, reading it over my shoulder. "Christ! You think there's a god out there who's going to read this and provide the perfect man? Ha!" I had internalized his voice as I had internalized my mother's. Now, the work became quieting that chorus in my head and moving forward anyway.

I continued online dating in pursuit of this goal. You have to treat it like any job you want to succeed at. Send out messages responding to the parts of a man's profile you like. Be willing to set up phone calls and coffee dates. Show up for the dates, overcome rejection, and recognize that being ignored is normal. I was stood up, was promised calls, and even witnessed a disappearance. A New York artist I'd been in contact with over the course of several weeks told me he had ordered my book and would take it with him when he flew to Paris for a show of his work. I never heard from him after that. Did he hate my book? Meet someone else? Fall off the planet? I'll never know. But that's online dating. I've never had tough skin, but I developed a thin coating of resilience in knowing that it wasn't personal. It couldn't be. They didn't even know me. I never once thought I'd prefer to be back in my marriage. This was better than that.

Sharing about it at meetings helped. People laughed, related their own successes and disasters with me, and mostly bolstered my ego and promised me I'd find my mate.

Although I didn't keep strict count, between online messages, phone calls, coffee dates, a couple of walks at Compo, and the occasional lunch or dinner, I interacted with scores of men. Dick assumed we were a "thing" after two dates. He liked that we could be Dick and Jane, but I explained to him when he called for a third date that my gut was telling me it wasn't right.

I liked two men very much. The businessman from Milford and I got to a second date and a kiss, but he didn't follow up after that. Another man, ten years younger and quite passionately in pursuit, was too busy working off his accumulated debt to fit me in.

Every day Match.com sends its paid members several profiles of potential mates whose algorithms have paired with theirs. Every day I dutifully emailed a cordial message to each match, noting that we shared an interest in NPR, PBS, or Doc Martin, referencing a tidbit from his profile. I might hear back from one in eight when I did that.

Not one to quit, I kept sending out positive messages and agreed to take the man's phone number (protocol), when offered, to dial him up, in order to get past the writing stage.

Out of habit, I responded to one gentleman's profile when it showed up as a match for me. He lived seventy miles north of Norwalk and had a full head of curly hair and a playful smile. I wasn't wild about the Hawaiian shirt he posed in, but Sandy warned me about prejudging. His screen name, 6Bandaid, aroused my curiosity. But the line that convinced me to reach out to him read, "Not only can I spell 'credenza,' I know what one is, and I can move yours."

I emailed him that night. By the next morning, I'd received a reply that included a couple of phone numbers where I might dial him the next day. Not knowing if it was a business line or a cell, I chose one and called it the next afternoon.

"Hi, you've reached the Mike line," his outgoing message said.

I made a judgment. Who refers to their phone number as the Mike line? If there were a copy of my voice mail, it would register a long pause before I made the decision to speak. I had almost hung up. Wide net, wide net!

Instead, I left a brief message, offering a time that evening when we could speak. Mike called me back that night.

As Maya Angelou tells us, we may forget what people say or do, but we remember how they make us feel. You could apply that to online-dating communications and judge your prospects by it. This man, of the Mike line and Hawaiian shirts, from our first phone call made me feel seen, heard, and appreciated. *From the first call.*

The Match.com mail interface was unwieldy and a nuisance. You had to sign on to the dating site just to visit your inbox there before checking to see if there were any messages. Clunky. One of the ways Mike took charge of the relationship from the beginning was to politely and cordially ask if he could have my regular email address in order to bypass Match's.

You learn quickly that when you pursue online dating you should have an anonymous email address and give out only your cell phone number, not your reverse-searchable landline, to avoid the crazies. After my first conversation with Mike, I was comfortable and trusting enough to make the strategic decision to give him my jane@janepollak.com address, knowing that it made me Google-able. I'd sent it to other men in the past, with no further mention. It was my subtle test. Would they take the time to look me up? It was also a calculated risk. If they didn't bother to look me up, would I count that against them?

We spoke a couple of days later. By this time, Mike had studied my website and read dozens or more of my blog posts. He asked me informed questions, listened intently to my responses, and created an exchange that deepened my comfort level.

"I'd like to meet you," he said toward the end of that call. "I know you live in Norwalk. The only place I know how to get to is the Maritime Center. I used to take my kids to the aquarium there when they were little. Can you pick a place to have dinner near there?"

For someone as choosy as I am, he scored big by registering where I lived, being willing to drive all the way to me, rather than meeting halfway, as most of my dates did, and mentioning that he had brought his children to a learning environment seventy miles away. Ding ding ding!

I picked Papaya Thai, where I'd be able to make a vegetarian selection at a reasonable price. I didn't know this man's means and didn't opt for the more expensive and coincidentally named Match restaurant farther down the street. Sandy, my dating-coach friend, advised allowing the man to pick up the check on the first date.

Because of our schedules, we arranged to meet that Sunday night. On Friday, I planned to have dinner with an old friend. Over a glass of wine with her, I mentioned that I was scared about meeting this guy Mike.

"Why?" she asked.

"I know this sounds ridiculous, but he's so nice. I like him already. He's showing a lot of interest in me, makes me laugh, and respects what I say. Why that's scary to me, I don't know, but it is."

"I had someone in my life like that, and I pushed him away. That was seven years ago, and I've been trying to replace him ever since."

I used to do that with boyfriends. Maybe it's what I did unconsciously with Ben. Here was an opportunity to do it differently.

On Sunday night, I picked out the sexiest outfit I had in my wardrobe. I wore a black pencil skirt, a dark gray camo top that showed a little cleavage, and a pair of strappy black heels.

Always early to events, I pulled into the Maritime Center parking lot ten minutes before I was scheduled to meet Mike. I tapped Sandy's name on speed dial.

"I thought you had a date tonight," she said upon picking up.

"Yeah, I do. I'm in the parking lot across the street. I'm nervous."

"Why?" she asked, as my other friend had.

Now I was even clearer about what the fear was. "Because this could be it."

I promised to call Sandy after the date to let her know how it had gone, restarted the engine, and drove across the street to the restaurant.

There was only one other vehicle in the parking lot, a gray Toyota pickup truck with a Cornwall Volunteer Fire Department license plate holder surrounding the Connecticut plate.

*A truck? He drives a truck?*

I remembered Sandy's advice, swallowed, and went up the stairs and into the restaurant. Moments later, I met the next love of my life.

# Chapter Eighteen

*I*n the 1960s TV comedy spy show *Get Smart*, there was a gadget called the Cone of Silence that enveloped Agent 86, aka Max, and Chief, his boss, when they discussed secrets of the highest order. It never worked properly and sometimes hit them on the head as it descended into place.

There was something in my childhood that I would liken to that fictional device. I'd name it the Cone of Motherly Love. It was more a psychological mechanism than a physical one. My mother often repeated this mantra: "No one will *ever* love you as much as I do." I'm sure she meant it to be affectionate and reassuring, something she may have wished to hear from an adult when she was growing up.

My brother responded immediately when I emailed my siblings to ask if they remembered her words. "She would use that line as a club more than a caress, and it still (to this day) feels hollow to me," he replied.

It was confusing. She told us about her great love for us kids, but once we'd grown into adolescence and adulthood, it no longer felt loving. It felt demanding, critical, and shaming.

Should I try to find a mate who would prove her wrong and love me more than she did? Ben may have briefly, but it faded once children entered our marriage.

I didn't know what it felt like to be truly loved by a man. My father's emotional unavailability was the norm, so I had no expectation of love from him. Guys tried. As a teenager, I rejected them outright. I couldn't accept loving gestures, even a box of Valentine's chocolates offered by a boy I had a crush on in eighth grade. As soon as he showed interest in me, it was over.

It made sense that I married someone who would not be demonstrative. It would have made me run in the opposite direction.

But as I got into therapy, self-help programs, and ultimately recovery, knowing that I was lovable and capable became absolute. After my divorce, I would not tolerate a relationship with anyone who wasn't as crazy about me as I'd grown to be about myself.

AS THE HOSTESS and I entered the dining room, Mike rose to his feet alongside the booth he occupied at Papaya Thai. He extended both of his arms toward me, taking my right hand between his two in a warm shake.

"It's so nice to meet you," he said, as he helped me remove the red wool jacket I wore. He placed it on the hook adjacent to my side of the booth.

I'd seen his photos but found him more attractive in person. He may have been the first man I dated with facial hair, a full beard, but I didn't object. It suited him and nicely complemented an abundant head of salt-and-pepper curls. He had on a tweed wool blazer, a sweater, and an Oxford button-down shirt. He was taller than I, and broader, too.

Ben's height wasn't a problem, but Mike's stature appealed to me. There I went, comparing again. But I liked the difference.

We quickly ordered and dispensed with any further waitress interference. I had a glass of wine and noticed Mike's request for a fruit juice mixture in lieu of alcohol.

"Driving," he acknowledged. He dittoed my order of tofu with vegetables over brown rice, a positive sign.

A conversation about food choices ensued, followed by topics as varied as our kids, our work, volunteer activities, friends, and ex-spouses. There was never a pause in the flow, and I felt like an equal participant throughout.

After nearly two hours of easy talk, Mike said he'd like to see me again. I appreciated how direct he was. I had come to the date knowing that I had scheduled a ten-day trip that would take me out of the country. I hoped he wouldn't perceive my immediate lack of availability as a turnoff.

"I'm leaving on Friday for a macrobiotic cruise through the Caribbean. I won't be able to get together again until . . ." I named a date two weeks in the future.

"That actually coincides with my busiest time at work," he said. "I'm leading a conference at the end of that week, so I'll be able to get everything organized and done by the time you return."

Then he leaned his torso across the dark-stained pine tabletop, took both of my hands in his, and said, "I'm sure my affection for you can sustain your absence until then."

Time stopped. I felt the warmth of his skin on mine. My face flushed, and my heartbeat sped. A big smile pulled up the edges of my mouth, and I bent my head forward over our joined hands.

We exited together on that freezing February night, but neither of us felt the chill.

"Oh, I have something for you," Mike said, opening the door of his truck. He pulled out a leaf-shaped glass bottle filled with amber liquid accented by a red wool crocheted cord. "Maple syrup," he clarified, offering it to me. "I tap my trees each year and make syrup with my friends who have a sugar shack."

Sweetness coursed through my veins as I received his gift.

"Er, I wasn't as prepared. But I do have something to give you, too." I popped open the trunk of my RAV4, where I kept a carton of my books, just in case I ever had the opportunity to hand one out. Presenting someone with a copy was more often to build up a commercial venture. But I thought Mike would appreciate receiving one anyway, even if it wasn't wrapped.

"Thank you," he said, pulling it to his chest.

We parted that night with a date on the calendar for when I got back. I liked this man and was happy that he expressed the same feeling toward me.

He followed up with a call from the Mike line soon after our Sunday night date. Turned out that "M-I-K-E" corresponded to the 6-4-5-3 in his phone number. Everyone in his small town shared the first three numbers for their phones. He'd made it simple for his friends by labeling his the Mike line.

Our communication was easy, reciprocal, and interesting. Whatever topic I brought up, Mike would contribute or listen eagerly, to learn more about what subjects mattered to me. He had read my entire book and mentioned commonalities he'd discovered.

Here was another human being offering me what I'd always longed for—notice and appreciation, not just once, but repeatedly and with intention. It sounds so simple, yet he was the first person who consistently and reliably brought that to a relationship with me. I'd always played that role. Mike was the first seeker I ever wanted to be sought by.

"I know that you're leaving on Friday and are busy packing and getting everything ready for your trip. But I also know that you always go for your three-mile walk no matter what." He'd actually listened to the description of my daily routine. "Would it work for me to come down and walk with you at Compo Beach on Thursday before you go?"

He was offering to drive ninety minutes each way to accompany me on a forty-five-minute walk. I could barely take in that anyone would value my company enough to do that. Truthfully, at the height of my codependency with Fran, I would have done the same thing. But I didn't view Mike's offer as codependent. It felt like courtship.

I wanted to see him, too, and said yes.

That March Thursday was freezing cold and windy, more so because we met by the sound. Both of us bundled up to brave the weather and complete the scenic three-mile loop.

"Would you like to get coffee?" I inquired, as we headed back to our vehicles.

"I was hoping you'd ask," Mike said, being careful not to overstay his welcome. It was late afternoon, and I was completely ready for my excursion. He followed me to a Crumbs bakery across from the Westport Library where we spent another hour together before driving back to our separate homes.

"I'd give you a big smooch, but I know I have coffee breath," Mike said, as we stood by our cars, preparing to say goodbye. He gave me a bear hug instead. That was good, because I wasn't ready for an on-the-lips kiss yet.

I took off on my journey the next day, flying to Florida, where I would board the cruise ship. There were long lines to navigate, administrative hurdles to leap while organizing passports, luggage, and cabin assignments. After a couple of hours of waiting and signing forms, I dropped off my backpack and headed to the deck where lunch was being served.

Though we were still in port, I was surprised when my cell phone rang. *Who could be calling me?* I wondered, and then noticed an 860 area code. Mike!

I felt touched and a little nervous. Could I handle this much attention? We spoke briefly, and I told my roommate seated next to me, "I just met this guy. That was him. Wow! I've never been pursued like this. Ever."

The good news was that I didn't need to process our interaction incessantly. I took a deep breath. I noticed the sensations in my body, without judging them as right or wrong, and then moved on. Thoughts of Mike came and went during the week I was away. There was a growing comfort that this area of my life was more filled in than it had been in a long time.

Back home a week later, I went to my PO box, where I received the majority of my mail. It was the address on my website and the one I gave out to all but my most intimate friends. When I turned my key in the lock of the small box, I opened its door to reveal a stack of cards and letters delivered in my absence.

The first pieces I noticed were postcards, all from Mike, with his bold black printing on the back. For every day that I'd been away, Mike had mailed a note to me reporting his hometown news and interesting details of his day.

Day two: "I'm stalking you online, unless there is another holistic cruise going on." His naming the behavior endeared it. His content was thoughtful, his interest in me and what I was doing so palpable, that I felt myself expanding and warming with each word.

Before I'd met Mike, I had kept my calendar full on the

weekends to avoid feeling lonely and dateless. Even though we both looked forward to seeing each other, it was a couple more weeks before I could fit him into my schedule again. We arranged to see each other on a future Sunday, midafternoon, subsequent to my son, Ryan's, running the New York City Half Marathon.

Mike accommodated my tight schedule, which I gradually allowed to open up after we met. I started to attach his name to my weekends. This particular Sunday, he met my train after the brunch so we could spend the rest of the day together, including another walk at Compo. This time, it was a sunny, warm afternoon with no snow on the ground. After a quick-paced first half of the forty-five-minute loop, we sat on a bench so I could retie my shoelaces.

We'd been holding hands throughout the walk. When we were seated facing the water, Mike put his arm around my shoulder and pulled me closer. Then he leaned over and kissed me on the lips. His were soft and sweet. I was eighteen again, limp in his arms but excited in my heart.

"I've been wanting to do that for a long time," Mike declared, and gave me another. "Do you know what a desirable woman you are?" he asked.

I didn't know how to answer his question. I did not know that I was desirable. How would I have known? Wouldn't some man somewhere have had to give me that message? Ben never had. Those words had never been applied to me before. I knew I was likable and pretty enough. But desirable? Quite the contrary, my mother's message was always *Keep your legs crossed. Make him buy the cow.*

Every cell in my body was performing the happy dance. I felt magnetized to this man, wanting to be one with him in that moment, a sensation I had never known before. At sixty-three, I welcomed this foreign awareness.

IN THE TWO hours between our walk and suppertime, it made sense for Mike to come back to my place and relax. We had not yet been to each other's homes. My apartment building had a community room with comfortable, contemporary decor, a big-screen TV, and a fireplace. I situated Mike there, telling him that I'd go up to my apartment, meditate, shower, and return when I was finished.

I wasn't ready to have him come all the way into my life just yet. Wonderful as that first kiss had been, I knew I needed time to savor it and process the relationship before we became more intimate.

The lobby area was close enough. I went upstairs, relaxed on my recliner, and practiced my afternoon meditation. Taking my time, I showered, changed, and put on a fresh coat of lipstick before going back downstairs to be with him.

When I got there, I was particularly excited to show him a photo I'd snapped that morning at Ryan's with my iPhone. "Mike," I said, walking toward him with my arm extended, device in hand, "I want to show you this!"

He had made himself at home on the couch, feet on the coffee table, a basketball game on the set. In his hands was a crochet project he was working on.

"Wait one second," he said. I fully expected to stand there until the play was completed or the quarter was over, as I had throughout my marriage. Talking to my ex-husband's profile while he watched a game was standard behavior.

Instead, Mike grabbed the remote, turned off the TV, placed his project on the table, and motioned with his left hand for me to sit down in the space he'd just cleared. "Show me," he said, and looked into my eyes.

The stone-walled fortress of resistance and defenses I'd

erected throughout my lifetime was slowly and gently being dismantled. With each whisper of attention Mike paid me, a layer of my personal boulder crumbled and fell away.

We had dinner a few miles from my place, at a Mexican restaurant in a strip mall on the Post Road, where Trader Joe's was the anchor store. Over chimichangas and fish tacos, Mike asked me who my oldest friends were. Aimee Garn and Cookie Russo immediately came to mind, women I'd met at Mount Holyoke when I was nineteen, and whom I still saw regularly. I loved the question and where it took our conversation.

After our meal, Mike asked if I wanted to pick up anything at Trader Joe's. It had become one of my favorite groceries, so there was always something I could use from there. Since his closest branch was twenty-five miles from his house, he was happy to take a few items back with him as well.

Pushing the cart down the fruit aisle, I heard someone call out, "Jane!" I looked toward the cash registers and spotted where it was coming from. It was Aimee, who had a second home in Westport.

"How often do you two bump into each other like this?" Mike asked.

"This is the first time ever," I said, finding yet another magical moment in this mystical day.

I made the introduction. "Mike, this is Aimee—who we were *just* talking about. Aimee, this is Mike Barton, my . . ." Was I actually going to say the next word? "Boyfriend!" I looked at Mike, then at Aimee, and burst out laughing that that word had passed my lips. Mike had a wide grin on his face, and Aimee gave me a hug.

Aimee and Mike connected immediately over his hometown of West Cornwall, where a favorite cousin-in-law of

Aimee's had lived. Watching Mike in action with my good friend further deepened my feelings about him.

Within weeks of that first date at Papaya Thai, Mike rolled toward me in bed one night and said, "I think I'm falling in love."

"I think I am, too," I echoed.

Soon we were both sure of it.

EVEN WHEN THE sunbeams and unicorns faded and disappeared, which happens in any relationship, we were able to talk about it. There was a brief set-to about the location of my hiking boots at Mike's home on a fall visit there a few months into our courtship. I became aware of the change in his tone and thought to myself, *If I don't say something now, I never will.*

"It felt like you yelled at me," I said in an even tone, without accusation. Just the facts.

He stopped, looked right at me, and said, "I'm so sorry. I wanted to catch a glimpse of my neighbor's baby before they passed the house, and didn't know what you were talking about. I promise it won't happen again."

Done. Confronted, then over. Quick recovery, and a relationship deepened.

THERE WERE NO parents to bring Mike home to meet. Instead, we introduced each other to our friends, siblings, and children over the next several months. Unfortunately, at our age, many of the occasions that brought us together were memorial services. The first of those was at the Columbia School of Journalism, for a neighboring family matriarch and friend of Mike's, where he gave a tribute. Bonnie, the daughter-in-law of the deceased, whispered in Mike's ear, "She's a keeper" after she and I had met briefly.

Mike joined me at a most unusual hospice gathering a few weeks later in Connecticut. We were invited to attend a party for a terminally ill man I knew. Rather than missing all his friends at his funeral, Philip was treated to a last bash, hosted by his family, while he was still well enough to enjoy the company.

A successful graphic designer and photographer, my friend arrived via a hospital bed from his semiprivate quarters into a sunny community room overlooking the Long Island Sound. One friend had arranged a collection of Phil's black-and-white images throughout the space there. Flower arrangements blossomed on several tables, and there was a gourmet spread for the dozens who attended. Phil held dominion from the bed, which had been cranked up to a seated position.

Not only did Mike get to meet many of my creative friends that afternoon, he also met Phil for the first and last time. Mike leaned over Phil's shoulder and delivered his favorite joke. which Phil fully appreciated. Kathryn, Phil's wife, later shared with me that that act of kindness was most memorable.

At Phil's service a couple of months later, "Home," by Edward Sharpe and the Magnetic Zeros, was the soundtrack for the charming and sentimental video his daughter Hannah had created. Mike nudged me as the tune began. In the habit of sending me a daily melody, he had selected that song's poignant lyrics as a recent choice.


BY LATE SPRING, Mike and I had made each other a priority and considered the other's calendar when making future plans. An avid amateur theater performer, Mike let me know that the Sharon Playhouse would be taking up much of his time that coming summer. I saw how engaged he was with the other actors and how much that association meant to him. It was fun to watch him sing and dance in the productions there.

He was cast in several small parts in *The Sound of Music* that July. Among them were the bishop who marries Maria and Captain von Trapp and a Nazi who delivers the captain's orders. I wondered out loud to him which of his roles my mother would have disliked more. One surprisingly pleasant outcome of that casting was that Mike needed to be clean-shaven. I never objected to the beard, but he was even more handsome without it. He's been shaving for me ever since.

Staying busy that summer was not an issue. Our lives dovetailed and connected frequently and respectfully. I continued to attend my meetings in Connecticut and had recently become a grandmother.

WHILE THE ROOMS had become my constant source of unconditional love, I was slowly able to let in Mike's boundless affection. I learned how to trust that, unlike in my childhood, love wouldn't be withheld or removed because of an infraction or a requirement on my part. That freedom opened more than my heart and soul. My body responded as never before, which at sixty-three was the most surprising gift of all.

Throughout those first few months, I had the constancy of my fellows to affirm what my heart was telling me. This was a good and safe man who loved me and wanted to support me in everything I did. My job was to receive his love, to offer mine, and to meet my daily fears with awareness and acceptance.

Chapter Nineteen

*B*efore I met Mike in February 2012, I attended a Broadway show with a friend who had moved from Wilton, Connecticut, into Manhattan a few years before. During intermission, after I'd updated her on the collapse of my marriage, she eyed me closely and asked, "What's keeping you in Connecticut?"

I looked back at her, paused, and was silent.

My friend's simple question provided the proverbial slap upside the head. What *was* keeping me in Connecticut? From that moment forward, I began the process of transitioning from suburban living to becoming a city girl, first mentally, then geographically.

Ever since my mother took her three daughters to see Mary Martin in *The Sound of Music* when I was eleven years old, I've been hooked on seeing shows. My professor in college told us majors that even if we didn't have a career in theater, we could be patrons—advice I took to heart by subscribing to several theater companies over the years.

After Ben had admitted to his infidelity and our divorce

proceedings had begun, I had moved out of the home I'd created for my family and into my apartment. The thought of moving to New York City had crossed my mind only fleetingly. My three grown children all lived there. Surely the supply of eligible men would be more ample than it was in the suburbs. My work was mostly virtual and could be done anywhere.

For me, New York City has always been the greatest city in the world, which is why I chose to live within fifty miles of it the majority of my life. I drove to the city or took the train there for frequent visits, on occasion commuting in several times during the same week. My trips to Manhattan always provided me with a fresh experience, increased energy, and enthusiasm for everything else in my life.

Being closer to Lucy, Ryan, and Lily was a major impetus for my wanting to move. Getting them out to Connecticut was increasingly difficult. There are few things to attract thirty somethings to the suburbs after they've left home. Once Ben and I no longer lived together, it became even harder. They would have to make two stops on their trip or, worse, decide which of their parents to visit.

Each of my children welcomed the news, saying, "That's great!" and, "Let me know when you want to look for apartments. I'll help you."

The only attachment I still had to Norwalk, after having lived in the state for forty years, was recovery, the rooms I'd been sitting in since 1989. I had graduated from every other group I'd been a member of prior to finding that community. Very few of the relationships I'd formed with parents during the tenure of those organizations lasted beyond their completion. I can count on one hand the women who remained in my life once my membership in their group diminished: Rosalea from La Leche League, Prudy from the Community Cooperative Nursery School, Aimee and Cookie from Mount Holyoke.

In twelve-step recovery, I had discovered an organization that I'd never outgrow. Although I had intimate and loving relationships with the people I met there, future rooms offered the promise of even more nonjudgmental, unconditionally loving, and safe environments for me to share myself. Difficult as it was to shift from fellowship to fellowship, each time I did try out a different group, there was the prospect of new individuals to become friends with.

By the early 2000s, I spent most of my social time with program fellows—meals, movies, coffee dates. It was my community, as well as my support system—my family of choice. While I couldn't select who had brought me into this world, I could now determine with whom and where to spend my time.

Every Saturday morning before my meeting for adult children, I met one woman for coffee and conversation. Following that gathering, my sponsor and I sat side by side on a cushioned window seat in a hallway of the church. There, I filled her in on the ups and downs of my week. She simply listened while I expounded on the interactions I'd had since we last met. She didn't judge, criticize, or offer advice; she let me go on until I didn't need to talk anymore.

This is the grace of the program. One of the things we do for each other is to serve as witnesses. Something transformative happens when you're beheld in this way. I have countless thoughts that live and die in my head. When I give voice to the ones that are most important, and another human being acknowledges that she's heard them, an act of kindness has transpired.

I knew that if I could just talk out my thoughts, I'd self-correct. In this particular sponsoring relationship, I felt the safety and acceptance that allowed me to fully express what I was thinking.

"I identify with everything you've told me," she'd say when I was finished. I felt a circle of love winding around my shoulders and silently embracing me. I'd been seen and heard, and I felt full.

Those three precious weekend hours kept me grounded, connected, and relieved of pressures that had built up over the previous seven days. I attended other meetings, occasionally made phone calls between, but that safety valve of Saturday mornings provided my spiritual anchor. Bring on life! I was equipped.

Telling my sponsor what I was up to regarding my move was the downside to my overall excitement. Her face, usually neutral and receptive, betrayed her the morning I revealed my plan. I saw it crumple slightly for a millisecond, but then a smile emerged.

"This makes so much sense, Jane," she said. "You love the city, and you'll get even more from living there." She commuted regularly and understood its draw for me. "This is really exciting."

The wheels of my move were already in motion by the time Mike and I started our relationship. The intention had been set. I wasn't sure where our relationship would be in six months, so I didn't feel any urgency to let him know and hadn't mentioned it. It was in my heart but hadn't surfaced in conversation yet.

Stopping at Lucy's on a cold, wet afternoon in late March, Mike and I sat on the floor of her living room, playing with my granddaughter, Chloe.

"Any progress on the apartment situation?" my daughter asked. She saw my eyebrows shoot up and my eyes dart toward Mike's face. "Oops! Was I not supposed to say anything?"

I could feel my blood rushing up my neck and into my cheeks.

"I haven't mentioned this," I said, turning toward my boyfriend, "but I'm planning to move into the city when my lease is up in Connecticut this September."

"I'll find you wherever you go," Mike responded. We'd been dating only a month, but this reassurance rippled my insides. He loved the city. Even though Norwalk and West Cornwall were in the same state, the drive to Manhattan would add only fifteen minutes to his travel time, since it was more direct as the crow flies. Plus, Mike said, "At the end of the ride, you're in New York!"

I hadn't feared that it would be a deal breaker, but I felt a surge of love upon hearing Mike's warm support. It made everything easier and more attainable.

It wasn't hard to figure out which neighborhood to investigate. I knew I'd want to be near the theater district and my kids. When I started my search, both Ryan and Lucy had apartments on the Upper West Side. Lily was in Queens, which wasn't on my radar.

I quickly made a list of a dozen apartments within my price range, called for appointments, and set up a day to get into Manhattan and look. Lucy attached Chloe to her chest with a strap-on carrier so she could easily get in and out of taxis as we began the hunt. There were three places we planned to look at together. Having lived in a half dozen apartments herself since she moved to New York after college, Lucy knew what questions to ask and what to look for during our tour.

I resigned myself to having less space, even than in my Norwalk apartment. I had downsized from house living without much angst. I'd need to pare down even more to fit myself into a New York City dwelling.

We visited several okay Upper West Side apartments in one afternoon. Our last stop that day was Sixty-Third and Riverside Boulevard—an extension of Riverside Drive—at a building called the Ashley. It had a few apartments in my price range, but it was the amenities that grabbed me.

The lobby was large and elegant, with a uniformed doorman and another gentleman, a concierge, behind the desk. Lucy, Chloe, and I waited on the modern sofa on the opposite side of the spacious entry while he dialed the building's leasing office.

The in-house agent greeted us, showed us two layouts on the third and sixth floors, and then guided us around the lower level, which housed a sports complex that featured a swimming pool with a well-appointed locker room, basketball and squash courts, state-of-the-art treadmills and workout equipment, a climbing wall, a simulated golf room, Ping-Pong and pool tables, and a bowling alley. But the pièce de résistance, around the corner from the lobby and adjacent to the building's social room, was a Kidville playroom with padded walls, a cushioned floor, and upholstered play shapes.

"If you take this place, Mom," Lucy promised, "we'll be here all the time."

I signed the contract that week.

While Mike was busy with his shows that summer, I got myself ready for my move in the fall. A professional organizer helped me measure my Sixty-Third Street space and showed me how the pieces I now owned would fit there.

Mike offered to store the overflow at his house and drove his truck down so that he could transport my recliner, dining room table, office cabinets, and desk units to his place until my next move, whenever that would be.

Hardly a day passes in my life when I don't have moments

of despair and hopelessness: a negative email response throws me off balance, or I get an unexpected rejection that creates a wave of nausea. But this major move, one of the biggest things I'd done in my life—change states, navigate New York real estate, bid goodbye to my home of thirty-five years—was almost effortless. I sweat the small stuff, but the big stuff seems to take care of itself.

The movers arrived as planned. The woman helping me through this effort accompanied me into the city and took charge as the workers hauled my pieces up from the van and into my new home. By 6:00 p.m., my organizer had arranged all of my furnishings, unpacked the cartons, and gotten my kitchen and office completely set up. Lucy and Chloe stopped by with a bouquet of yellow calla lilies just as my helper was leaving. I was now officially a New Yorker.

Apartment 602 was 575 square feet, not a lot bigger than the dorm room I'd occupied at Whittier Hall in 1970 at Columbia, but worlds apart in every other respect. Then, I was a single young woman looking for a life path, a mate, and a home. I was living in a furnished room on the edge of Harlem well before it gentrified into the desirable location it has become.

In 2012, I was again single but no longer alone. All of my major questions had been answered. I'd created a family and carved out a satisfying career. Now I was renting space in a luxury building along the Hudson River. Before the organizer left that night, she hung a handmade banner I'd brought from my old apartment. It was a string of flags, which she tacked up over the front door. On each of the four panels was one word. The entire message read, DESIRE WHAT YOU HAVE. It captured perfectly how I felt that crisp October night, living again in the greatest city in the world.

I was hungry by the time everyone left, but didn't know

where to go to eat. I wandered a few blocks up to Tenth Avenue and chose the first place that wasn't a diner but had fast food that met my needs, a falafel hole in the wall, where I sat at the counter and wondered how long it would be before I felt like I belonged.

WHEN BEN AND I first moved to Connecticut, I searched the classifieds for tag sales, pulled out my Hagstrom map, buckled Lucy into her car seat, and felt my way around my new neighborhood. That was well before people had the Internet, Google Maps, and the ability to zero in on what they're looking to find. At twenty-seven, I didn't know what I wanted. By sixty-three, I did know. I wanted to meet like-minded people, i.e., in recovery, and sought out the meetings closest to my apartment building. I was no longer looking over my shoulder to see if Ben approved. My gut was giving me the necessary signals now.

The morning after I moved in, I headed straight for a twelve-step meeting nearby, found easily after a keyword search. My group in Connecticut had given me a going-away party before I'd moved. We took a photo so I'd have it with me as I leaped into my future. I knew I couldn't replace the love, friendships, and support I had there, but I would at least put myself in a place where it could be available again. I'd learned to turn around from holding on to the bars of a jail cell in my mind and walk out among the open fields surrounding those thoughts.

Because I wore the expression of someone who didn't know where she was headed, the guard behind the reception desk asked if I needed help. When I mentioned the recovery group's name, he gestured over his shoulder to a room down the hall.

There was a rectangular formation of folding tables and chairs, with six seats on each of the four sides and double rows of chairs on opposite ends of the room. I sat against the far wall of the room, facing the doors and a couple of seats in from the end. There were already a few men and women there when I entered. Over the course of the hour, every chair at the connecting tables was taken and most of the others filled in as well. By 8:00 a.m., more than thirty people were in attendance, at least double the size I was used to.

The person presiding started promptly at 7:30 a.m., I was happy to see. The group had made it through over two decades without my help. It felt good to know that my recovery would not make or break this room. Yet, I wanted people to know that I had lots of twenty-four hours and would make a solid contribution. How would I let them know that today? Even after all my years in the rooms, I still cared about the impression I'd made. Even with a loving boyfriend and a solid career, and living in the best city in the world, I felt that old twinge of urgency to be seen.

There was a break in the action at 8:00 a.m., when announcements were made and an envelope passed around for contributions.

"Is there anyone visiting from out of town or new to this meeting?" the leader read from the formatted notes. I raised my hand.

"Hi, I'm Jane," I announced.

"Hi, Jane! Welcome!" came the anticipated choral response.

"I moved here from Connecticut," I continued, and paused for impact. "Yesterday." I felt a warm response as a few people laughed.

"If you're so inclined," I added, "I'd be grateful for phone numbers." I said it, and I let it go, not knowing if by the end of the meeting anyone would still remember I'd asked. I knew the important thing was asking.

Two people moved toward me once the final Serenity Prayer was spoken. One, a tall blondish-white-haired man with a close crew cut and a big smile, handed me a folded piece of paper. "I'm so glad you made that request. My sponsor just told me I should use the phone more, and then you made your announcement. Don't you love how that works?"

I liked him already.

A woman stood behind him. As he walked away, she, too, extended a small, creased note in my direction. "Welcome! It's good to have you here," she said. "I'd love to have coffee." She was also tall, and very pretty, with long, dark hair.

Those two gestures made me feel immediately embraced by the room. I often think I need a red carpet rolled out, but all it actually takes is knowing I've been seen.

HUMORIST JEANNE ROBERTSON tells her audiences, "People don't go to Denny's. They end up at Denny's." It gets a laugh and made me think about my move to New York City, Manhattan particularly, in exactly the opposite terms. People don't end up in Manhattan. They go there with intention. It's a wonderfully formidable place to be.

I met Ben in the city in 1970, moved to Connecticut and had a union with him for nearly forty years, and molded myself into a lifestyle that no longer fit me. I never had the courage to leave, but once released, I flew.

Chapter Twenty

*I* didn't realize that my son, Ryan, had an agenda when he suggested a lunch date in mid-March 2013. Everyone in the family was excited that he and Anne were expecting their first child that August. Ryan was in the city for an appointment and arranged to see me. I was happy anytime one of my children took the initiative to get together.

I say that everyone was excited, but I had little idea how Ben felt about the pregnancy. He and I had had zero communication since our day in court, March 17, 2011, when we'd gotten divorced. I'd been receiving my alimony check reliably each month. There was always a sentence or two jotted on Ben's personalized beige stationery: "Jane—for January 2012" or "Jane —great news about Ryan and Anne." There was never a closing or signature, just my name, the month the payment was for, and an occasional reference to family news.

He knew that I'd received the checks, because I deposited them. But I didn't write back. I had nothing to say.

Aside from those mailings, neither of us had any contact with the other. It was a bit weird. This man whom I'd shared the past thirty-eight years with was now absent from my life. I didn't miss him, though. I'd felt invisible and neglected for many of those last years. What was there to miss?

Throughout my life, I'd read manuals and operating guides to find the right school, marriage, doctor, and career. Now, I had no interest in finding out how to be well divorced. My new existence felt as though a magician had pulled the tablecloth of my perfect life out from a completely set table. Instead of everything remaining exactly as it was while the cloth underneath was whisked away, every dish, glass, and candle was thrust into the air and scattered helter-skelter.

Online wisdom suggests keeping postdivorce communication limited, impersonal, and to the point. We were definitely following protocol on that front. But when it came to who should reach out to whom for any personal relationship, I followed the slogan I'd learned to rely on: "When in doubt, don't."

I did wonder about who or what would break the silence—an event, illness, death? It wasn't something I gave a lot of thought to, but it occurred to me that it was an unusual behavior pattern to be in. It was almost as though it had never been any other way—until this afternoon when my son pointed it out.

Ryan and my lunch destination was Candle Cafe, a favorite restaurant of mine on the Upper East Side. It was a drenching March day, the kind when spring still feels like a remote destination.

I had no trouble deciding what to order—ginger stir-fry with tofu. But Ryan, I heard later in the meal, was not a lover of vegetarian restaurants. He'd accommodated my choice of venues and decided on a pasta dish that wasn't too offensive or kale-y for him.

After the waitress had taken our order, Ryan got down to business.

"Anne and I were talking about the birth experience we want with our baby. It's making us both anxious that you and Dad aren't talking to each other," he said. "We don't want to have to worry about who arrives at the hospital when."

I jumped in. "We're not intentionally *not* talking to each other. There's nothing preventing us from speaking. We just haven't."

Why was I being so defensive? Ryan hadn't accused me of anything. He was simply stating how he and his wife wanted it to be.

"We don't want a repeat of what happened when Chloe was born," he continued, referencing the birth of my first grandchild, two years earlier. My older daughter had scheduled it so that I would arrive the night of the birth and Ben would show up the next day. I had anticipated that Ben and I might bump into each other at the hospital, but Lucy had arranged it so we wouldn't.

"It would stress us out," Ryan told me.

The waitress brought our entrées and placed my bowl of piping-hot vegetables on the table in front of me. Ryan picked up his fork and pierced the penne he'd been served.

"What are you suggesting?" I ventured.

"I'd like you to connect with Dad," he responded.

My inner four-year-old rebelled. *Why do I always have to be the one? Why aren't* you *asking Dad? It's not my job. He's the one who left the marriage. Why don't you make* him *pick up the phone?*

I chewed my mouthful of brown rice slowly and thoroughly.

"I'd be fine seeing Dad," I said, trying to dislodge a piece of celery caught between my teeth.

Ryan refolded his napkin into a small square and wiped his mouth. "Can you call him?"

"If you're so concerned, why don't *you* have us both over for dinner before the baby is born? I'd be fine with that. I've always been the one to make the first move. I don't want to do that anymore," I said, furthering my cause.

"I shouldn't have to," Ryan replied. "You know *he* never will."

"*You* know *he* never will?" I echoed, surprised that my child saw the bigger picture as clearly as I did. I must have thought it was some kind of secret that only I carried. Of course he knew that Ben was no risk taker. Things eventually came to him if he waited, or they didn't. The biggest thing Ben had ever done in his life since I'd known him was leave our marriage. And even then, he'd had to ask me, "Do you think I should move out?"

Ryan nodded his head in response to my echoed question. Just then, his cell phone, which had been sitting near the edge of the table, began to vibrate.

"That's him," he said, as he pointed toward his device.

I chopsticked a piece of tofu and placed it between my teeth. Ryan took another bite from his dish.

The phone went to black.

"I'll text him," I said.

Bluster. I'd known I'd do it the second he'd asked me. I was having a mini-tantrum. I still wanted to be sought after and didn't think I should have to take the initiative. I'm not proud of this.

What bothered me in the moment but stands out in retrospect was my not acknowledging the courage it took Ryan to initiate this conversation. I gave him a hard time. I'd leaned out from him, instead of in.

I had a long talk with my sponsor the next day. I hate to be wrong, but my behavior was wrong in this situation. With time and perspective, I can see that now, and wish I'd had a loving presence pointing out to me how brave my son was. That I had raised this fine young man to have the maturity and wisdom to take care of himself.

I'm sorry I didn't take Ryan's hand across the table and say to him, "This must be really hard for you. Thank you for thinking this through, knowing what you want from me, and making this request."

The way I wish my mother had all those years ago. Or Ben. I'm learning this only now, though I thought it was a birthright.

WITHIN A WEEK of our lunch, I texted Ben a simple message: "Ryan wants us to connect. R u available for that?"

To which I received an immediate response: "Absolutely."

I continued to share my process at my morning meetings. "I'm walking through uncharted territory here. I don't know how to behave. There's no formula for this kind of get-together."

I listened intently for others who mentioned similar reunions and noted what aspects of their experience could help me. Keep it light. Stay away from anything accusatory or personal. If it's hysterical, it's historical.

A friend in Connecticut described how she erected a pop-up tent in her backyard and hung a sign over its entrance, naming it the Place of Not Knowing.

"It helps me to have somewhere to go when I don't know what to do, to have an actual spot where I can be in the unknown." I imitated her example and sat with my feelings, not in a tent but in a designated spot where I could get still and call upon something higher for guidance. I've heard a better name for creating this pause. It's called grace.

DURING MY SHARE on the day of Ben's visit, I asked for help. "Please keep me in your thoughts this afternoon, and anyone who can give me a hug after the meeting, I'd love to receive it."

I think of my home group as my mosh pit of love. I visualize myself being supported by the men and women who fill the seats there every day, their extended arms holding me up, as I traverse my way across these emotional hurdles. Then I take the next step, show up, and have a new experience.

Ben drove into Manhattan to meet me at my building. I was expecting his arrival. Pedro, the concierge, called my apartment when Ben approached the desk, saying he had come to see me. Rather than saying, "Send him up," as I usually did when guests arrived, I told Pedro, "I'll be right down."

I'd gotten to know and love the staff of my building. I'd actually confided in the afternoon attendant, "My ex-husband is coming to see me. I haven't seen or spoken to him in two years."

"Want me to look out for you?" he asked sweetly. It must've sounded as strange to him as it did to me.

Ben was chatting with Pedro at the desk when I got to the first floor. He immediately turned away from the desk, came toward me, and opened his arms for an embrace. It was as though he'd just gotten back from work, like in our newlywed days when we still kissed upon his arrival home.

Like nothing had happened between us that might prevent this show of affection. I responded as I would have if I received a hug from a distant relative: politely and formally. I experienced no physical reaction to his touch. My only awareness was slight curiosity.

The library on the first floor of my building provided a neutral place to sit and talk. We walked to the couch opposite the mounted television screen and sat beside each other.

He asked me a lot of questions about the Ashley. What were the other residents like? How was it living in the city? Did I have friends in the building? Could he have a tour?

It was a friendly conversation and not the least bit difficult. Nothing of substance was discussed, and I didn't broach any topics that might have changed the tenor of the visit. I made no mention of Mike, nor did I ask about his involvement with the woman in Maine. Someday I might thank her for my release, but keeping her as not really a person was self-protection. Stay out of harm's way, my sponsor would say. What would knowing more about her accomplish? I preferred anonymity.

Within an hour or so, Ben said he had to go. That was it.


THAT JULY, WHEN Chloe was turning two, Lucy asked if she could hold her birthday party in my building. She wanted to entertain the tots in the Kidville playroom. The courtyard was a protected outdoor place where they could serve cake and beverages to the children and their parents. I was happy to be a part of the planning.

Seeing Ben there, now that we'd broken the ice a few months earlier, was easy and comfortable. Mike attended the party as well, so there was that introduction to be made. Being the thoughtful man he is, Mike composed his greeting to Ben. When they shook hands the day of the festivities, Mike said, "Hello! I want you to know I'm a big fan of your kids" and extended his hand.

This was the first time that our whole family had been together since that dreadful Thanksgiving in 2009, four years before. We didn't assemble for a group photo, but I had the sense of peace that mothers have when their brood is all in one place.

Lily pulled me aside after the party to say, "It made me so happy to see you and Dad talking."

It's not that I never thought about the impact of our divorce on the kids. I did. I was just ill-equipped to figure out how to operate once Ben left the house. I had enough difficulty with the complete disruption of my existence.

We didn't do any counseling with them, although Ryan suggested it at one point. I can't remember why we didn't pursue that. It was something I would have been in favor of. Maybe I was too distraught to try to get Ben to agree.

Also, since they were in their late twenties and early thirties, they were capable of seeking their own help. No one acted out. There was only resigned acceptance and sadness. We didn't talk about it.

Lily's words grabbed my heart and held it. There was so much beneath that sentence that must have been stepped over in the interim. What had she been thinking? What had they all been thinking?

I had said to Ryan that 2009 Thanksgiving afternoon that we'd been through the hardest part: the shocking demise of our family unit. But as the months and years passed, it got worse. What was once a strong, happy, and united household no longer existed.

Friends said it was possible to reconfigure. I read an article about how Larry David and his family had amicable Friday-night dinners years after he and his wife divorced. That still feels far from taking place.

When Ryan completed law school and passed the bar exam in 2006, before any of this happened, Ben and I treated him and Anne to a celebratory weekend in Boston. We stayed at a downtown hotel and were going out for dinner on Saturday night. As our elevator descended into the lobby area and the doors opened, we witnessed a bridal party about to make its entrance into the ballroom nearby.

The bride was standing erect in a slim white gown. Her expression was hard to read. On her right, we surmised, was her mother, looking elegant in a taupe satin dress. The two women's arms were entwined, but the older woman was gazing to her right and into the distance. To the bride's left was a dapper, balding gentleman in a tuxedo, his arm inserted through the daughter's as well. His eyes were fixed on a nearby pillar. The tableau reflected a sense of frozen turmoil, not what you'd expect on the happiest day of this young woman's life.

Anne and I shared our observations as we left the hotel for the restaurant. "Not a happy-looking bride," I ventured, wondering if she was having second thoughts.

"I bet her parents are divorced," Anne said. In an instant, I sensed she was right and what a sad situation that must be for the young woman caught between the divided parties.

That isolated moment from years before occurred to me as a now-divorced woman. Might that bride, who perhaps also did her shopping at Crate & Barrel in preparation for this new chapter of her life, find herself there again one day for another passage? I hoped that my reaching out to Ben would prevent a moment like that for our unmarried daughter. I know that I will be fine in his presence and that we can both be joyful for our child's happiness. I had taken the first step of the mending process, not only for me, but for my children as well.

# Epilogue

For Ben's fortieth birthday in November 1986, I surprised him with plane tickets to London. Neither of us had ever gone abroad. A hop across the pond seemed to be a safe, entry-level trip to attempt together. The British spoke our language, we could visit Buckingham Palace, and the food wouldn't be completely unfamiliar.

When I handed him a slim wrapped box, he opened it at the table, surrounded by me, the kids, my brother, and my sister-in-law. Up until that moment, it had been festive, warm, and joyful in the dining room.

As soon as he took the gift paper off, opened the flat box, and lifted out the tissue-covered passport holder, his expression changed, along with the sentiment of the room.

"What's this?" he asked, fixing his eyes on me.

"I got us tickets to go to London," I said, trying to lighten his darkening mood.

"When?"

"During your April vacation," I answered.

"How long is the flight?"

"About five hours."

"Who's going to stay with the kids?"

It went on like this for a few more minutes, until my brother suggested that they had better leave, stood up to go, and made a quick exit.

I cleared the table and began the bedtime routine with the kids. Ben and I barely spoke before going to bed.

The next few months were hard as his anxiety about the upcoming journey rose and fell. Eventually he adjusted to the idea, relaxed, and enjoyed himself once abroad.

Looking back, after years of recovery, I can see my side of the street more clearly. Ben hated surprises. I wanted him to want to travel. I wanted him to be different than who he was. I wanted to get him out of his goddamn box—that safe space a couples' counselor had described early in our marriage—of watching sports in his comfortable chair, drinking soda, and holding the remote.

No one can make anyone else change. I'd tried to change Ben. I'd tried to change my mother. I was a living example of insanity.

I tried to make them happy. To get them to see, understand, and accept me. I never succeeded.

The only one I am able to change is myself. Over the years, I went from being an obedient daughter, student, and wife to being a woman who challenged the beliefs and rules I'd blindly adhered to until they no longer worked in my life.

Eventually, my slow, incremental transformation must have made being in the box with me too uncomfortable for Ben, and he sought someone else's company.

Once I discovered the rooms of recovery, there was a place where I could always be seen, heard, accepted, and loved. My part was to show up, raise my hand, and let the others know I was there, what I was thinking and feeling. The response was always the same: "Thank you, Jane."

In that environment of unconditional acceptance, I grew to love myself enough to attract a man whose generous heart and spirit matched mine. Someone who could share me with the rest of the world and did.

Two years after Mike and I met, I embarked without him, in January 2014, on a round-the-world voyage sponsored by Semester at Sea, a study-abroad program that a friend in Al-Anon had mentioned to me when I started attending meetings on the West Side.

It was not only a world-circling travel adventure but also an opportunity to enter life in motion on the high seas. I didn't know another soul onboard. The voyage was a tabula rasa. I could create whatever story I wanted for three months.

In addition to bringing a backpack and duffel bag containing all the clothing and supplies I'd need, I also brought what I'd learned in my two and a half decades repeating the Serenity Prayer: to accept the things I cannot change, to possess the courage to change the things I can, and to have the wisdom to know the difference. These served me well as I explored eleven countries, most of which were vastly different than the United States, including Vietnam, Myanmar, India, and Ghana, to name my favorites.

It's daring to go on a trip around the world, to figure out currencies, maps, and customs particular to each country. I did safe, touristy things with large expeditions from the ship, like visiting the Great Wall of China, the Taj Mahal in India, and Robben Island in South Africa, where Nelson Mandela was imprisoned for eighteen of the twenty-seven years before he was freed.

I also took risks on my own or in small groups, hiring a

driver to show me the less traveled gems of Fort Kochi, India, spending a night in a hut in a remote village in Ghana, and walking through an impoverished township in South Africa with only one other American and a guide.

My attitude was the best traveling companion I could have had. Whether I was afraid (crossing the insanely trafficked streets of Ho Chi Minh City), dumbstruck (that the capital of an African country didn't have sidewalks), or grateful (traveling with new shipboard friends in Marrakech), everything I learned in the rooms supported me and enhanced the journey in every port. I used my program, prayed to my higher power, and sent messages to fellows asking for their support when I felt alone.

Mike and I communicated daily via the ship's email connection. The Internet was less than spotty while we sailed, but, curiously, emails found their way out and in easily, even on the high seas. He was charting my travels and often let me know where I was before I knew myself.

"Lost at sea" is a cliché for a reason. While we were moving, there was little to mark our progress across the ocean or where we were in the world. I couldn't keep track either because I was focused on the experience that day on the ship. Mike's constancy provided even more than the love and support I came to rely on. He was my guide.

From "Hey there, Strait of Malacca Mama" to "Howdy, Bay of Bengal Traveler," he ensured that I never felt alone. It would have been a different adventure without the grounding piece that came naturally to Mike.

I believe that all my life I have been looking for someone to have my back. Many fortunate people are born into families who offer this quality in abundance. While my parents gave me multiple gifts, a sense of being fully supported was something I needed to discover for myself. It took me forty-one years of trying it my own way to show up in the rooms, but, having been there for twenty-eight years as of 2018, I know that connection is mine as long as I keep up my daily practices. The strength of the support I feel is directly interdependent with my spiritual condition.

Attached to feeling supported and loved is the freedom to continue to grow, welcome new people into my realm, bless those who need to leave, and marvel at the countless miracles life offers. I didn't know that if you weren't born this way, it is still possible to attain a loving community. Now I'm convinced of it, because that's exactly what happened for me.

# Acknowledgments

This book was conceived during Ann Randolph's extraordinary workshop called *Write Your Life for the Page and the Stage* at Kripalu in June 2014. Her powerful leadership, gentle guidance, and rapt attention to each reader's words provided the invitation for me to go further. Her wise assistant, Kate Brenton, was my guide over the next three months, coaching me from Hawaii and leading me further into the process.

I knew I wanted even more instruction, accountability, and peer motivation. This led me to sign up for memoir classes at the creative home for writers, Gotham Writers Workshop, where I studied with Cullen Thomas and Melissa Petro. During one particularly strenuous feedback session, as I was shrinking into myself, Cullen reminded me that "all I want to do is make you a better writer." I took that to heart, not as criticism, but as instruction, accepted his direction and applied it. Melissa, my second teacher at Gotham, continued to work with me as my writing coach. We often met virtually face-to-face via zoom.us several times. I'll never forget her expression when I finally took her guidance and made the revisions she suggested. She came onto the screen after reading my homework with a huge grin and nodded her head. "You got it!" The encouragement of these teachers propelled me through the process.

Sue Shapiro's classes energized me and helped me see my work going out to a bigger audience. She's a living example of a prolific writer, teacher, and advocate for all of us who wish to be widely published.

In between classes and coaching sessions I formed my own writers group. I did this by asking women I'd heard mentioning words like editor, publisher, or newsletter in conversation, to join me for a sample session. The four of us took to each other immediately and have been together since July 2014. Thank you, Kathleen Frazier, whose memoir *Sleepwalker* came out the next year, for being that many steps ahead of me so I could learn from you. Jenny Brown and Ruth Josimovich have been my guardian angels throughout the process. Their gentle coaxing when I went off-course, their deep encouragement and appreciation when I stayed on track, and their warmth and love throughout this arduous process were lifelines for me over the years it took to birth this book.

I have two other teams I meet with regularly who have been my witnesses, advocates, and truth-tellers. Jacyntha Kamor, Mark Boquist, and I meet monthly to share our challenges and goals. Their deep affection, spirit, and wisdom have fed and nourished my soul since our first gathering four years ago.

Harvey Weinstein, Matt Shapiro, and I get together every other week specifically to talk about our visions for our careers and lives. Their steadfast belief in me, affirmation that I'm staying the course, and laughter when I say I want to get a job at Starbucks, continues to sustain me on a daily basis.

Then there are the thousands of men and women, who shall remain anonymous, who continue to sit on folding chairs with me in church basements, hear my stories, rants, and successes. By listening to my shares, you've helped me to develop my voice, find my soul and let go of all that bound me one day at a time.

Thank you, Paulina Eisenbeis, for introducing me to Hafiz. His poem so resonated that I wanted everyone who reads my memoir to read it too.

I'm grateful to my first listeners who signed up to hear me present a webinar where I showed storyboard images from my book and read an abbreviated version over the phone for an hour. Kathy Ball-Toncic, Patti Tower (who listened in from India!), Gwen Morgan, Nancy Collamer, Marisabina Russo, Pam Toner, Julianne Stirling, Janis Bowersox, Jerilyn Deveau, and Barbara Heffernan. Thank you for the encouragement and the honor of having you listen to my words.

There were also my first readers to whom I am indebted: Park Bodie, Heather Habelka, Tom Cotton, Jim Urbom, Suzanne Ste Therese, Maria Kahn (who asked me who I would cast as myself in the film—that kept me going for a month!), Sandy Weiner, Gillian Anderson, the Munder women—Diane, Laura and Marilyn, Prudy Barton, and Carol Schneider. I feel so privileged to have had your attention and support.

To my siblings—Meredith, Barbara, and Andy—thank you for being early readers and helping me remember the details of life at 19 Easton Avenue, even if we disagreed on where our Ginny doll games were played.

To further understand who my audience would be, I asked if anyone would create a reading salon for me. I'm indebted to these women for coming forward to not only give their support, but also for their generosity and superb skills as hostesses: Rebecca Welz, Emily Neustadt, Aimee Garn, Kathy Ball-Toncic, Deborah Bonnell, Rosalea Fisher, Lucy Hedrick, and Abby Marks-Beale. Thanks also to Lisa Corrado and Belinda Wasser for providing the time and platform for me to do a reading at the Entrepreneurial Women's Club in Connecticut.

Though less than a decade old, She Writes Press has created a haven for women authors. A huge shout-out to Brooke Warner and her talented company for they've contributed throughout this expedition. I experienced continuing love and support throughout my relationship with them and my sister writers. Thank you, all!

If I haven't named you, it isn't because I'm not grateful for all you've contributed to my life and growth, but sheer oversight. Please know that I appreciate everyone who has touched my life and acknowledged me along this journey.

# About the Author

JANE POLLAK was born in the heart of the Midwest, in Columbus, Ohio, but she inherited the city gene from her New York City–native parents. When she was five, they returned the family to a neighboring suburb, White Plains, where Pollak grew up. She graduated from Mount Holyoke College with a BA in studio art and theatre and an MA in art education from Columbia University Teachers College. Her first book, *Decorating Eggs: Exquisite Designs with Wax & Dye*, was recently republished by Schiffer Publishing. Her second book, *Soul Proprietor: 101 Lessons from a Lifestyle Entrepreneur* (Crossing Press, 2001), shares what she learned as a home-based business owner who successfully turned her passion into a thriving company. When Pollak's marriage ended in 2011, she moved back to Manhattan, where she currently resides contentedly single, seeing her beloved significant other every weekend. She has three grown children and three grandchildren.